Mint Chocolate

5

Mami Orikasa

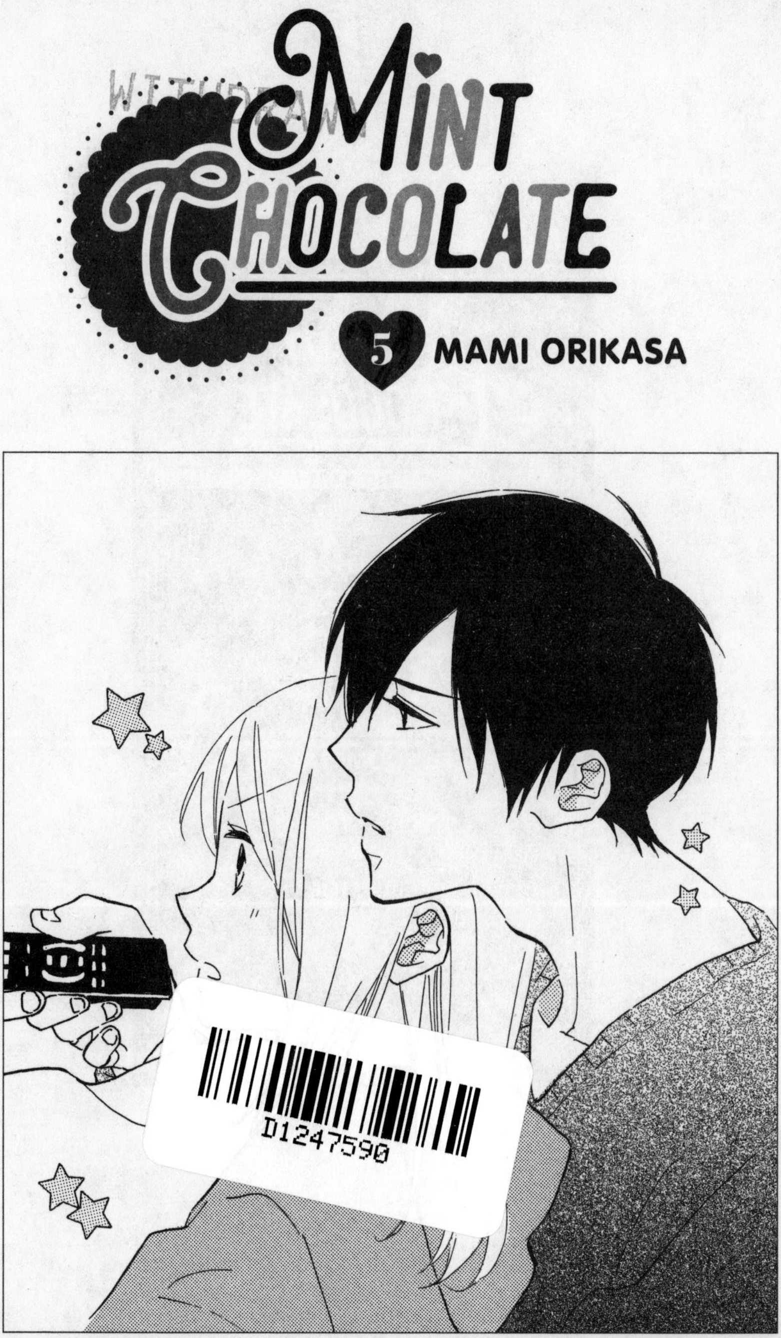

MINT CHOCOLATE

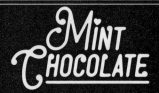

CONTENTS

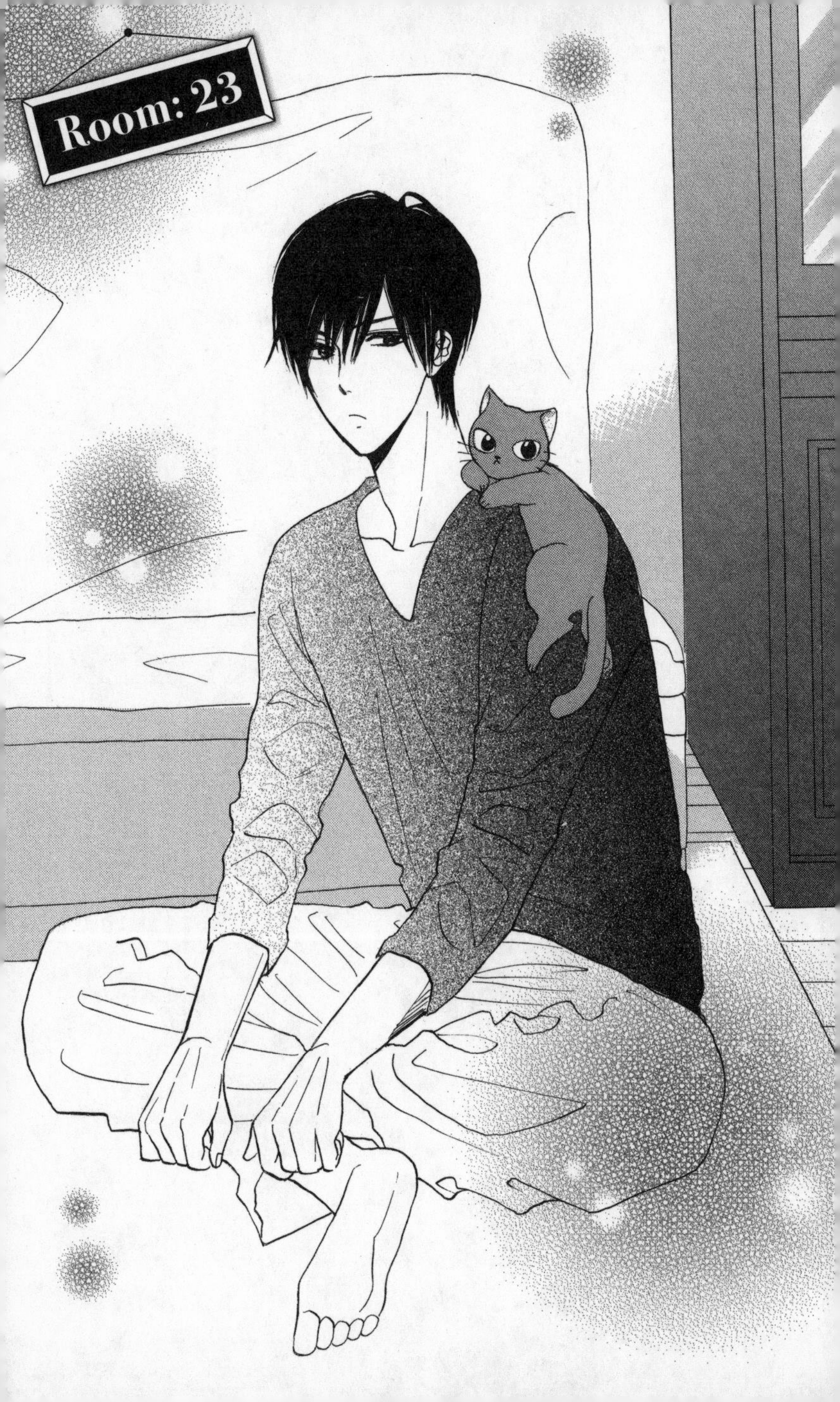
Room: 23

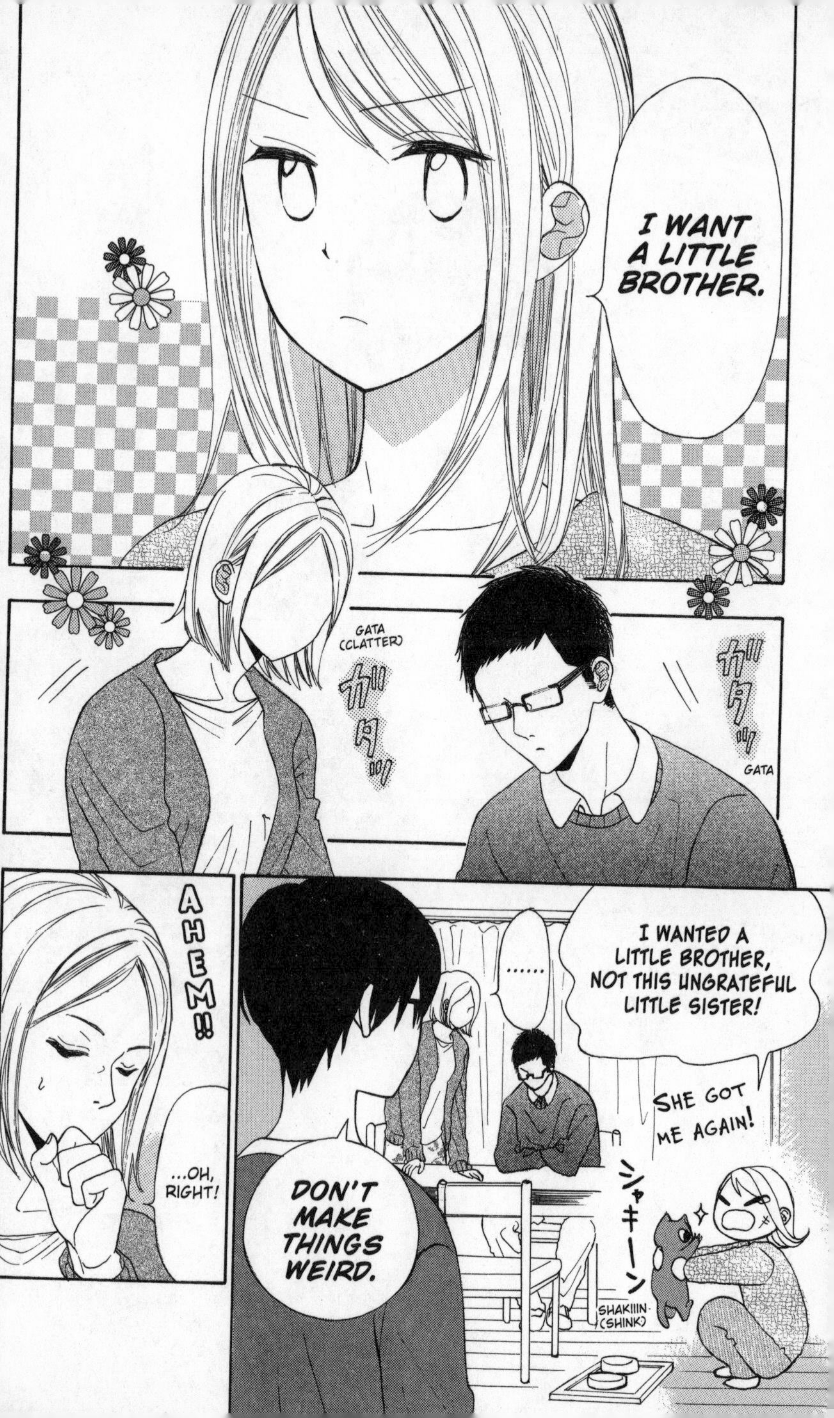
I WANT A LITTLE BROTHER.
ガタッ
GATA
GATA (CLATTER)
ガタッ
I WANTED A LITTLE BROTHER, NOT THIS UNGRATEFUL LITTLE SISTER!
......
SHE GOT ME AGAIN!
シャキーン
SHAKIIIN (SHINK)
DON'T MAKE THINGS WEIRD.
AHEM!!
...OH, RIGHT!

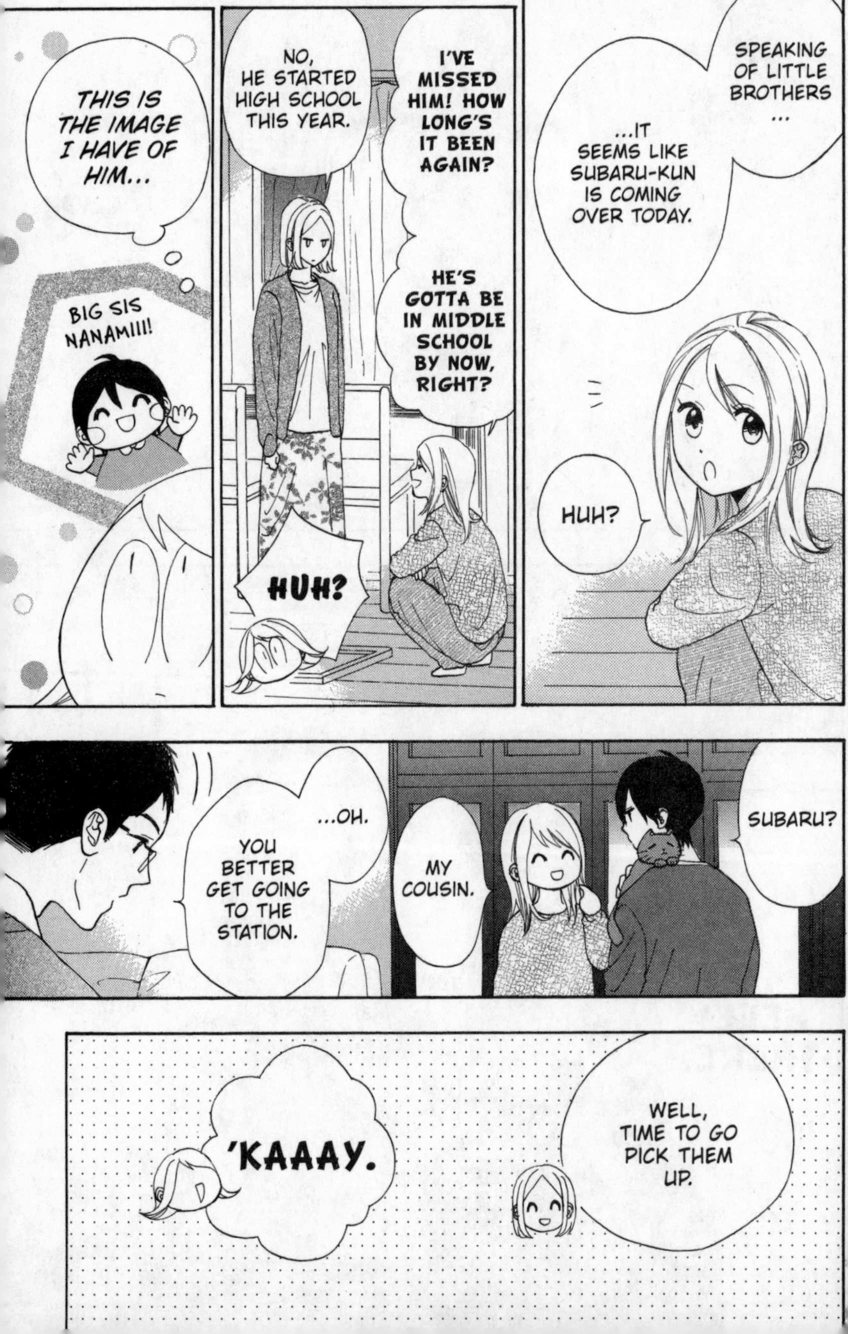
SPEAKING OF LITTLE BROTHERS ...
...IT SEEMS LIKE SUBARU-KUN IS COMING OVER TODAY.
HUH?
I'VE MISSED HIM! HOW LONG'S IT BEEN AGAIN?
HE'S GOTTA BE IN MIDDLE SCHOOL BY NOW, RIGHT?
NO, HE STARTED HIGH SCHOOL THIS YEAR.
HUH?
THIS IS THE IMAGE I HAVE OF HIM...
BIG SIS NANAMIII!
SUBARU?
MY COUSIN.
...OH.
YOU BETTER GET GOING TO THE STATION.
WELL, TIME TO GO PICK THEM UP.
'KAAAY.

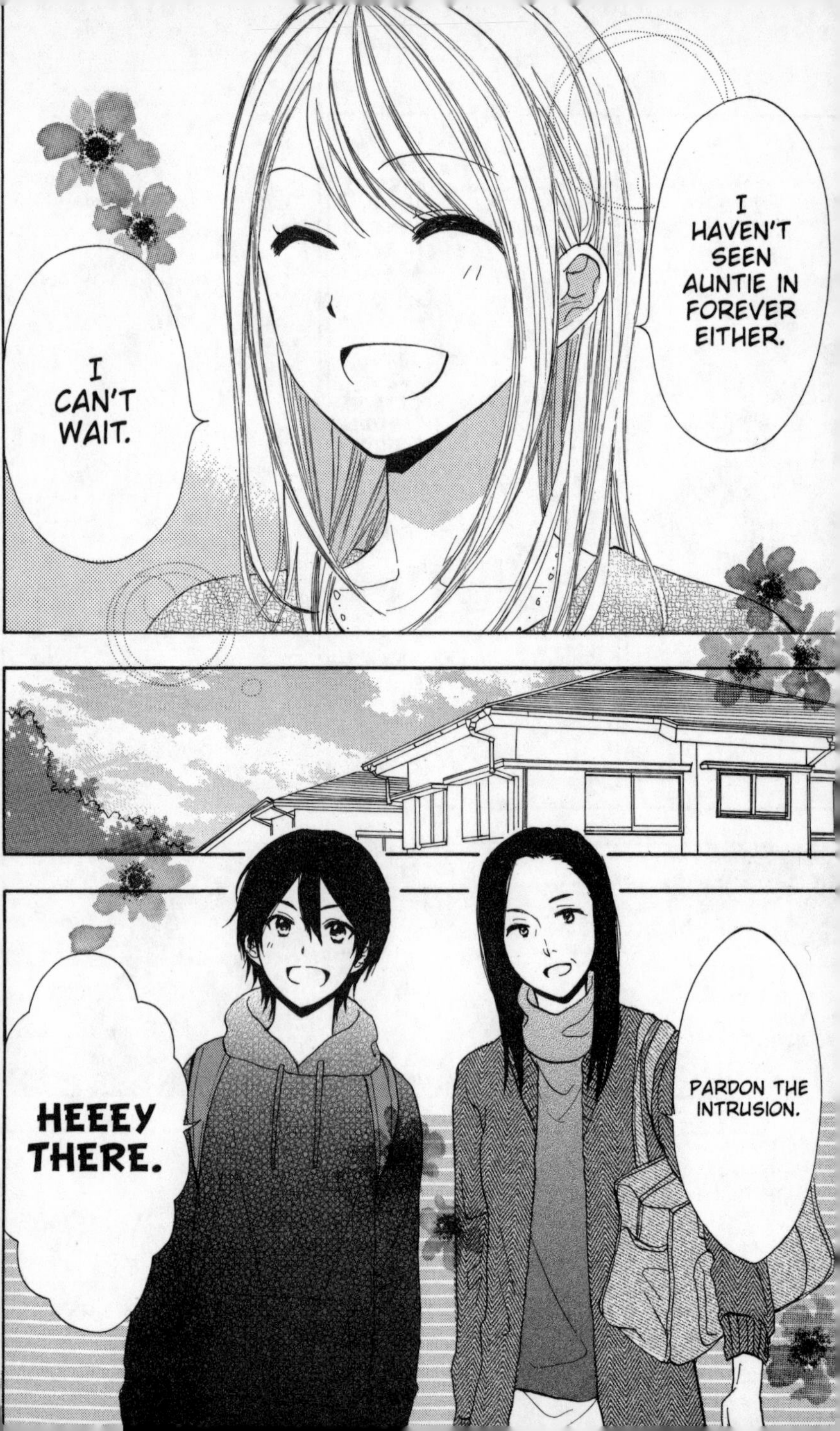
I HAVEN'T SEEN AUNTIE IN FOREVER EITHER.
I CAN'T WAIT.
PARDON THE INTRUSION.
HEEEY THERE.

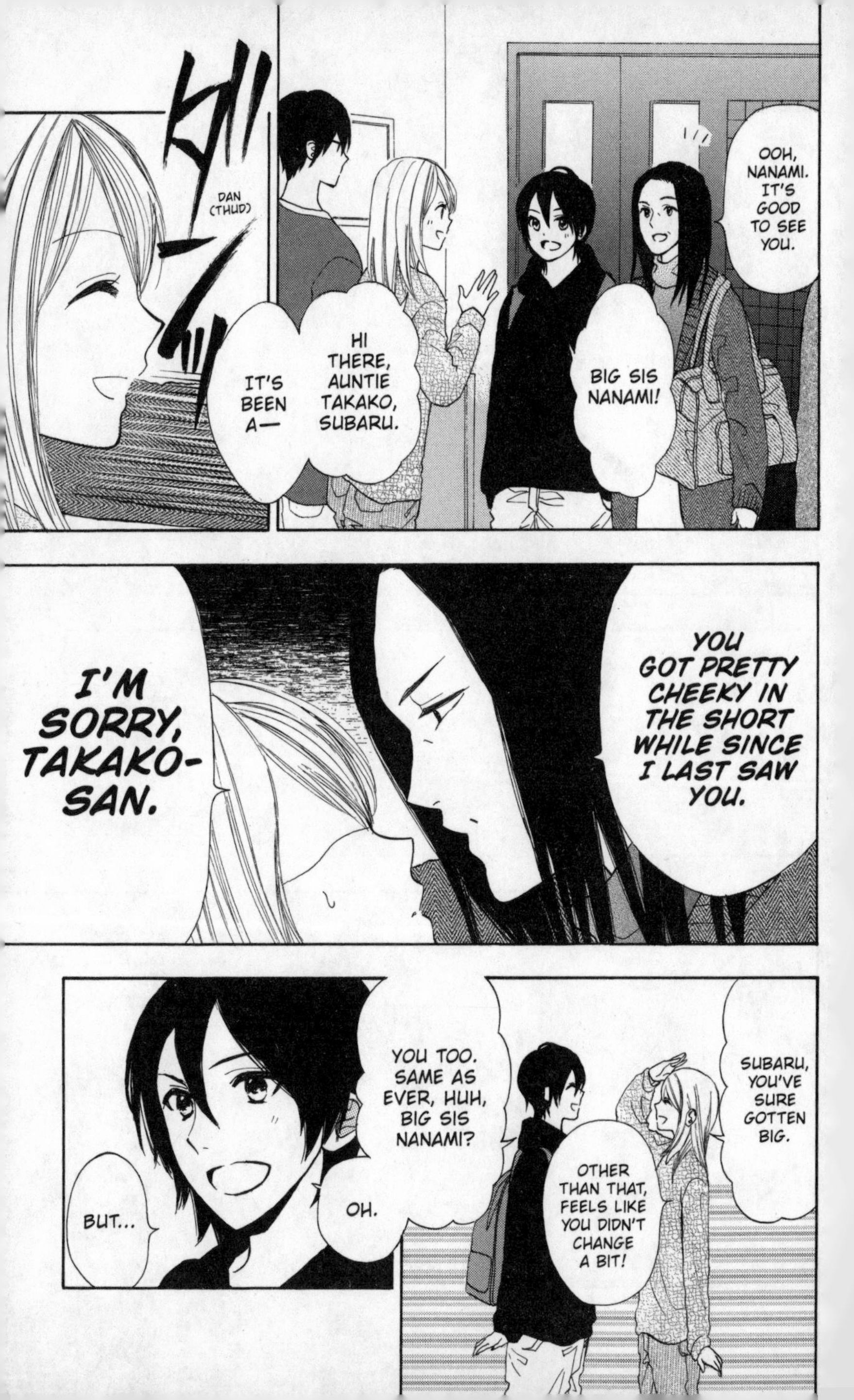
OOH, NANAMI. IT'S GOOD TO SEE YOU.
BIG SIS NANAMI!
HI THERE, AUNTIE TAKAKO, SUBARU.
IT'S BEEN A—
DAN (THUD)
YOU GOT PRETTY CHEEKY IN THE SHORT WHILE SINCE I LAST SAW YOU.
I'M SORRY, TAKAKO-SAN.
SUBARU, YOU'VE SURE GOTTEN BIG.
OTHER THAN THAT, FEELS LIKE YOU DIDN'T CHANGE A BIT!
YOU TOO. SAME AS EVER, HUH, BIG SIS NANAMI?
OH.
BUT...

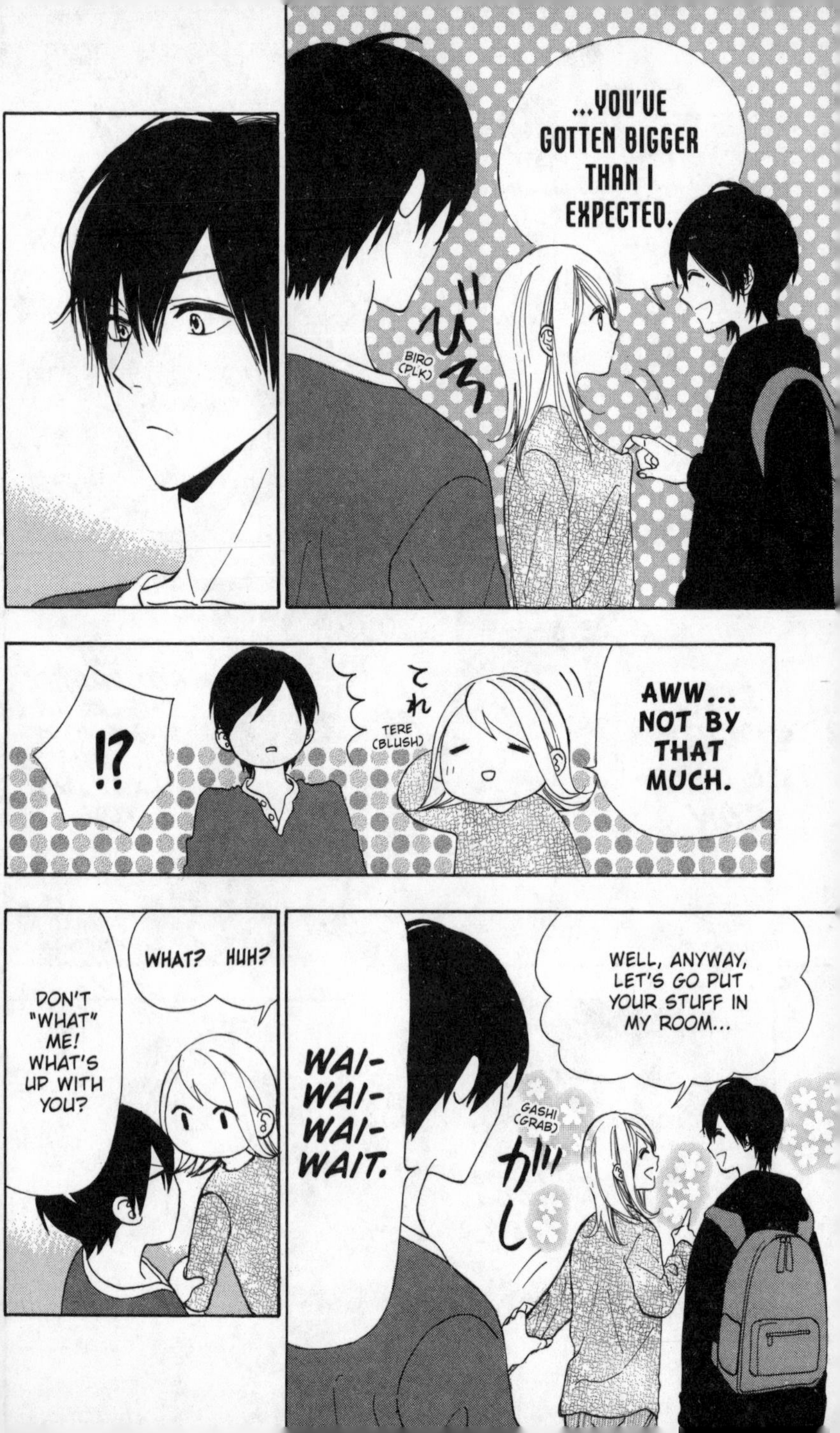
...YOU'VE GOTTEN BIGGER THAN I EXPECTED.
びろ
BIRO (PLK)
AWW... NOT BY THAT MUCH.
てれ
TERE (BLUSH)
!?
WELL, ANYWAY, LET'S GO PUT YOUR STUFF IN MY ROOM...
がし
GASHI (GRAB)
WAI-WAI-WAI-WAIT.
WHAT? HUH?
DON'T "WHAT" ME! WHAT'S UP WITH YOU?

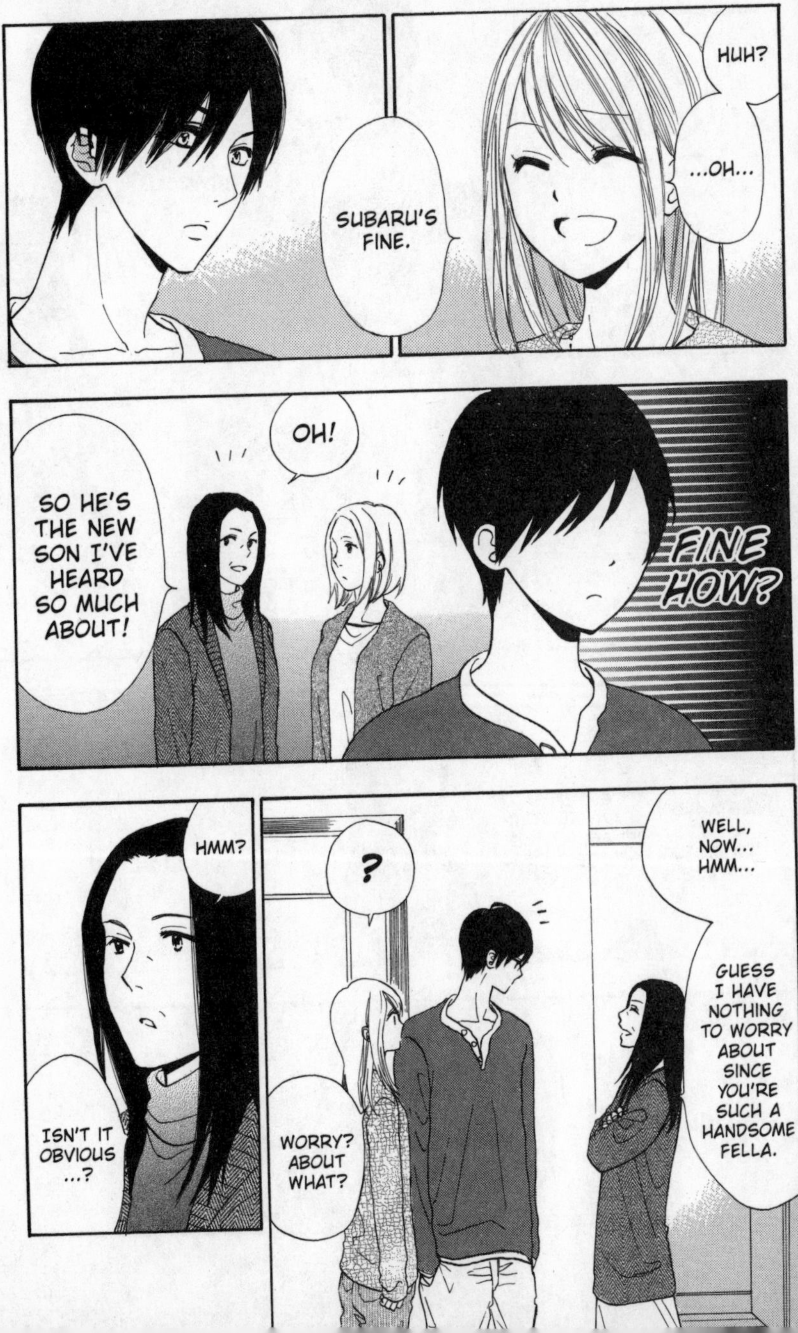
HUH?
...OH...
SUBARU'S FINE.
FINE HOW?
OH!
SO HE'S THE NEW SON I'VE HEARD SO MUCH ABOUT!
WELL, NOW... HMM...
GUESS I HAVE NOTHING TO WORRY ABOUT SINCE YOU'RE SUCH A HANDSOME FELLA.
?
WORRY? ABOUT WHAT?
HMM?
ISN'T IT OBVIOUS ...?

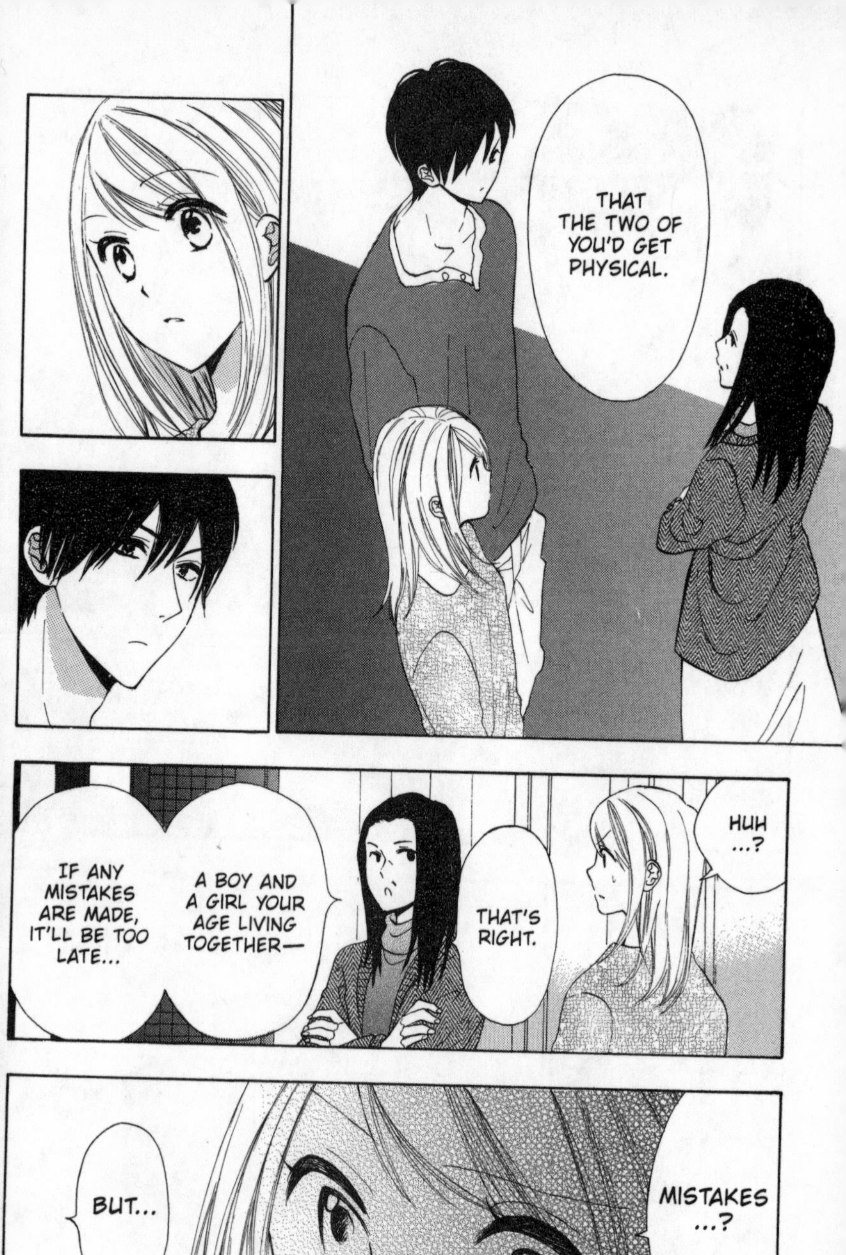
THAT THE TWO OF YOU'D GET PHYSICAL.
HUH ...?
THAT'S RIGHT.
A BOY AND A GIRL YOUR AGE LIVING TOGETHER—
IF ANY MISTAKES ARE MADE, IT'LL BE TOO LATE...
MISTAKES ...?
BUT...

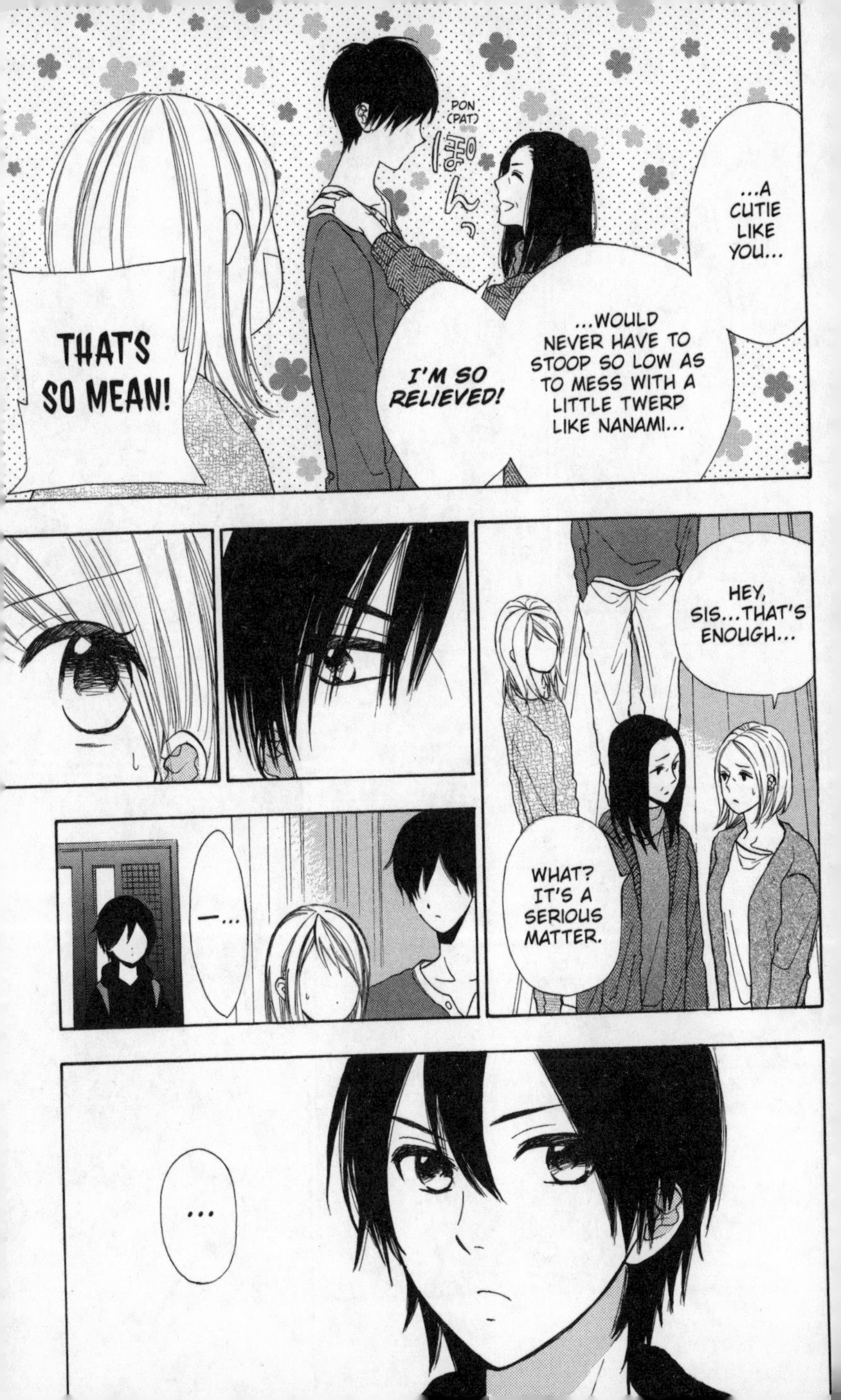
...A CUTIE LIKE YOU...
PON (PAT)
ぽん～っ
...WOULD NEVER HAVE TO STOOP SO LOW AS TO MESS WITH A LITTLE TWERP LIKE NANAMI...
I'M SO RELIEVED!
THAT'S SO MEAN!
HEY, SIS...THAT'S ENOUGH...
WHAT? IT'S A SERIOUS MATTER.
—...
...

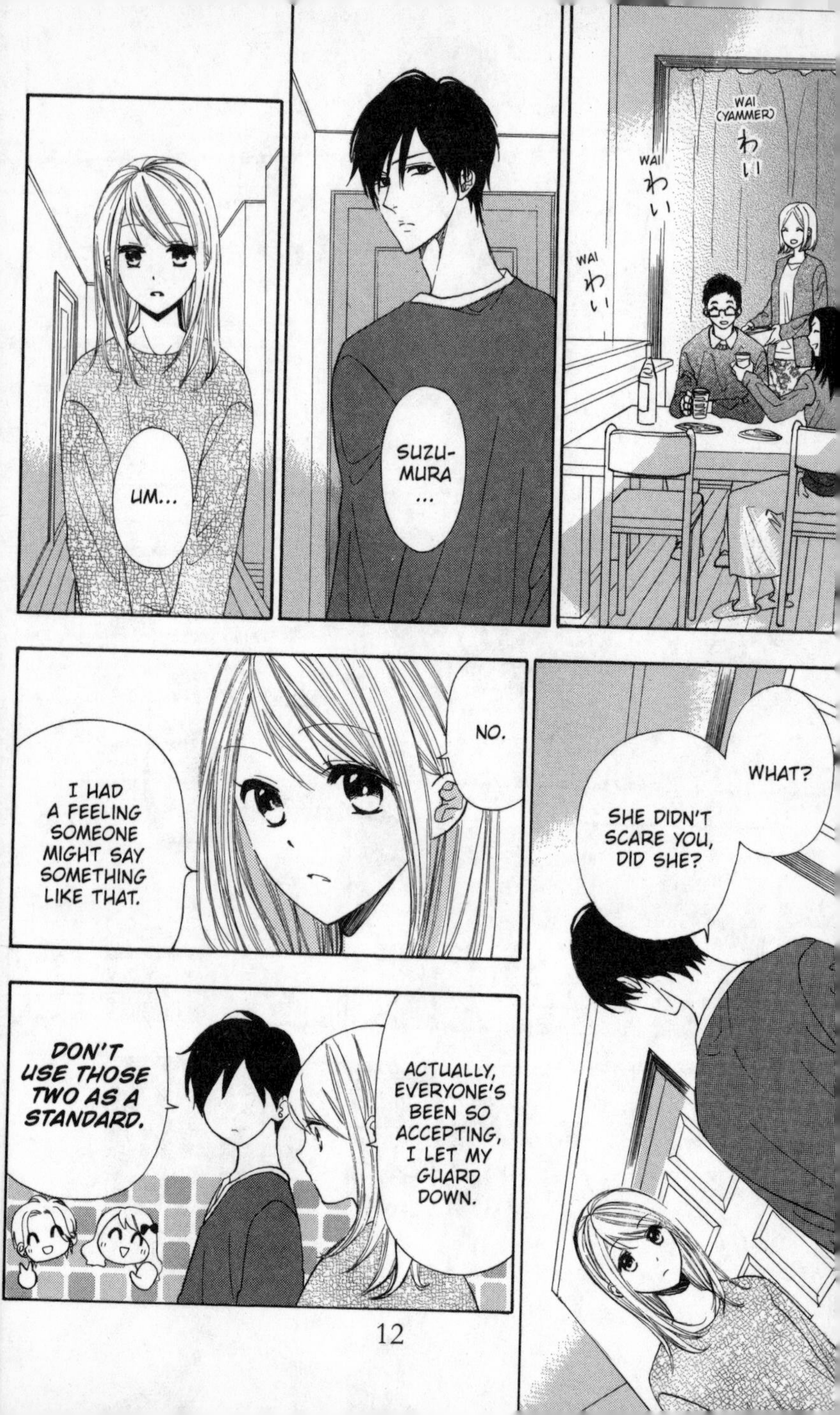

WAI (YAMMER) わい
WAI わい
WAI わい
SUZU-MURA...
UM...
WHAT?
SHE DIDN'T SCARE YOU, DID SHE?
NO.
I HAD A FEELING SOMEONE MIGHT SAY SOMETHING LIKE THAT.
ACTUALLY, EVERYONE'S BEEN SO ACCEPTING, I LET MY GUARD DOWN.
DON'T USE THOSE TWO AS A STANDARD.

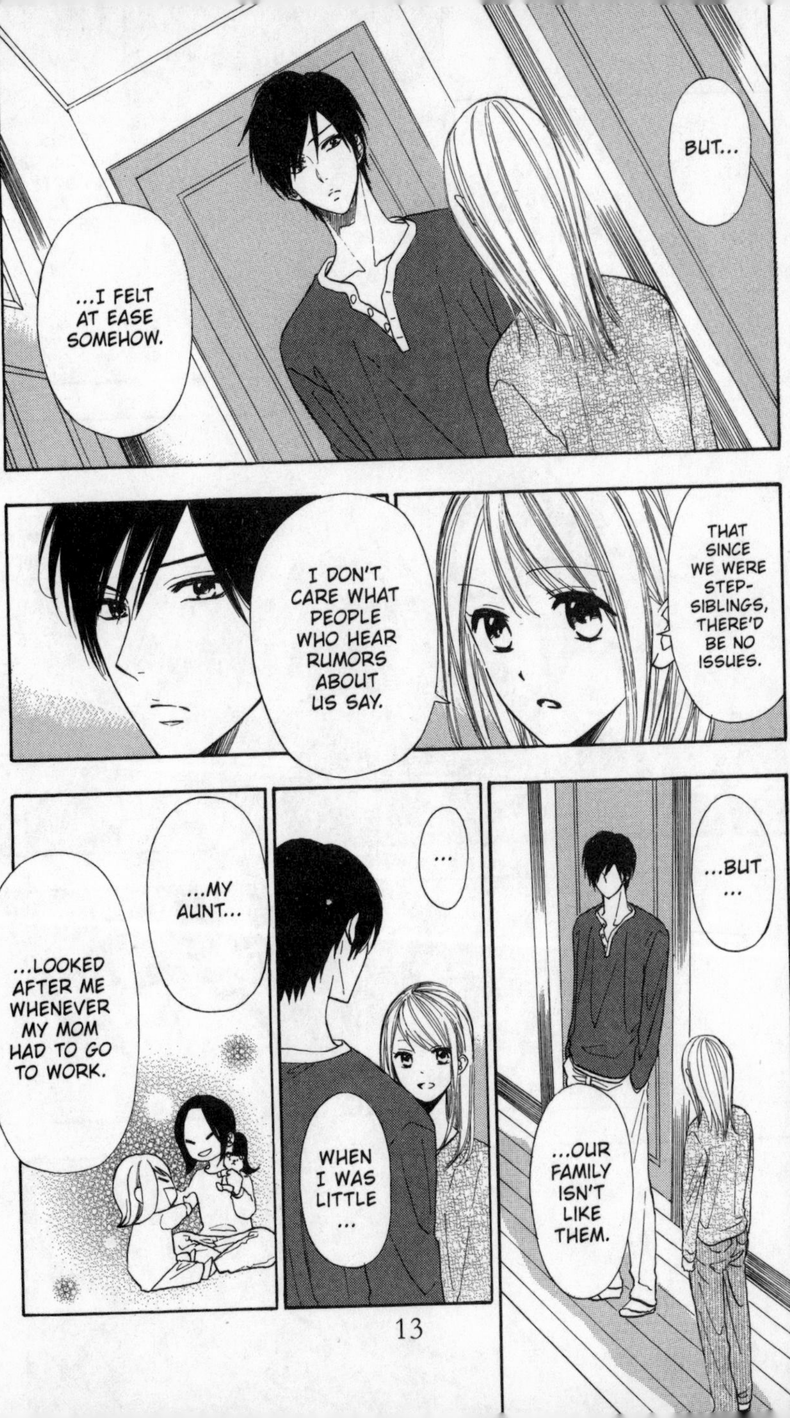

BUT...
...I FELT AT EASE SOMEHOW.
THAT SINCE WE WERE STEP-SIBLINGS, THERE'D BE NO ISSUES.
I DON'T CARE WHAT PEOPLE WHO HEAR RUMORS ABOUT US SAY.
...BUT...
...OUR FAMILY ISN'T LIKE THEM.
...
WHEN I WAS LITTLE...
...MY AUNT...
...LOOKED AFTER ME WHENEVER MY MOM HAD TO GO TO WORK.

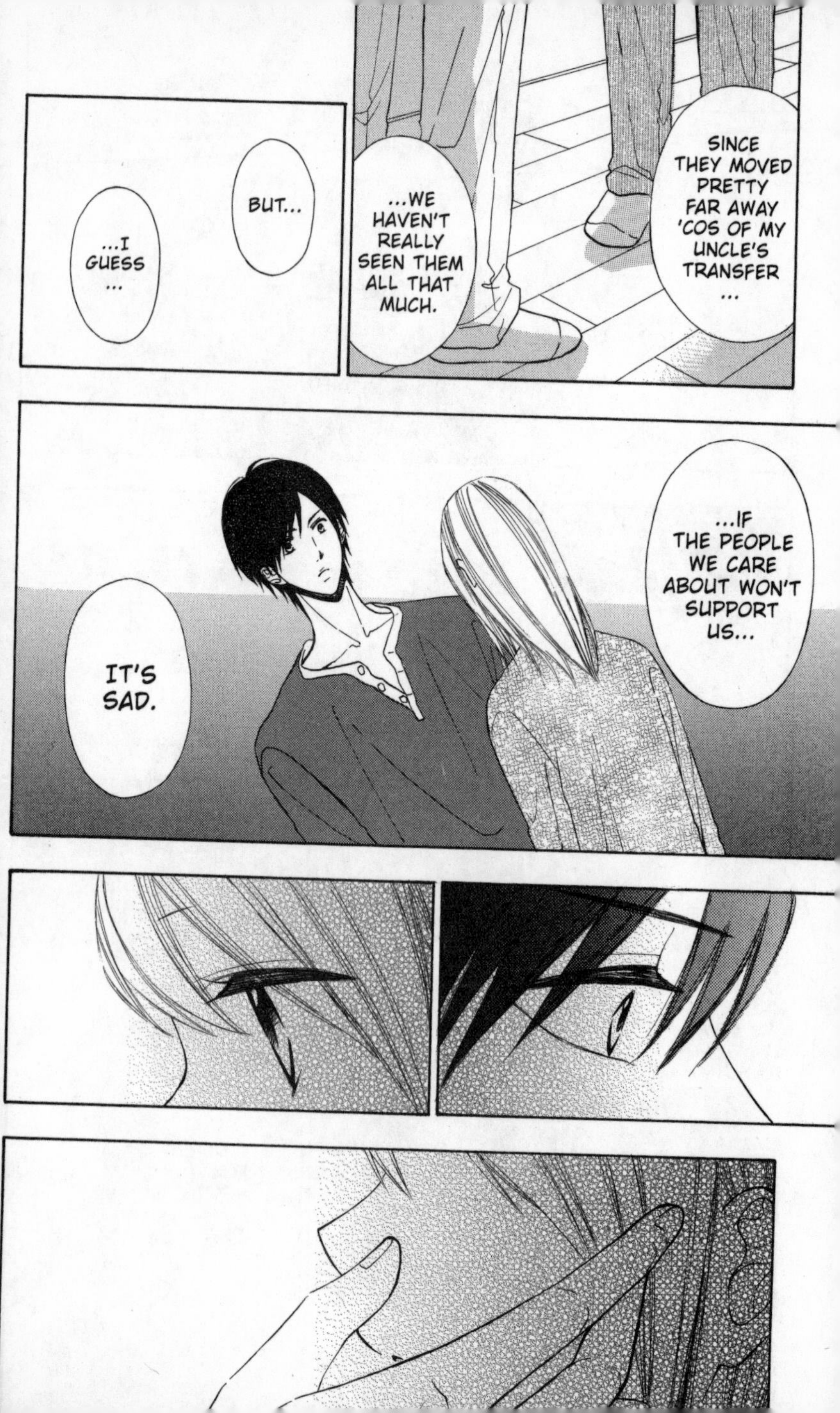
SINCE THEY MOVED PRETTY FAR AWAY 'COS OF MY UNCLE'S TRANSFER...
...WE HAVEN'T REALLY SEEN THEM ALL THAT MUCH.
BUT...
...I GUESS...
...IF THE PEOPLE WE CARE ABOUT WON'T SUPPORT US...
IT'S SAD.

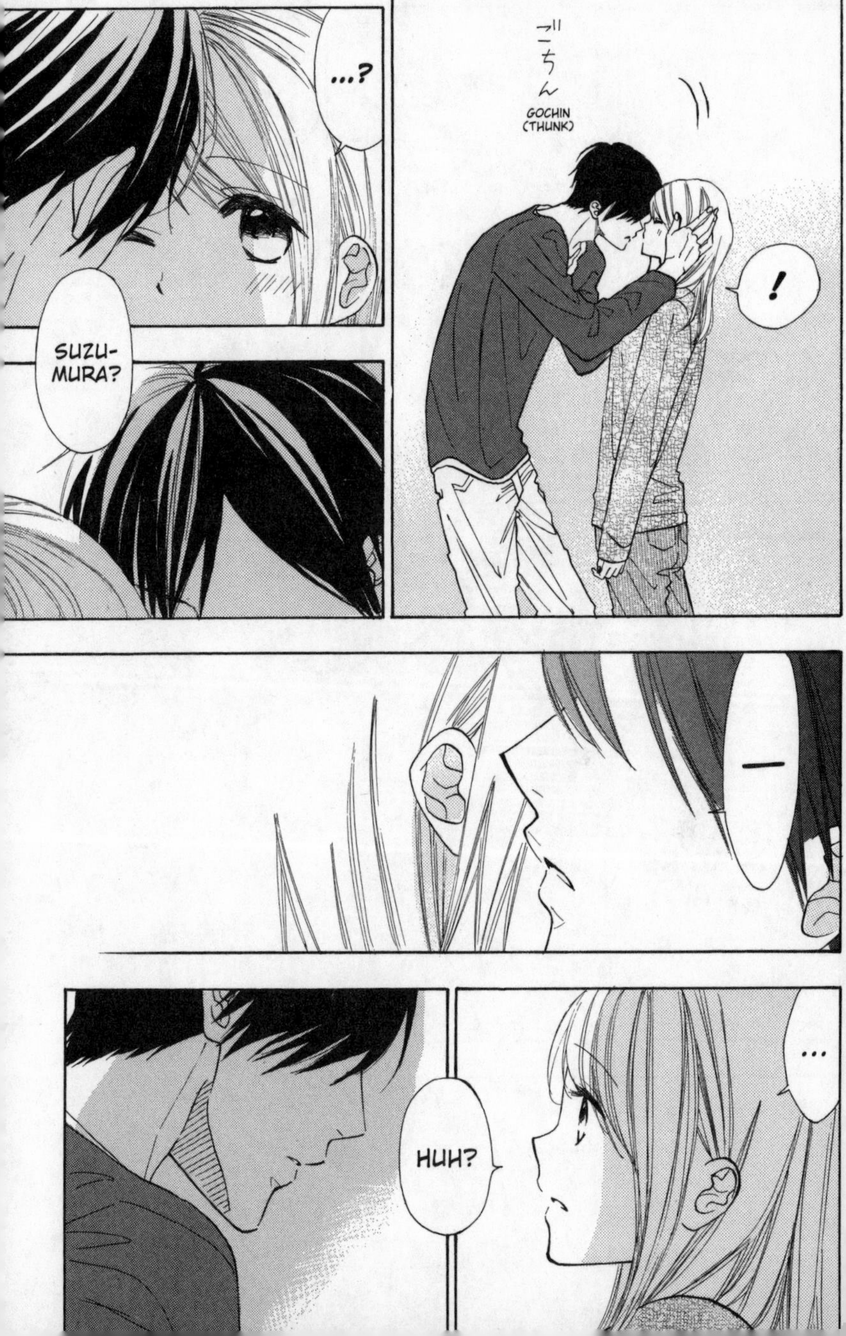
ごちん
GOCHIN (THUNK)
!
...?
SUZU-MURA?
...
HUH?

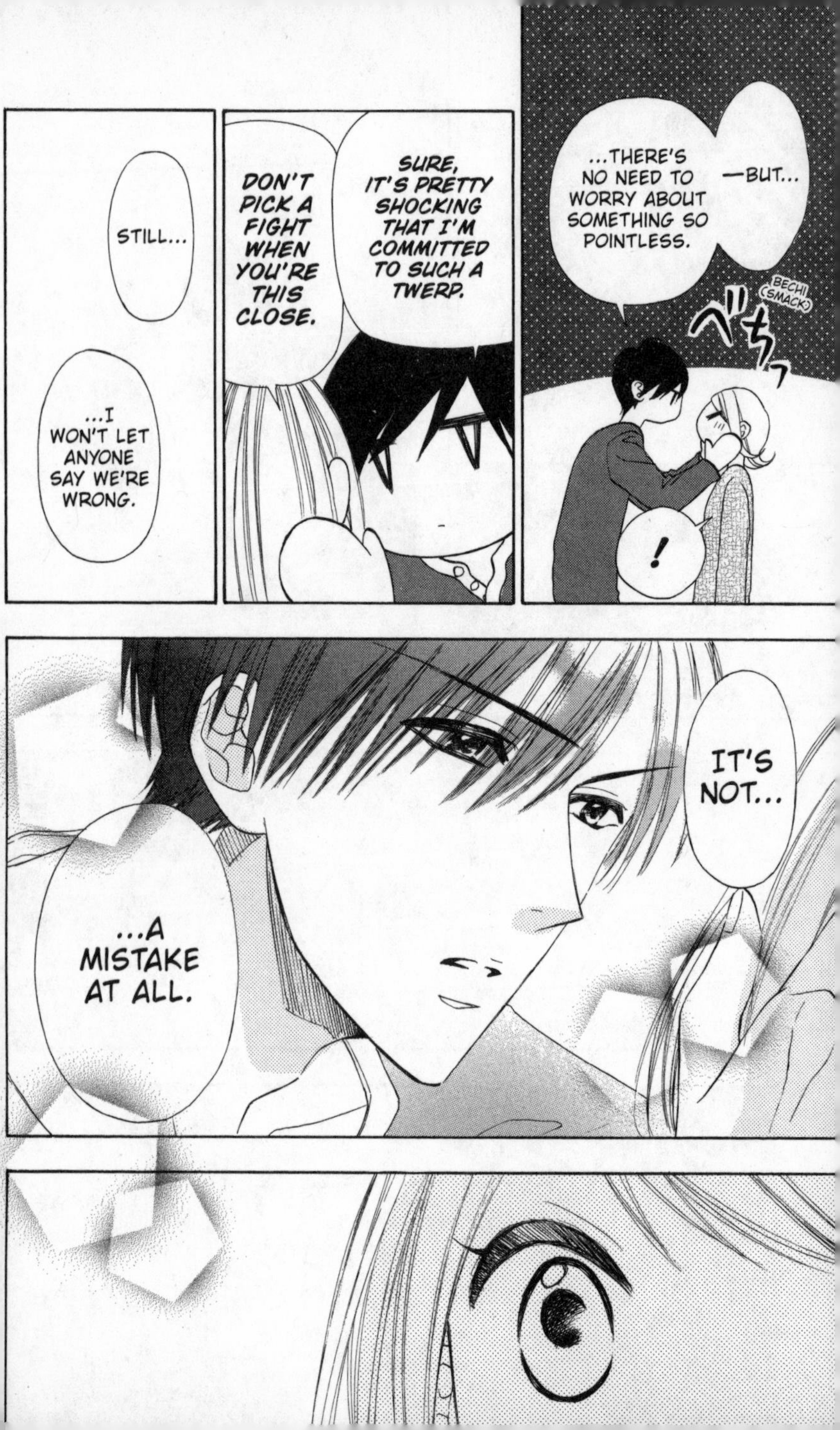
—BUT...
...THERE'S NO NEED TO WORRY ABOUT SOMETHING SO POINTLESS.
BECHI (SMACK)
!
SURE, IT'S PRETTY SHOCKING THAT I'M COMMITTED TO SUCH A TWERP.
DON'T PICK A FIGHT WHEN YOU'RE THIS CLOSE.
STILL...
...I WON'T LET ANYONE SAY WE'RE WRONG.
IT'S NOT...
...A MISTAKE AT ALL.

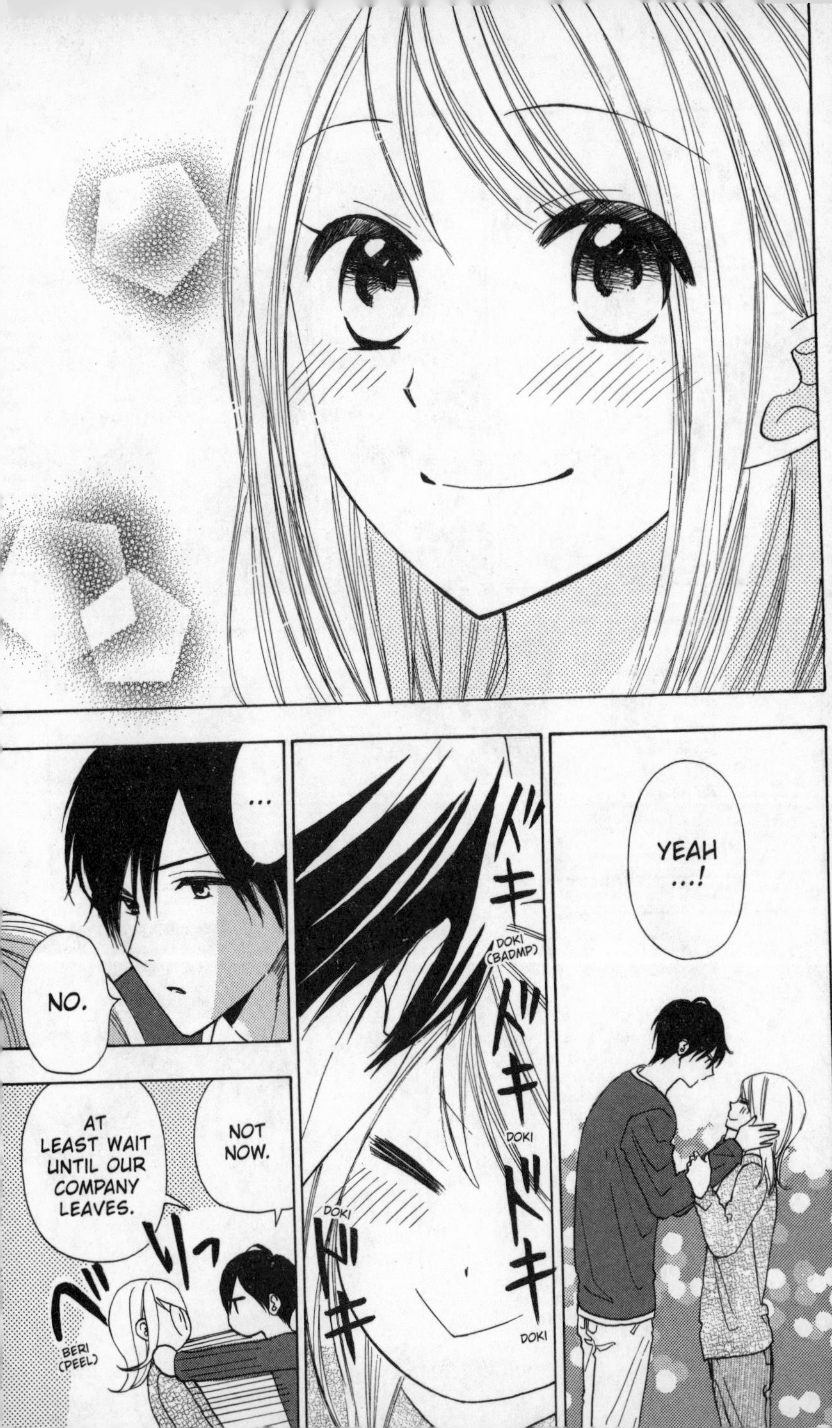
YEAH ...!
DOKI (BADMP)
DOKI
DOKI
DOKI
...
NO.
NOT NOW.
AT LEAST WAIT UNTIL OUR COMPANY LEAVES.
BERI (PEEL)

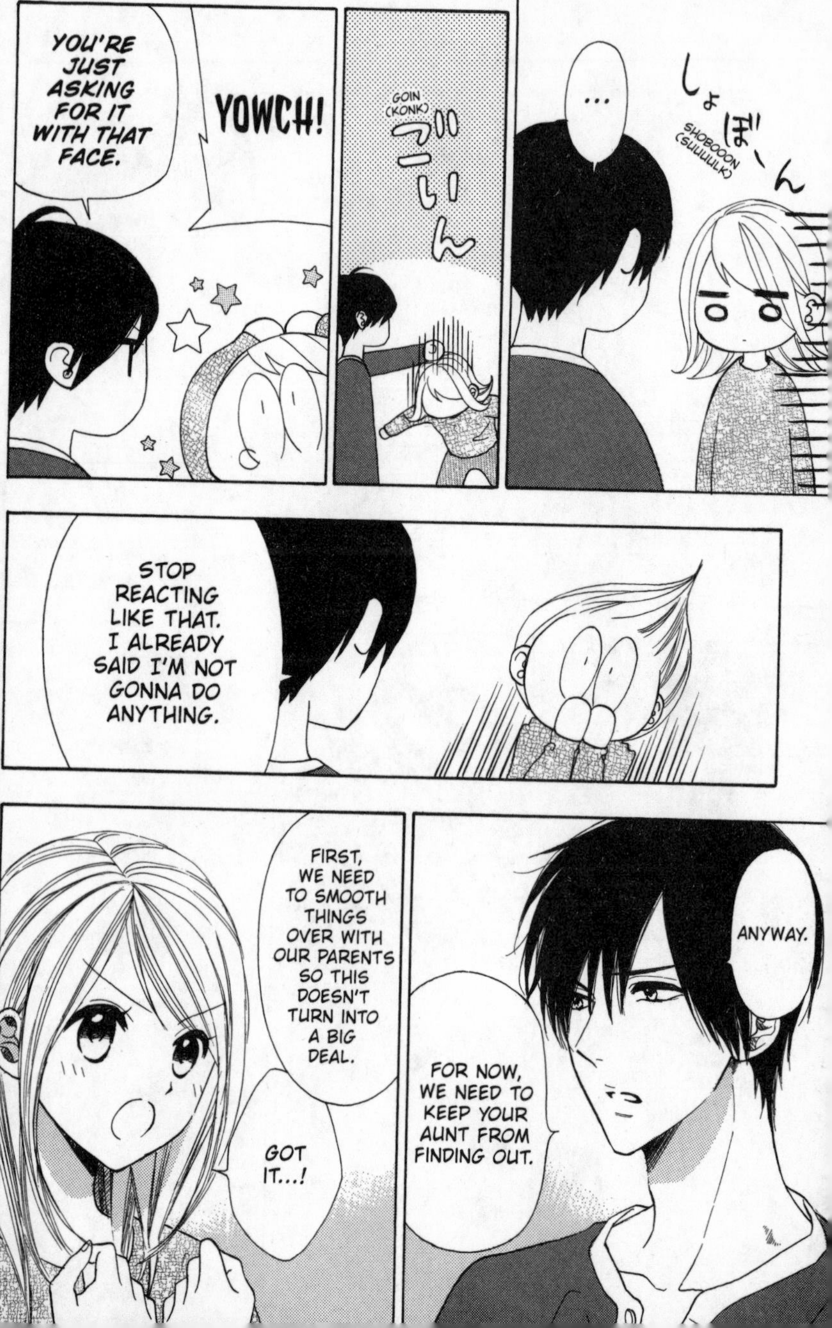
...
しょぼーん
SHOBOOON (SUUUULK)
ごいーん
GOIN (KONK)
YOWCH!
YOU'RE JUST ASKING FOR IT WITH THAT FACE.
STOP REACTING LIKE THAT. I ALREADY SAID I'M NOT GONNA DO ANYTHING.
ANYWAY.
FOR NOW, WE NEED TO KEEP YOUR AUNT FROM FINDING OUT.
FIRST, WE NEED TO SMOOTH THINGS OVER WITH OUR PARENTS SO THIS DOESN'T TURN INTO A BIG DEAL.
GOT IT...!

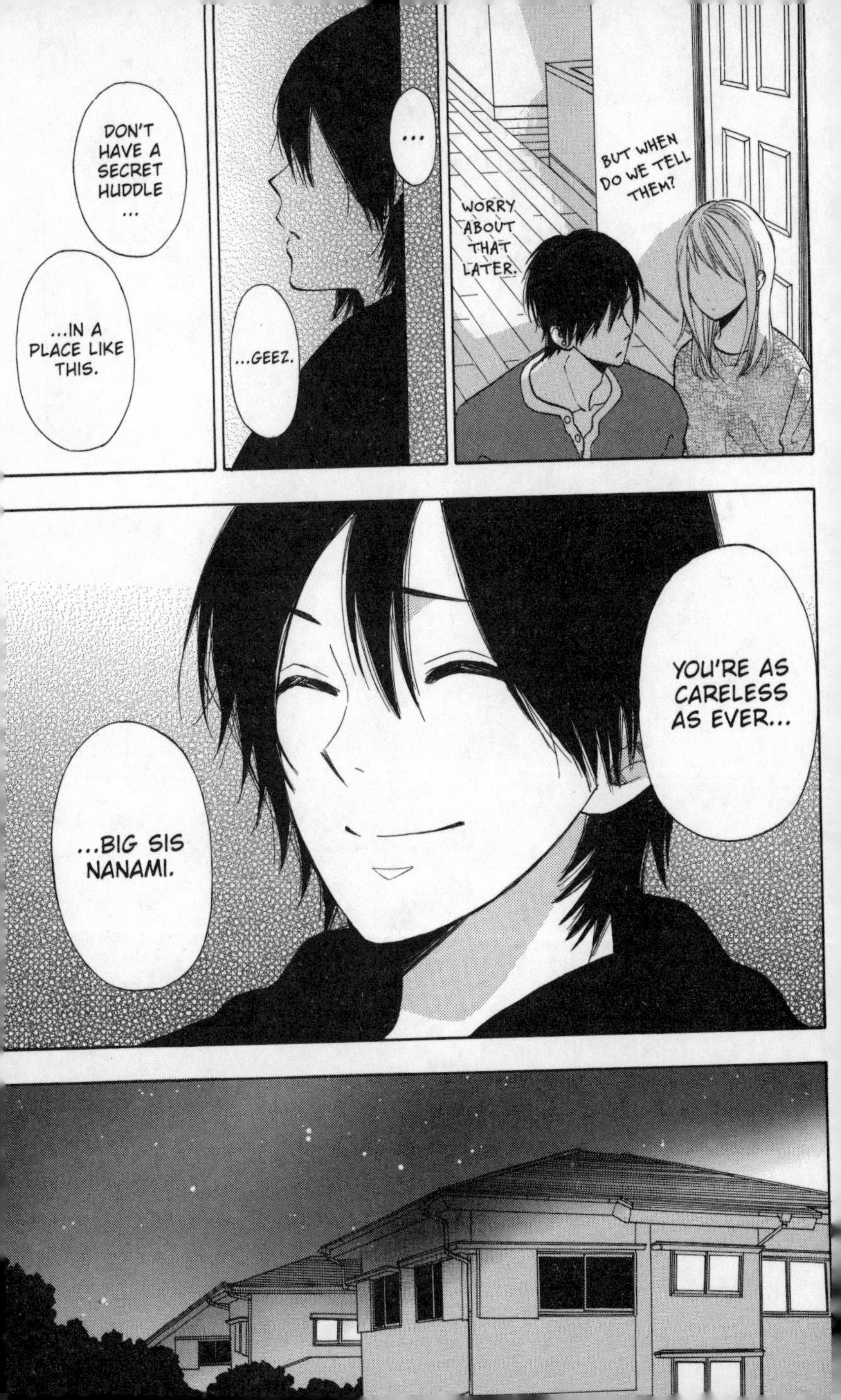
BUT WHEN DO WE TELL THEM?
WORRY ABOUT THAT LATER.
...
...GEEZ.
DON'T HAVE A SECRET HUDDLE ...
...IN A PLACE LIKE THIS.
YOU'RE AS CARELESS AS EVER...
...BIG SIS NANAMI.

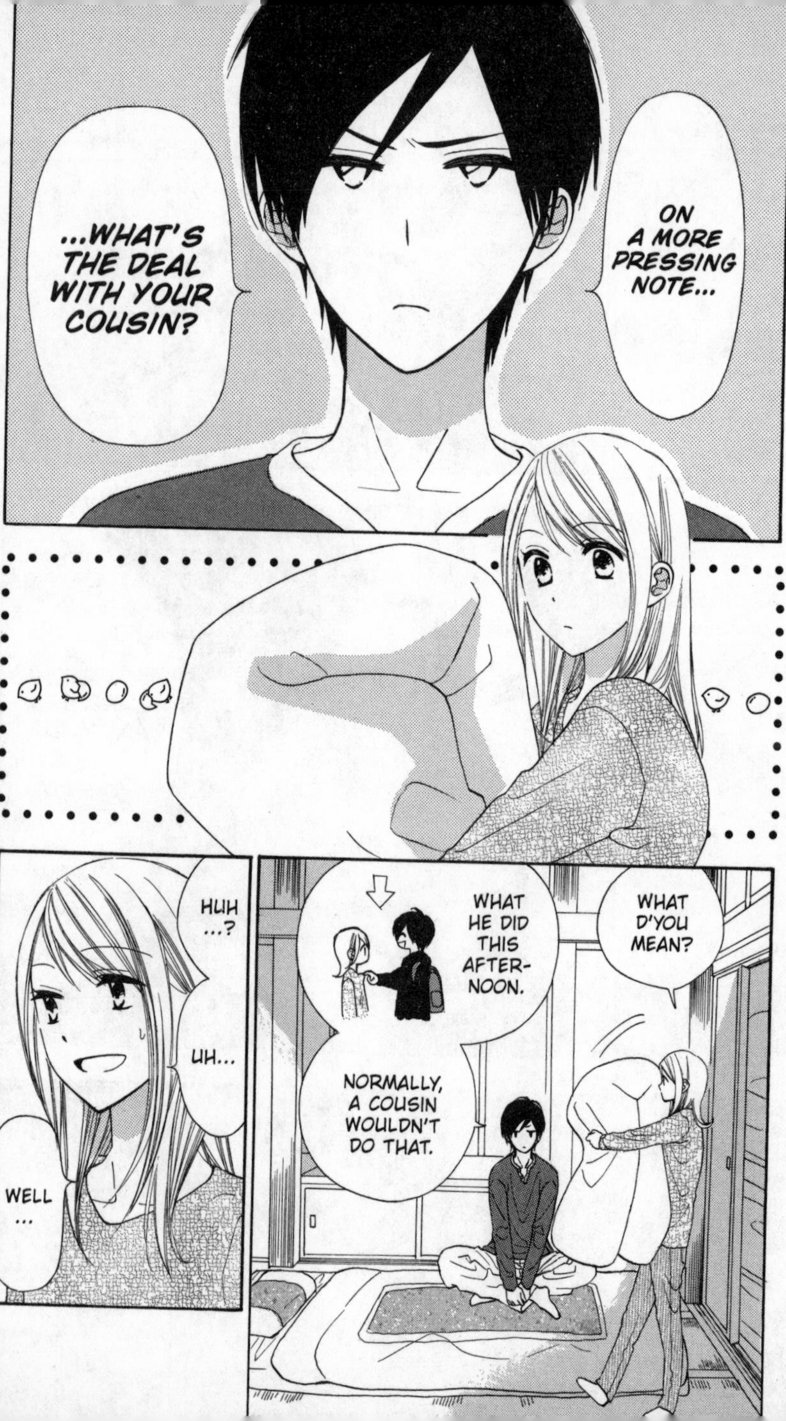
ON A MORE PRESSING NOTE...
...WHAT'S THE DEAL WITH YOUR COUSIN?
WHAT D'YOU MEAN?
WHAT HE DID THIS AFTER-NOON.
NORMALLY, A COUSIN WOULDN'T DO THAT.
HUH ...?
UH...
WELL ...

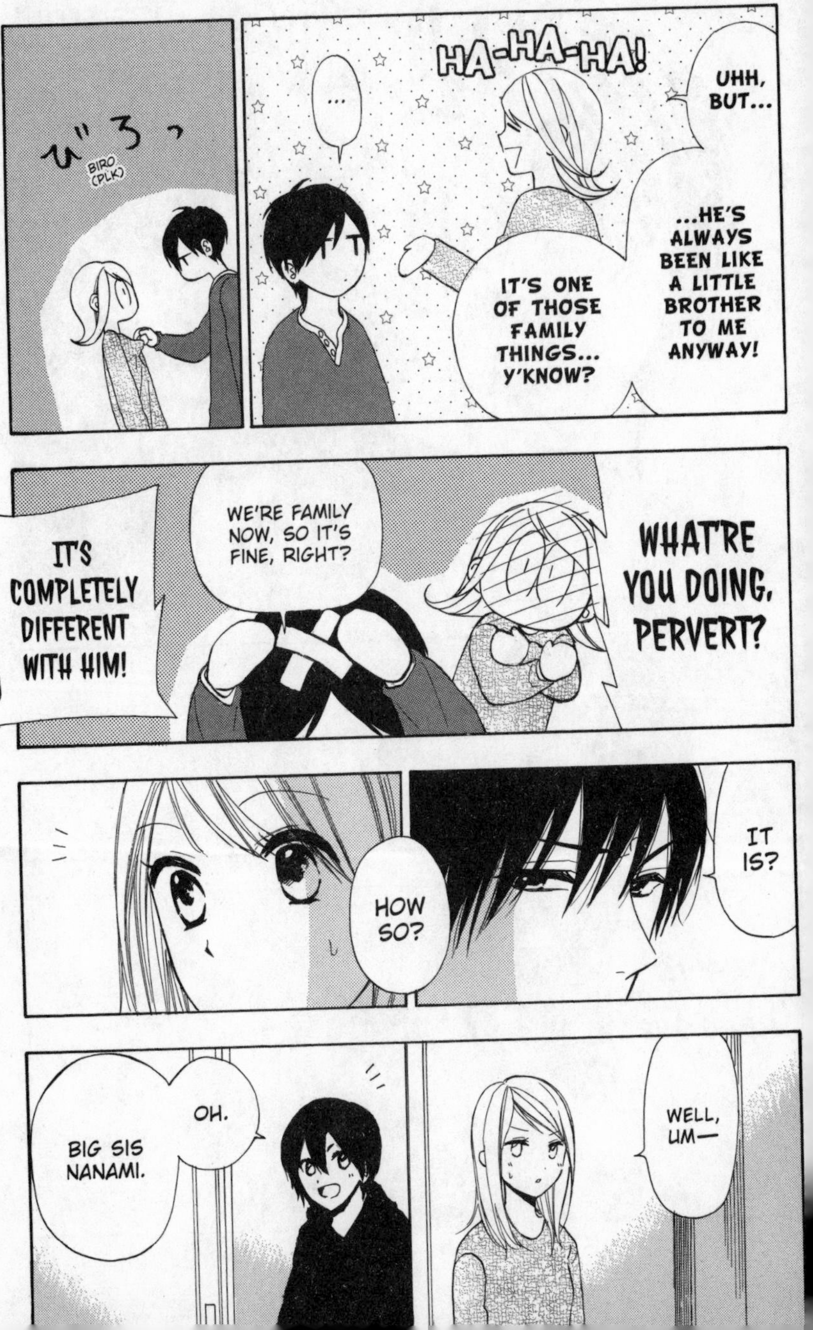
UHH, BUT...
HA-HA-HA!
...HE'S ALWAYS BEEN LIKE A LITTLE BROTHER TO ME ANYWAY!
IT'S ONE OF THOSE FAMILY THINGS... Y'KNOW?
...
びろっ
BIRO (PLK)
WHAT'RE YOU DOING, PERVERT?
WE'RE FAMILY NOW, SO IT'S FINE, RIGHT?
IT'S COMPLETELY DIFFERENT WITH HIM!
IT IS?
HOW SO?
WELL, UM—
OH.
BIG SIS NANAMI.

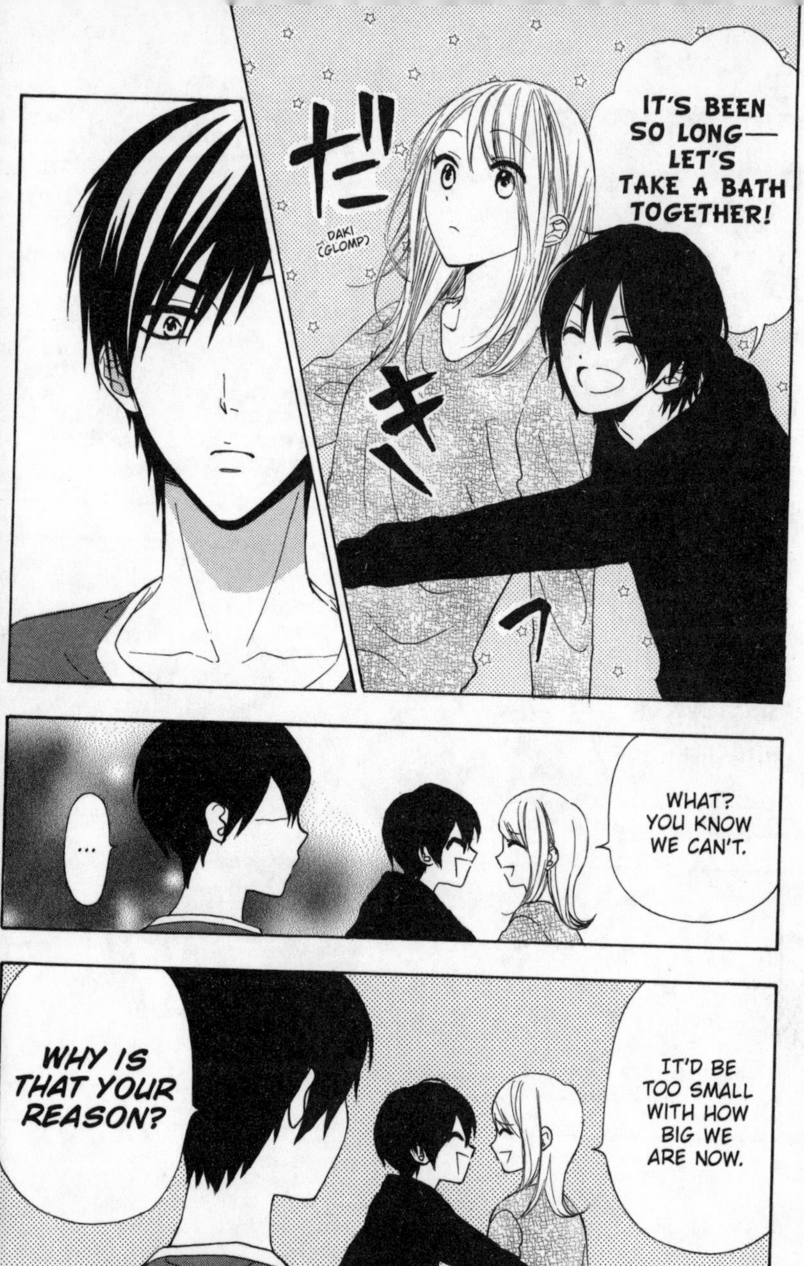
IT'S BEEN SO LONG—LET'S TAKE A BATH TOGETHER!
DAKI (GLOMP)
WHAT? YOU KNOW WE CAN'T.
...
IT'D BE TOO SMALL WITH HOW BIG WE ARE NOW.
WHY IS THAT YOUR REASON?

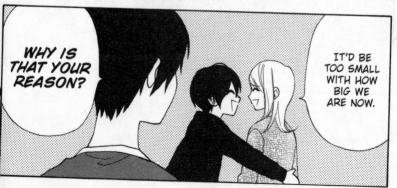

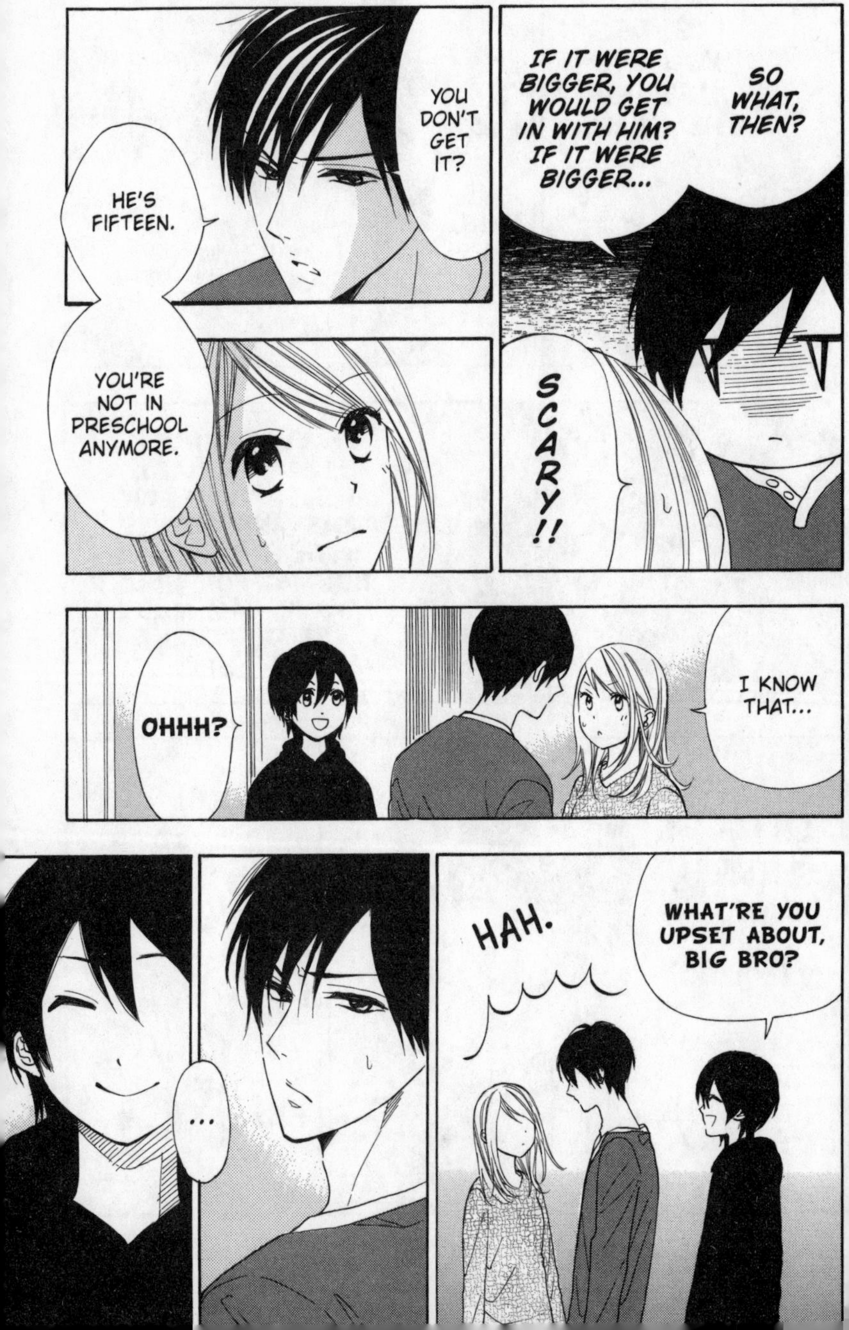
SO WHAT, THEN?
IF IT WERE BIGGER, YOU WOULD GET IN WITH HIM? IF IT WERE BIGGER...
SCARY!!
YOU DON'T GET IT?
HE'S FIFTEEN.
YOU'RE NOT IN PRESCHOOL ANYMORE.
I KNOW THAT...
OHHH?
WHAT'RE YOU UPSET ABOUT, BIG BRO?
HAH.
...

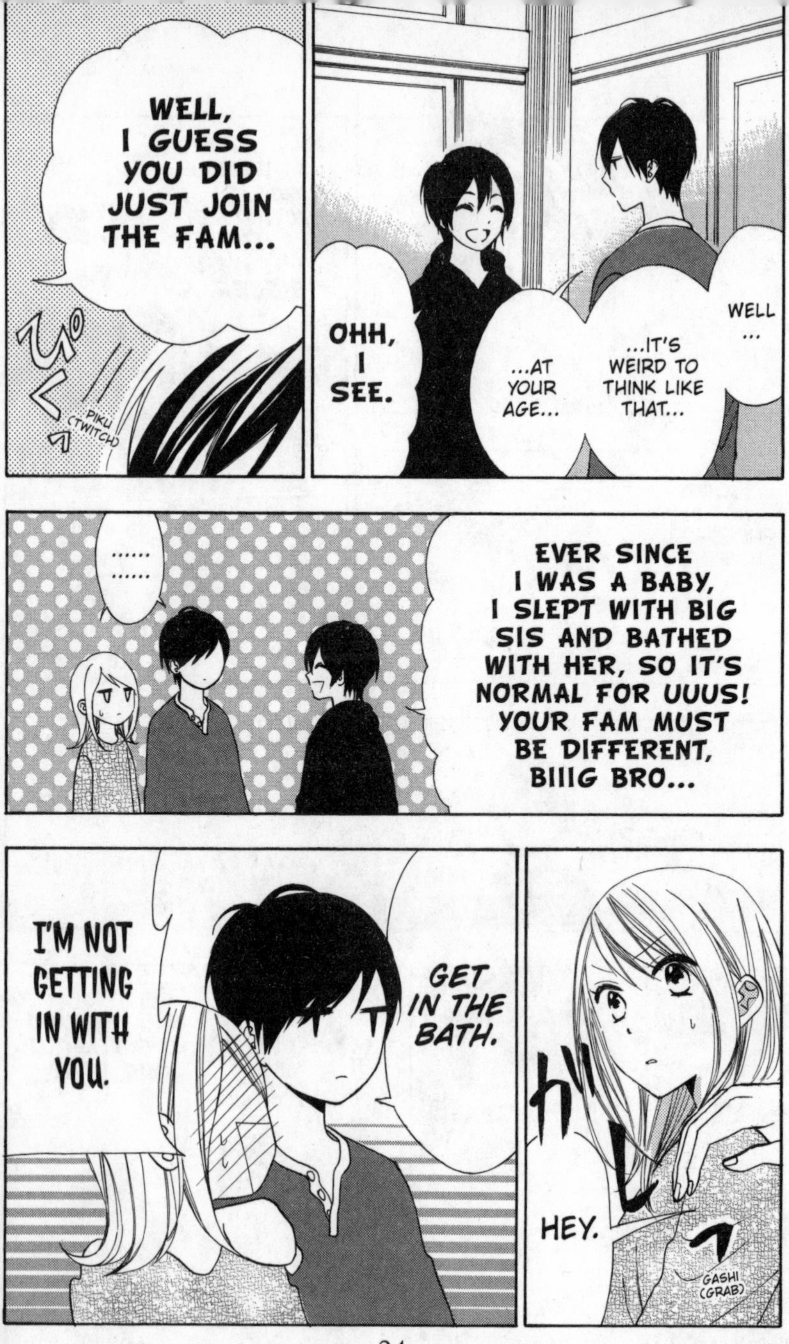
WELL...
...IT'S WEIRD TO THINK LIKE THAT...
...AT YOUR AGE...
OHH, I SEE.
WELL, I GUESS YOU DID JUST JOIN THE FAM...
PIKU (TWITCH)
EVER SINCE I WAS A BABY, I SLEPT WITH BIG SIS AND BATHED WITH HER, SO IT'S NORMAL FOR UUUS! YOUR FAM MUST BE DIFFERENT, BIIIG BRO...
......
......
HEY.
GASHI (GRAB)
GET IN THE BATH.
I'M NOT GETTING IN WITH YOU.

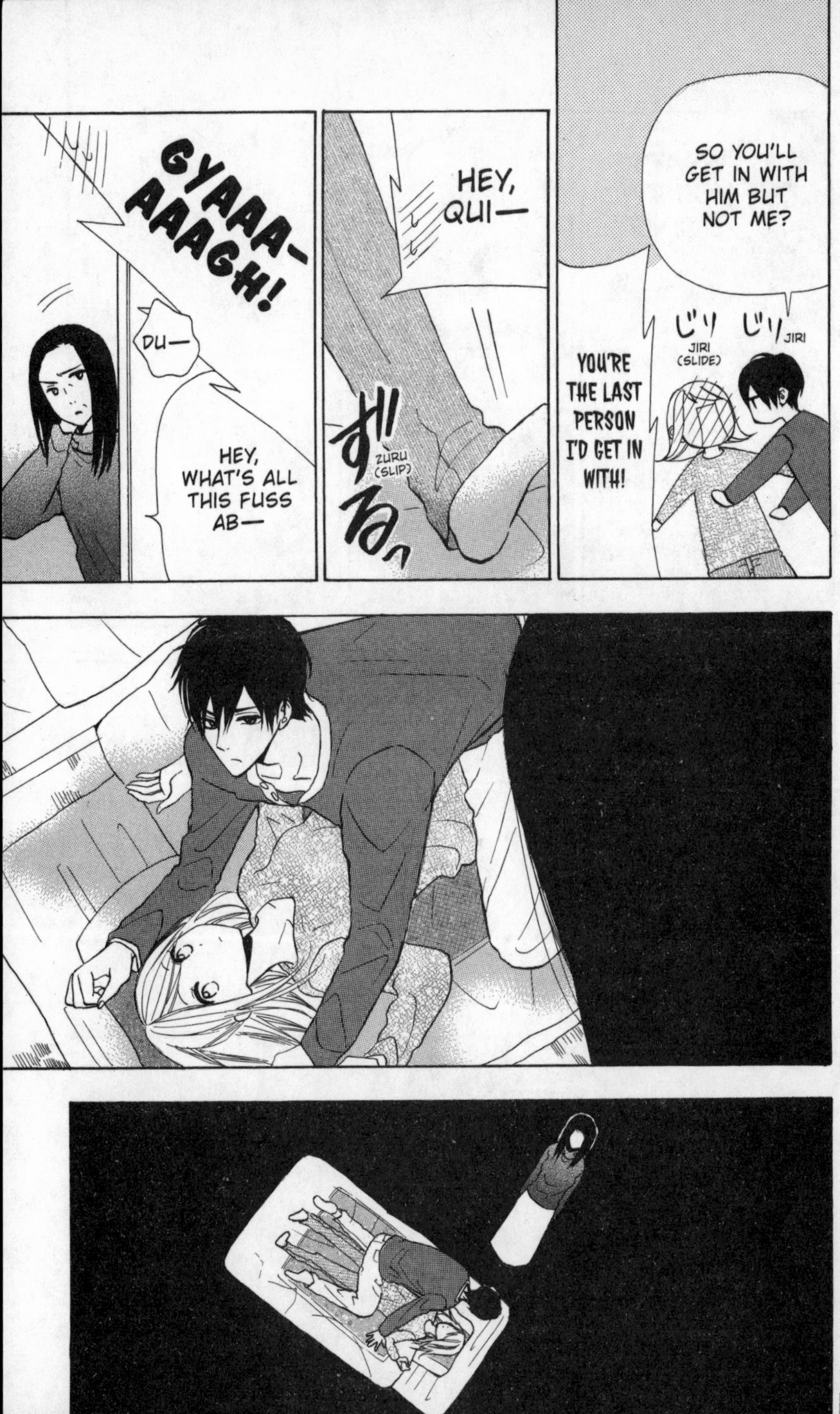
SO YOU'LL GET IN WITH HIM BUT NOT ME?
じり
JIRI (SLIDE)
じり
JIRI
YOU'RE THE LAST PERSON I'D GET IN WITH!
HEY, QUI—
ずる
ZURU (SLIP)
GYAAAA-AAAGH!
DU—
HEY, WHAT'S ALL THIS FUSS AB—

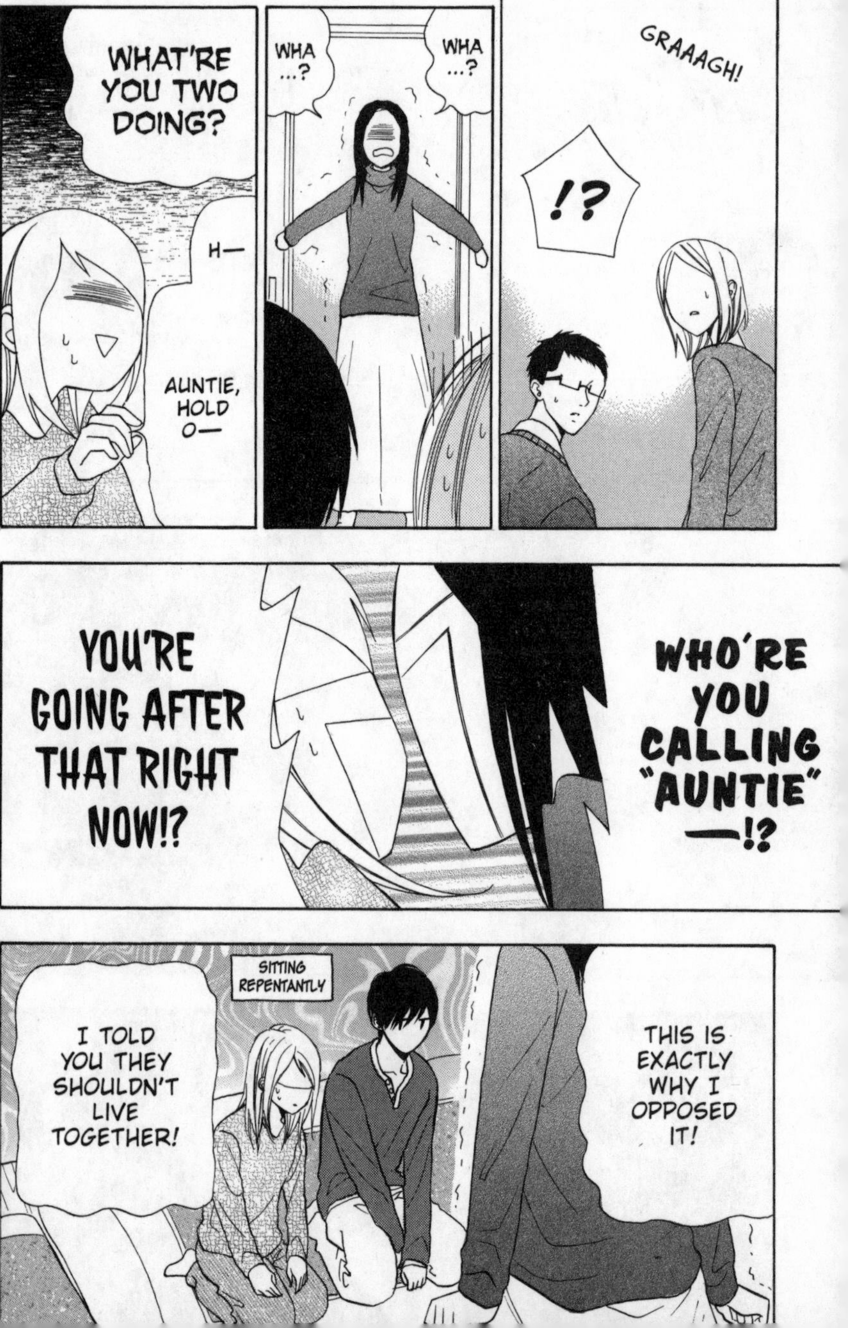
GRAAAGH!
!?
WHA ...?
WHA ...?
WHAT'RE YOU TWO DOING?
H—
AUNTIE, HOLD O—
WHO'RE YOU CALLING "AUNTIE" —!?
YOU'RE GOING AFTER THAT RIGHT NOW!?
THIS IS EXACTLY WHY I OPPOSED IT!
SITTING REPENTANTLY
I TOLD YOU THEY SHOULDN'T LIVE TOGETHER!

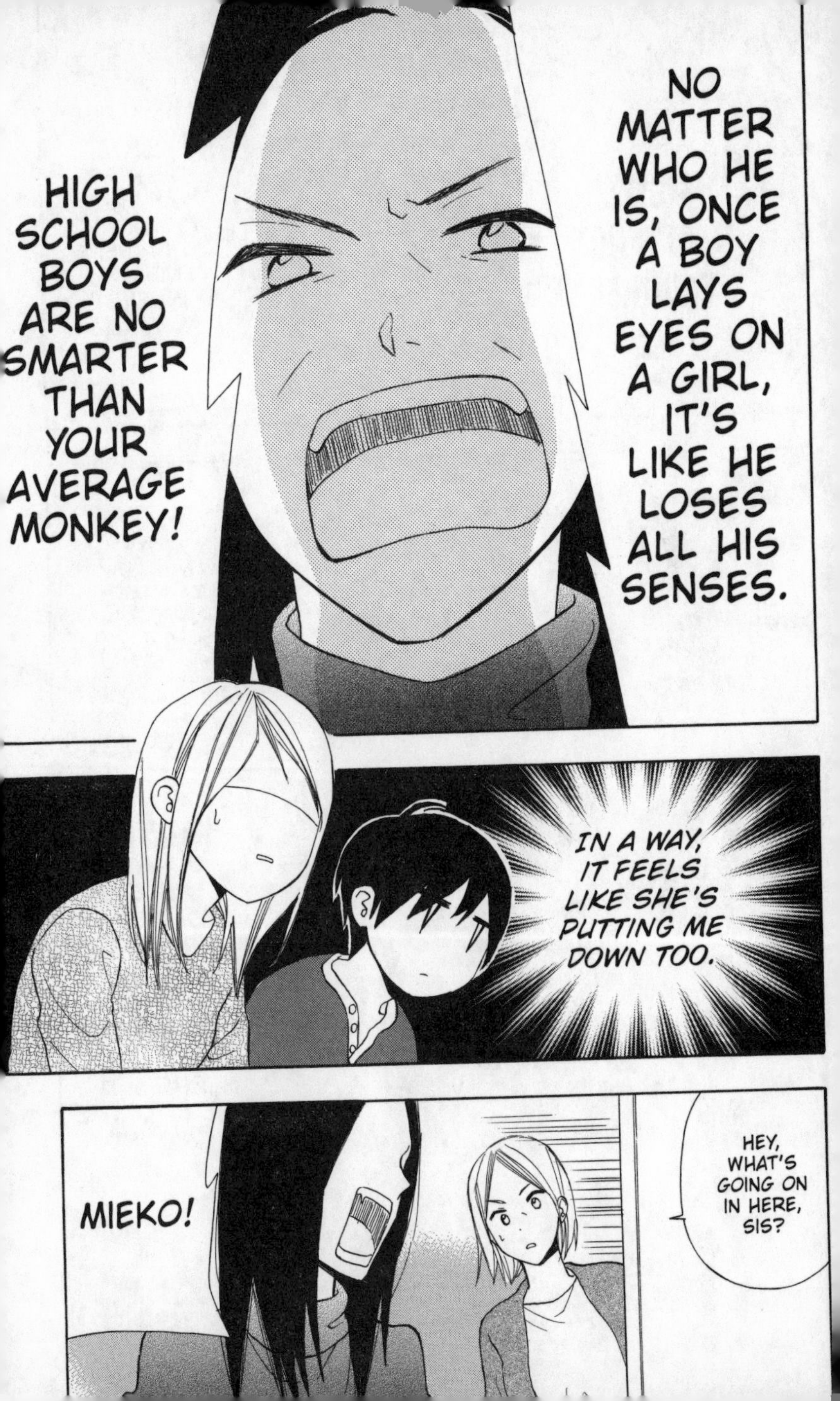
NO MATTER WHO HE IS, ONCE A BOY LAYS EYES ON A GIRL, IT'S LIKE HE LOSES ALL HIS SENSES.
HIGH SCHOOL BOYS ARE NO SMARTER THAN YOUR AVERAGE MONKEY!
IN A WAY, IT FEELS LIKE SHE'S PUTTING ME DOWN TOO.
HEY, WHAT'S GOING ON IN HERE, SIS?
MIEKO!

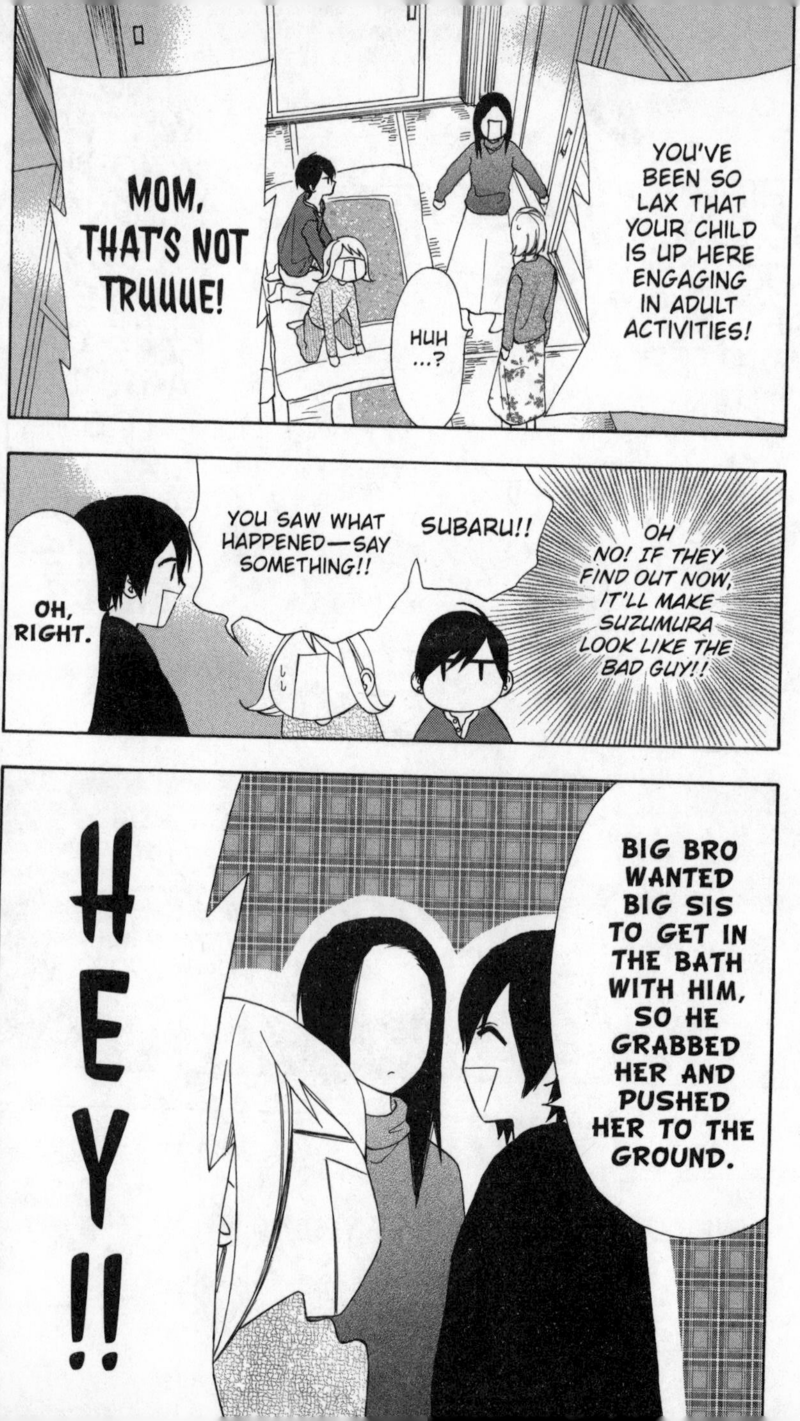
YOU'VE BEEN SO LAX THAT YOUR CHILD IS UP HERE ENGAGING IN ADULT ACTIVITIES!
HUH ...?
MOM, THAT'S NOT TRUUUE!
OH NO! IF THEY FIND OUT NOW, IT'LL MAKE SUZUMURA LOOK LIKE THE BAD GUY!!
SUBARU!!
YOU SAW WHAT HAPPENED—SAY SOMETHING!!
OH, RIGHT.
BIG BRO WANTED BIG SIS TO GET IN THE BATH WITH HIM, SO HE GRABBED HER AND PUSHED HER TO THE GROUND.
HEY!!

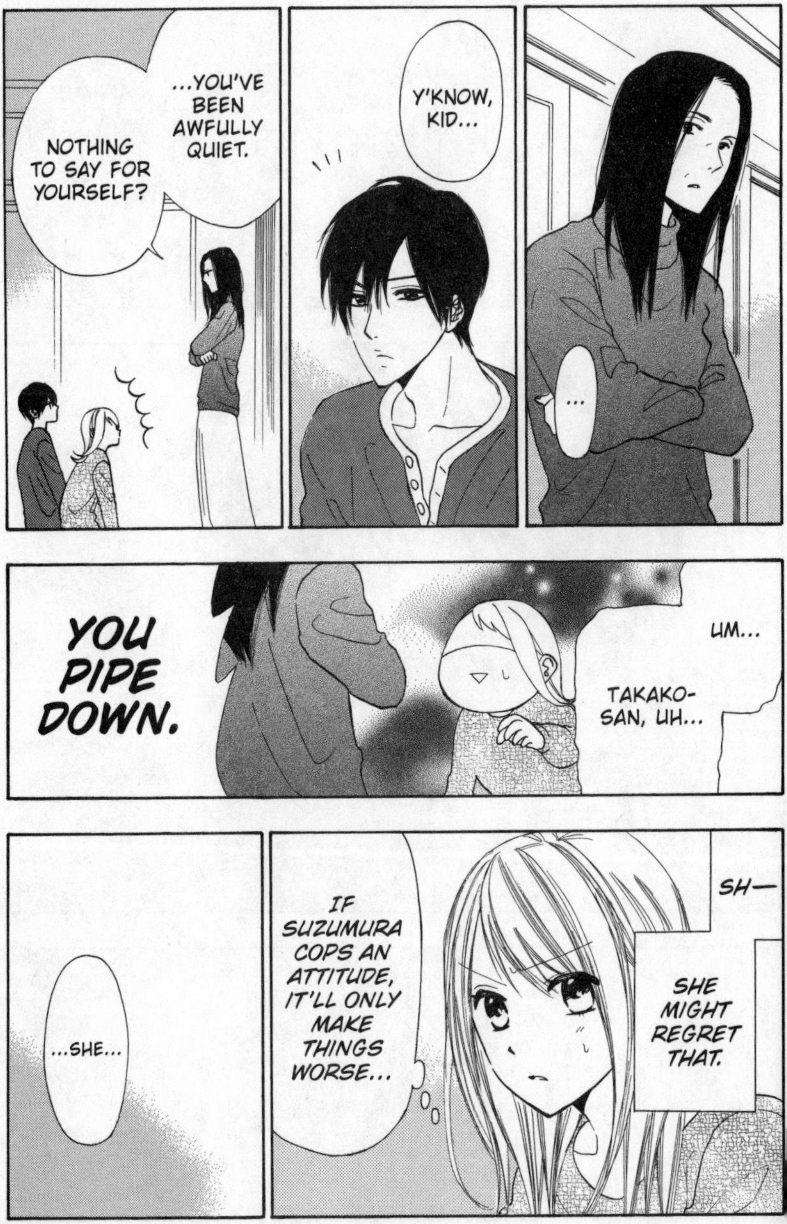
...
Y'KNOW, KID...
...YOU'VE BEEN AWFULLY QUIET.
NOTHING TO SAY FOR YOURSELF?
UM...
TAKAKO-SAN, UH...
YOU PIPE DOWN.
SH—
SHE MIGHT REGRET THAT.
IF SUZUMURA COPS AN ATTITUDE, IT'LL ONLY MAKE THINGS WORSE...
...SHE...

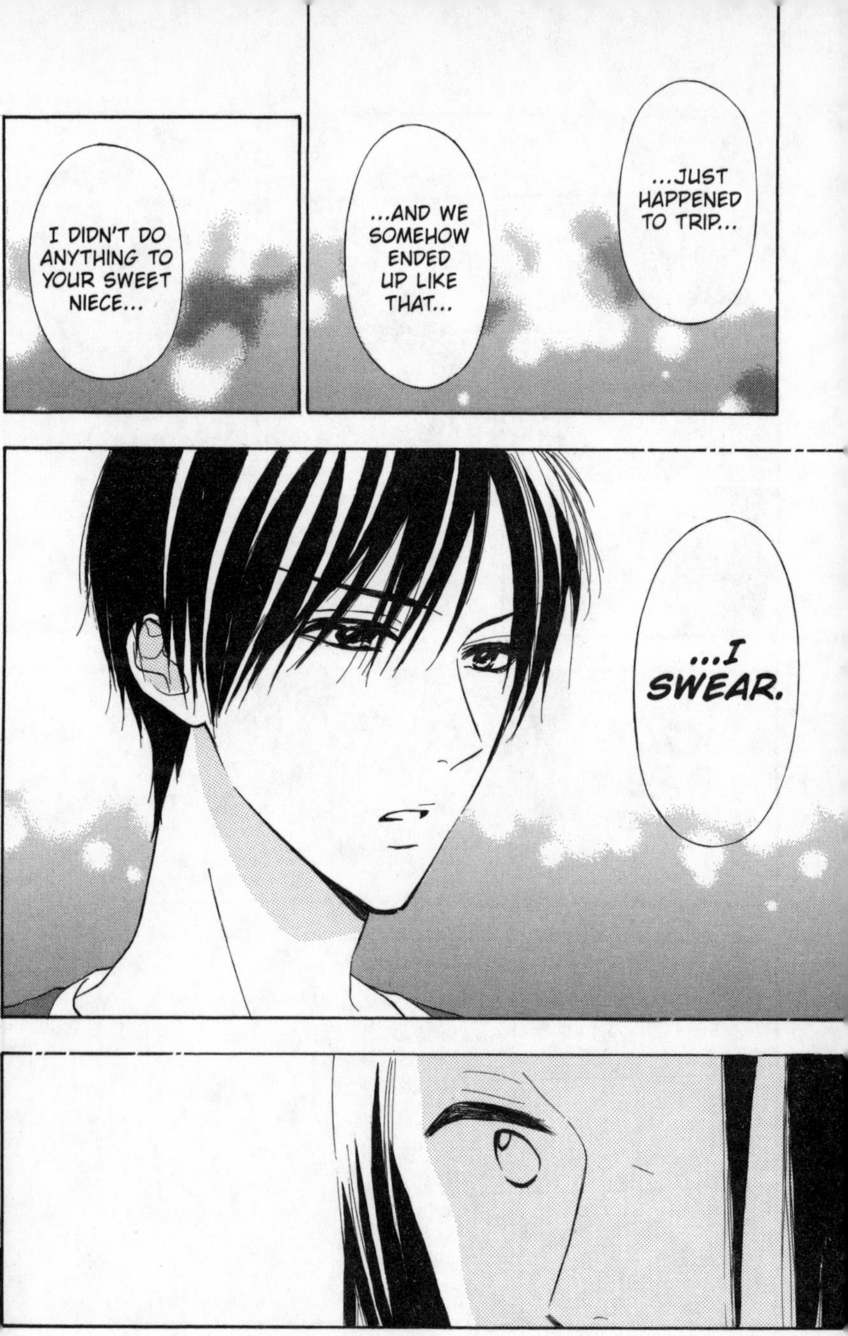
...JUST HAPPENED TO TRIP...
...AND WE SOMEHOW ENDED UP LIKE THAT...
I DIDN'T DO ANYTHING TO YOUR SWEET NIECE...
...I SWEAR.

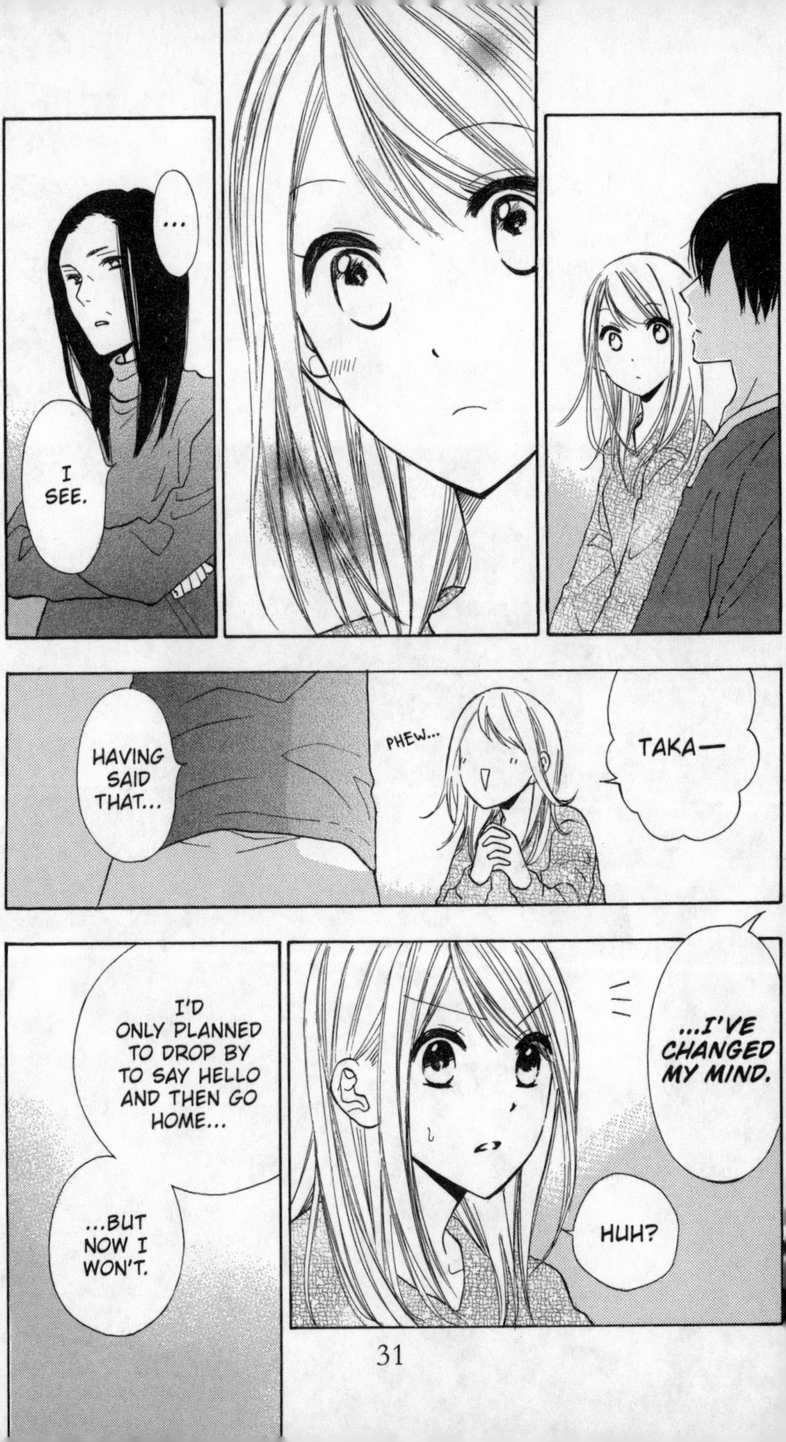
...
I SEE.
TAKA—
PHEW...
HAVING SAID THAT...
...I'VE CHANGED MY MIND.
HUH?
I'D ONLY PLANNED TO DROP BY TO SAY HELLO AND THEN GO HOME...
...BUT NOW I WON'T.

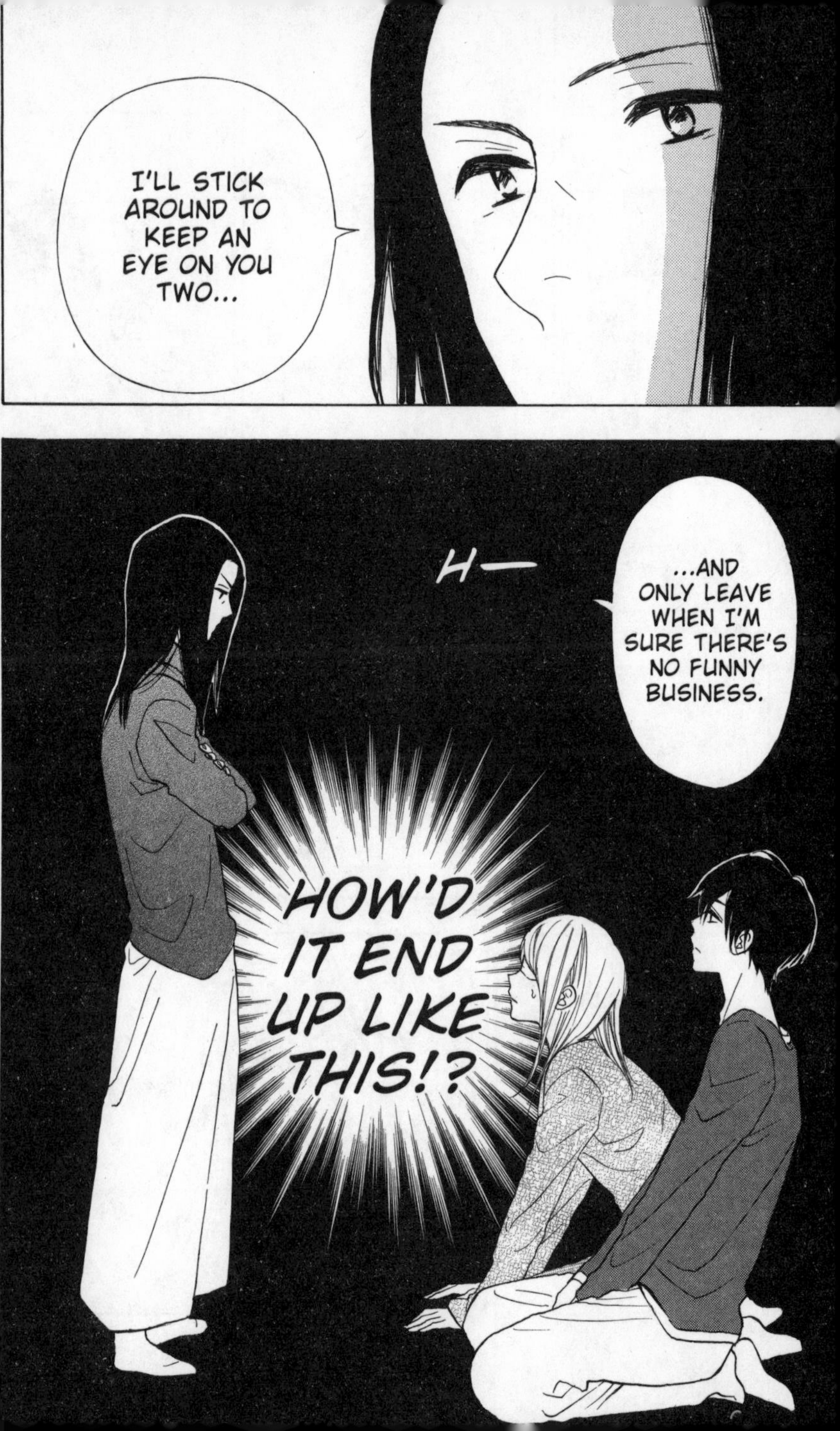
I'LL STICK AROUND TO KEEP AN EYE ON YOU TWO...
...AND ONLY LEAVE WHEN I'M SURE THERE'S NO FUNNY BUSINESS.
H—
HOW'D IT END UP LIKE THIS!?

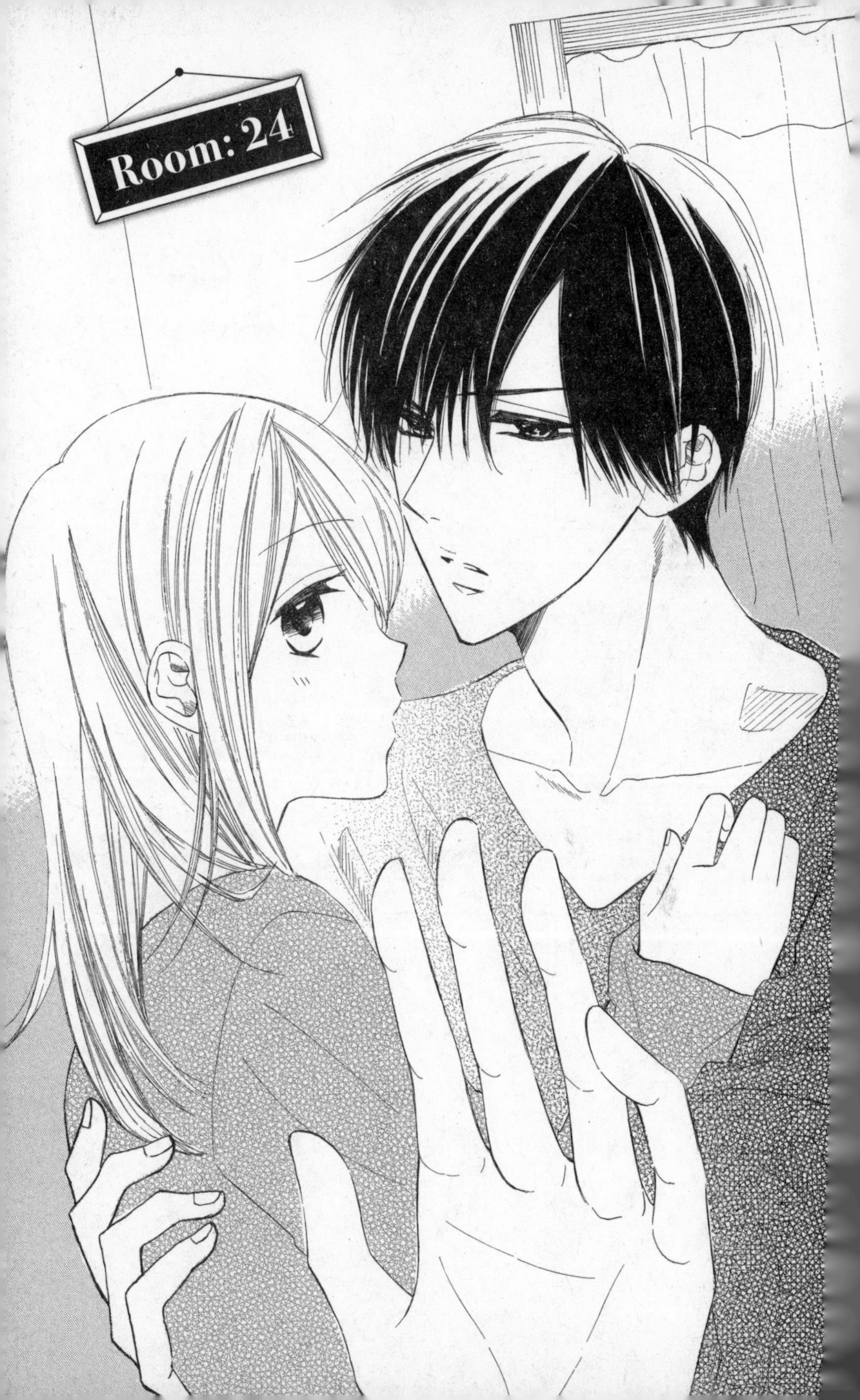
Room: 24

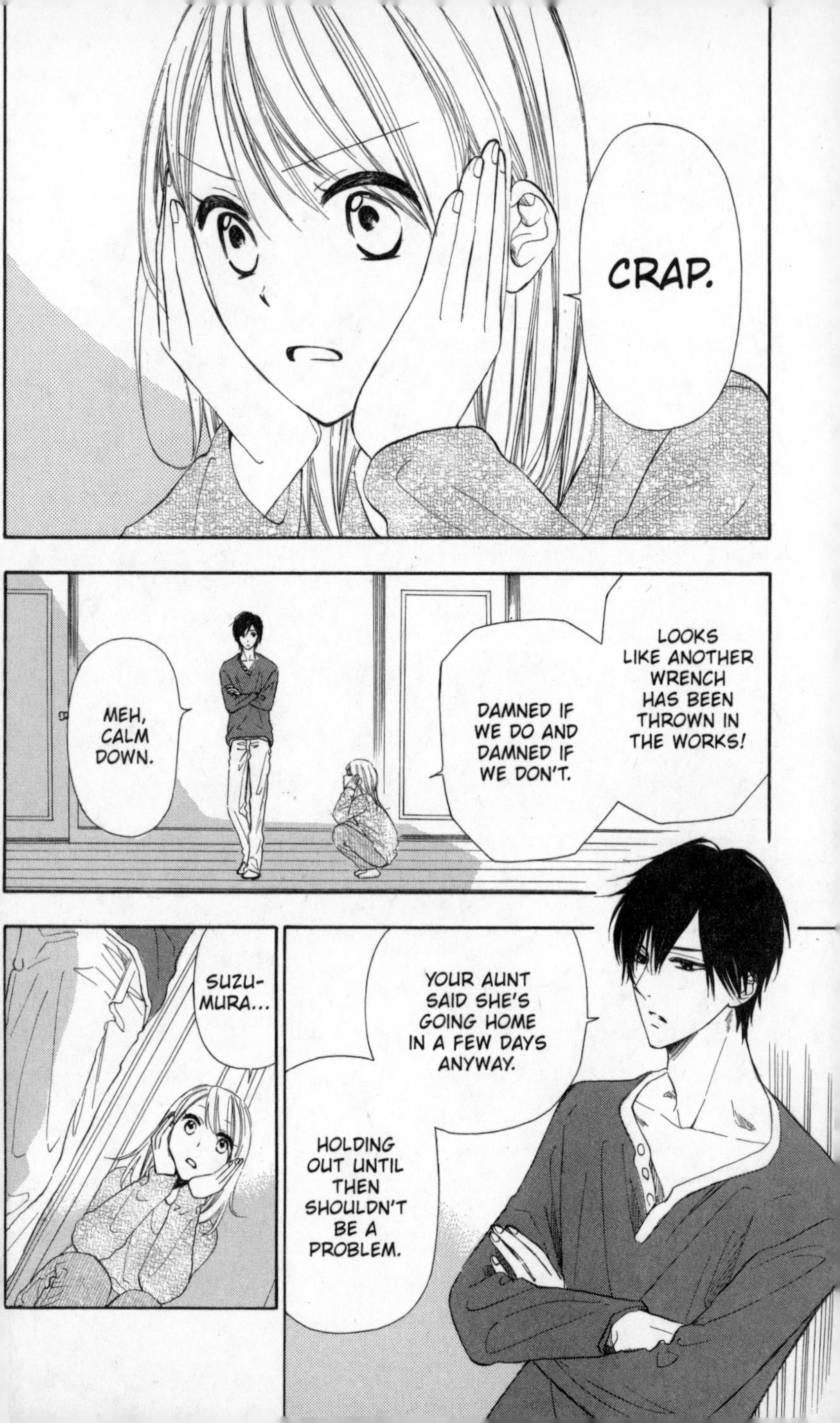
CRAP.
LOOKS LIKE ANOTHER WRENCH HAS BEEN THROWN IN THE WORKS!
DAMNED IF WE DO AND DAMNED IF WE DON'T.
MEH, CALM DOWN.
YOUR AUNT SAID SHE'S GOING HOME IN A FEW DAYS ANYWAY.
HOLDING OUT UNTIL THEN SHOULDN'T BE A PROBLEM.
SUZU-MURA...

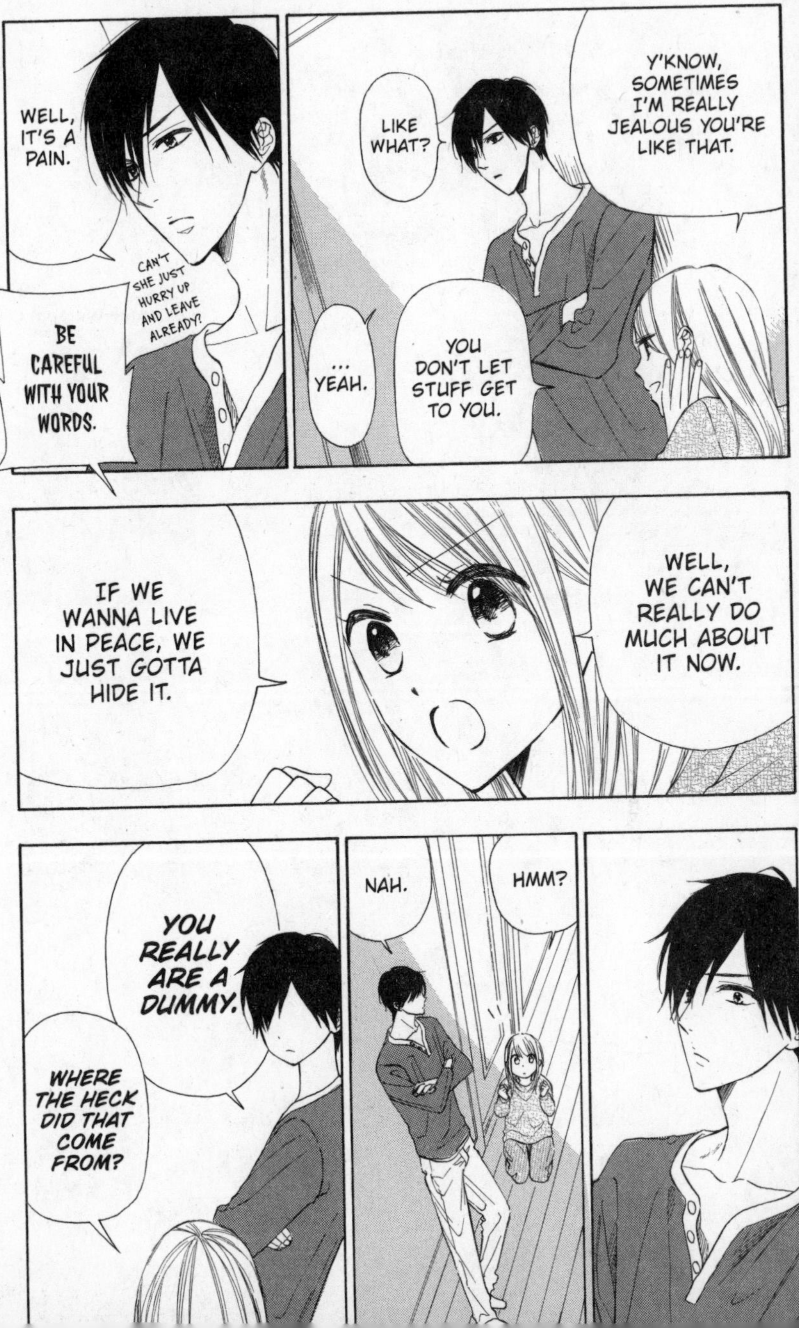
Y'KNOW, SOMETIMES I'M REALLY JEALOUS YOU'RE LIKE THAT.
LIKE WHAT?
YOU DON'T LET STUFF GET TO YOU.
... YEAH.
WELL, IT'S A PAIN.
CAN'T SHE JUST HURRY UP AND LEAVE ALREADY?
BE CAREFUL WITH YOUR WORDS.
WELL, WE CAN'T REALLY DO MUCH ABOUT IT NOW.
IF WE WANNA LIVE IN PEACE, WE JUST GOTTA HIDE IT.
HMM?
NAH.
YOU REALLY ARE A DUMMY.
WHERE THE HECK DID THAT COME FROM?

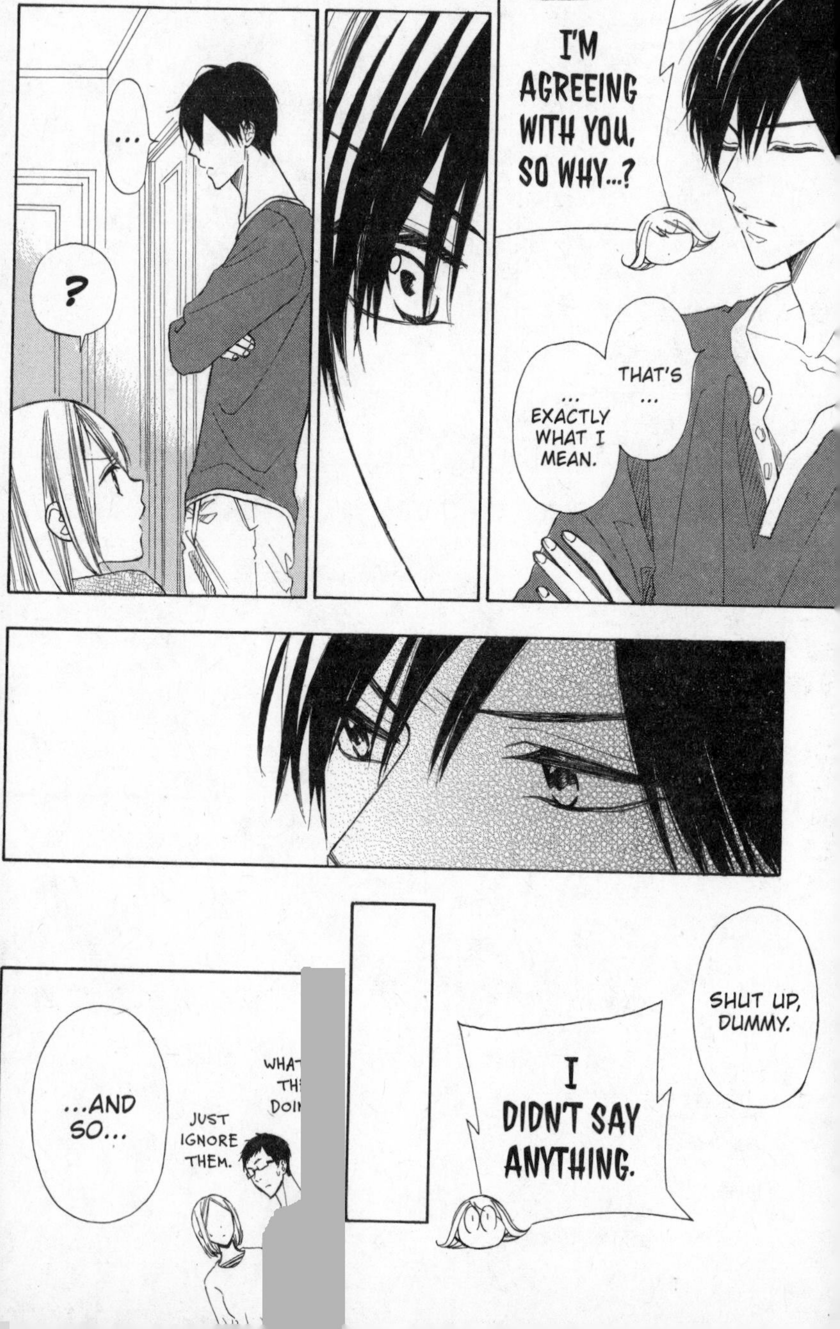

I'M AGREEING WITH YOU, SO WHY...?
THAT'S ... ... EXACTLY WHAT I MEAN.
...
?
SHUT UP, DUMMY.
I DIDN'T SAY ANYTHING.
...AND SO...
JUST IGNORE THEM.

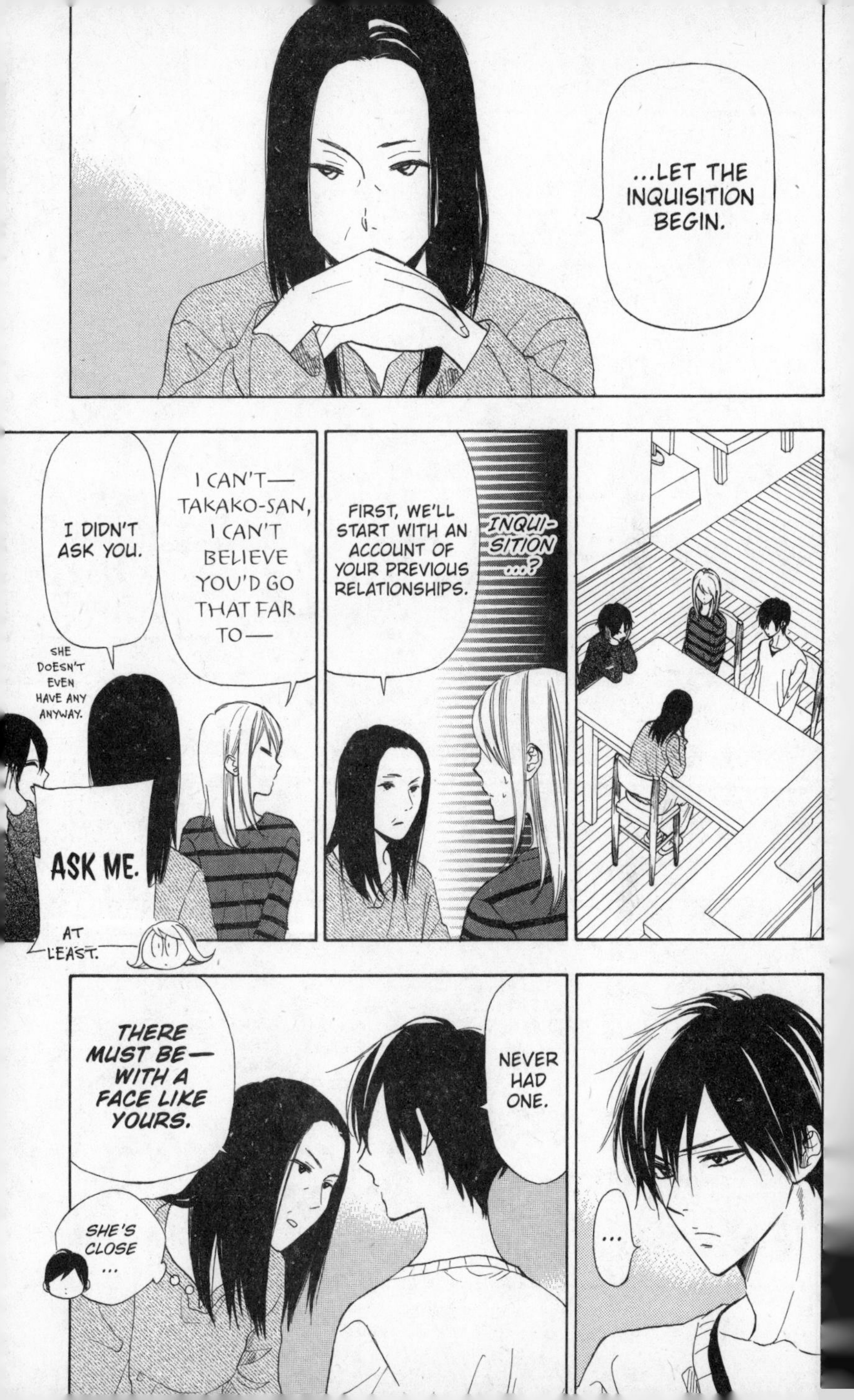
...LET THE INQUISITION BEGIN.
INQUISITION ...?
FIRST, WE'LL START WITH AN ACCOUNT OF YOUR PREVIOUS RELATIONSHIPS.
I CAN'T— TAKAKO-SAN, I CAN'T BELIEVE YOU'D GO THAT FAR TO—
I DIDN'T ASK YOU.
SHE DOESN'T EVEN HAVE ANY ANYWAY.
ASK ME.
AT LEAST.
...
NEVER HAD ONE.
THERE MUST BE— WITH A FACE LIKE YOURS.
SHE'S CLOSE ...

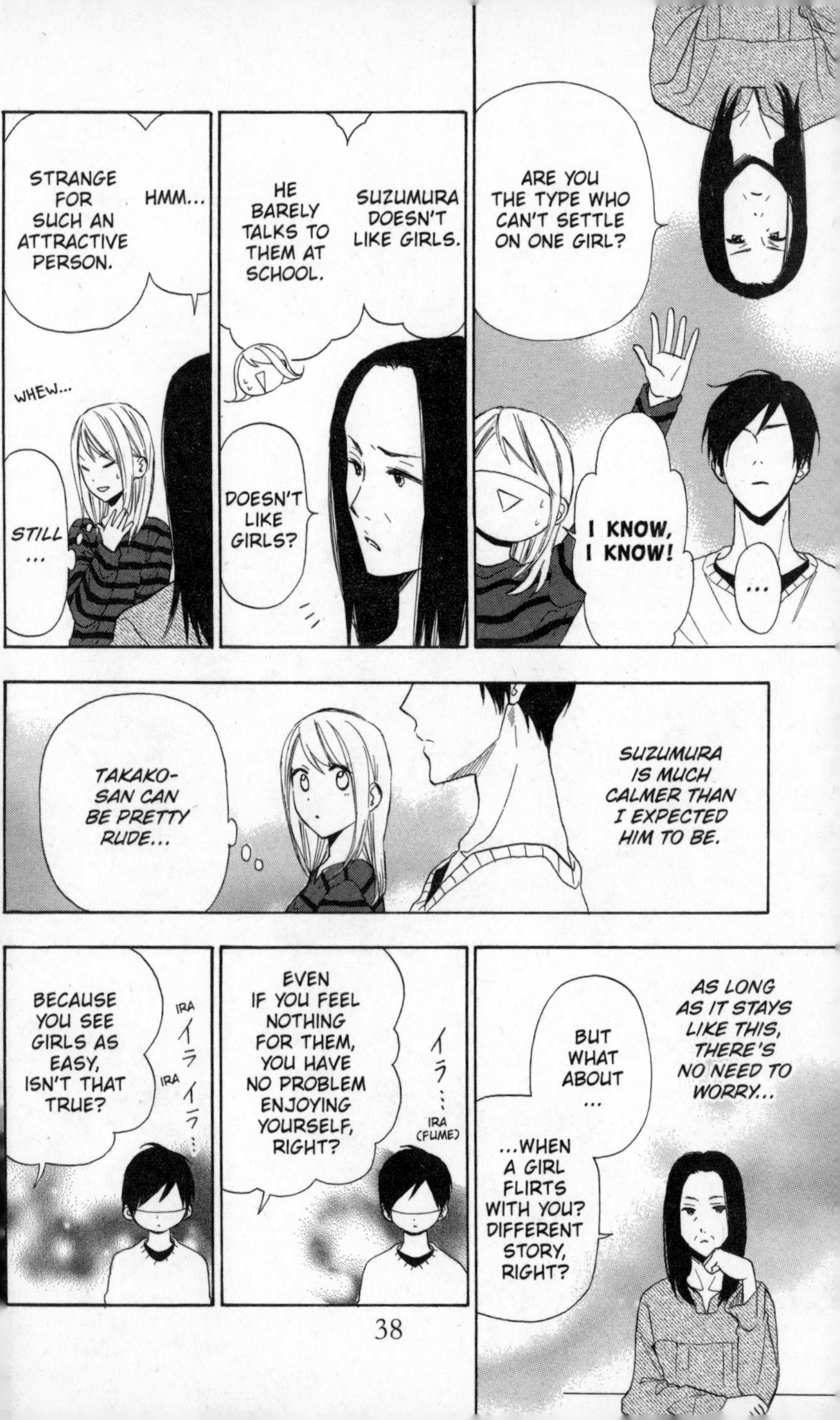
ARE YOU THE TYPE WHO CAN'T SETTLE ON ONE GIRL?
I KNOW, I KNOW!
...
SUZUMURA DOESN'T LIKE GIRLS.
HE BARELY TALKS TO THEM AT SCHOOL.
DOESN'T LIKE GIRLS?
HMM...
STRANGE FOR SUCH AN ATTRACTIVE PERSON.
WHEW...
STILL ...
SUZUMURA IS MUCH CALMER THAN I EXPECTED HIM TO BE.
TAKAKO-SAN CAN BE PRETTY RUDE...
AS LONG AS IT STAYS LIKE THIS, THERE'S NO NEED TO WORRY...
BUT WHAT ABOUT ...
...WHEN A GIRL FLIRTS WITH YOU? DIFFERENT STORY, RIGHT?
EVEN IF YOU FEEL NOTHING FOR THEM, YOU HAVE NO PROBLEM ENJOYING YOURSELF, RIGHT?
イラ...
IRA (FUME)
BECAUSE YOU SEE GIRLS AS EASY, ISN'T THAT TRUE?
IRA イラ
IRA イラ...

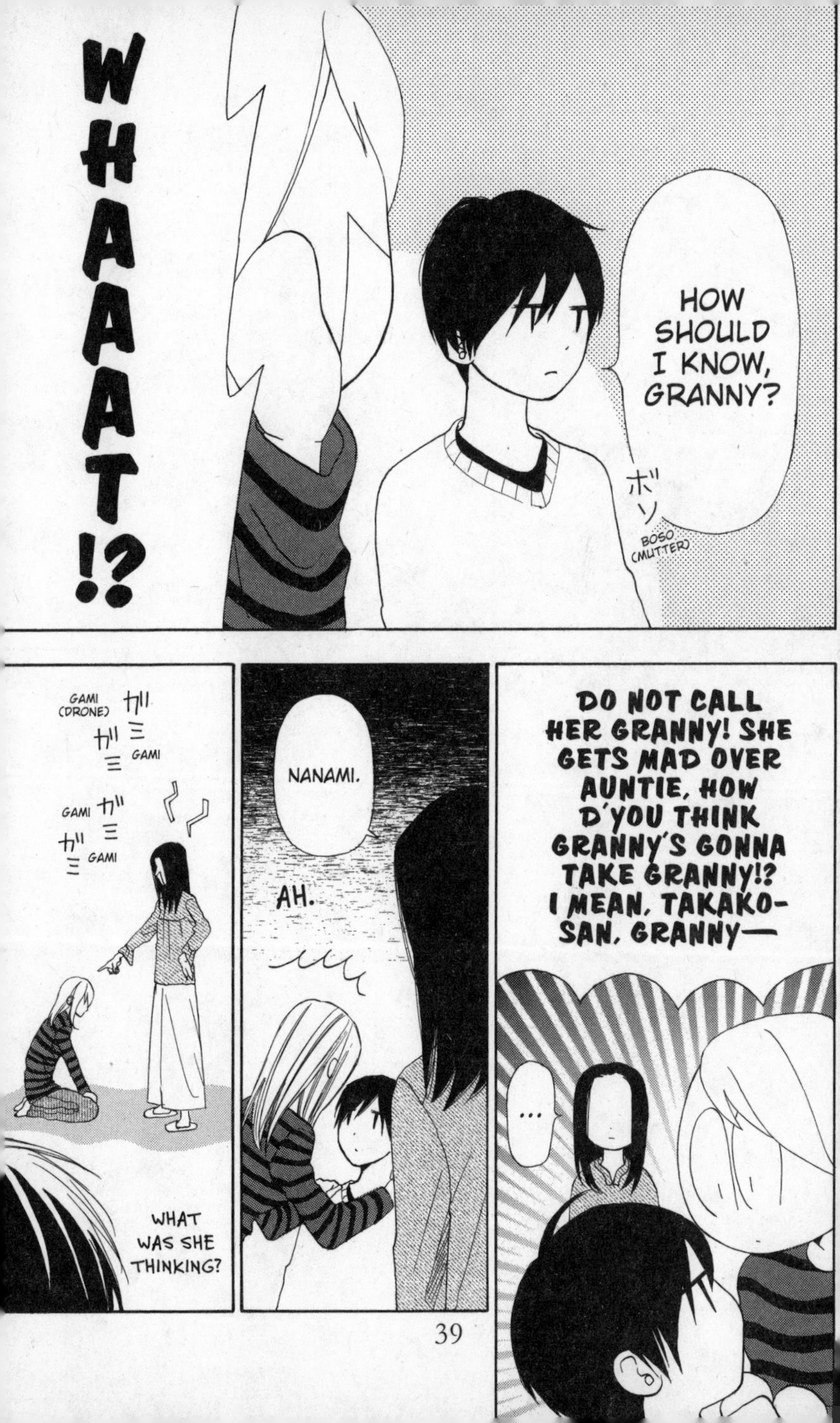
HOW SHOULD I KNOW, GRANNY?
ボソ
BOSO (MUTTER)
WHAAAT!?
DO NOT CALL HER GRANNY! SHE GETS MAD OVER AUNTIE, HOW D'YOU THINK GRANNY'S GONNA TAKE GRANNY!? I MEAN, TAKAKO-SAN, GRANNY—
...
NANAMI.
AH.
GAMI (DRONE) ガミ
ガミ GAMI
GAMI ガミ
ガミ GAMI
WHAT WAS SHE THINKING?

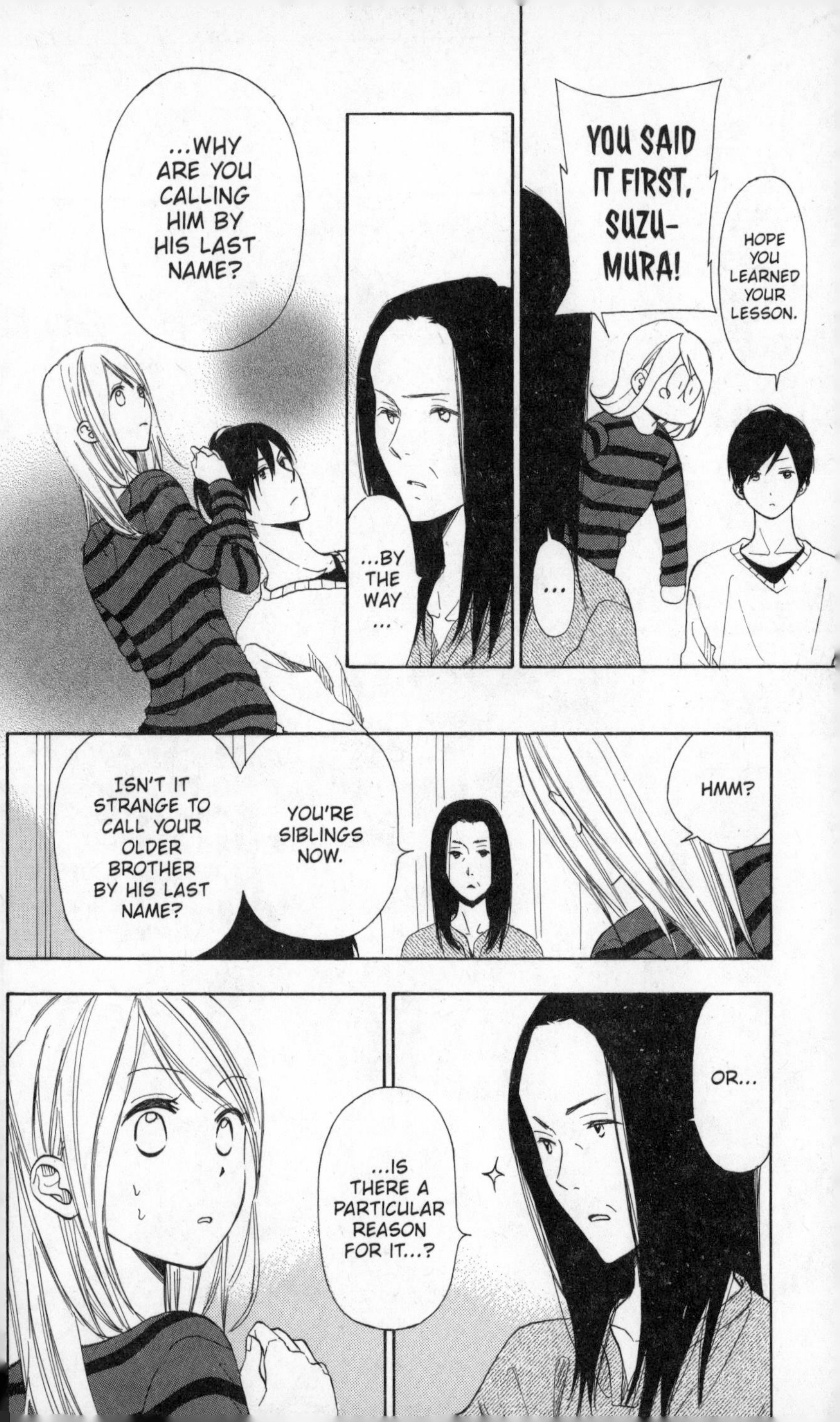
YOU SAID IT FIRST, SUZU-MURA!
HOPE YOU LEARNED YOUR LESSON.
...
...BY THE WAY...
...WHY ARE YOU CALLING HIM BY HIS LAST NAME?
HMM?
YOU'RE SIBLINGS NOW.
ISN'T IT STRANGE TO CALL YOUR OLDER BROTHER BY HIS LAST NAME?
OR...
...IS THERE A PARTICULAR REASON FOR IT...?

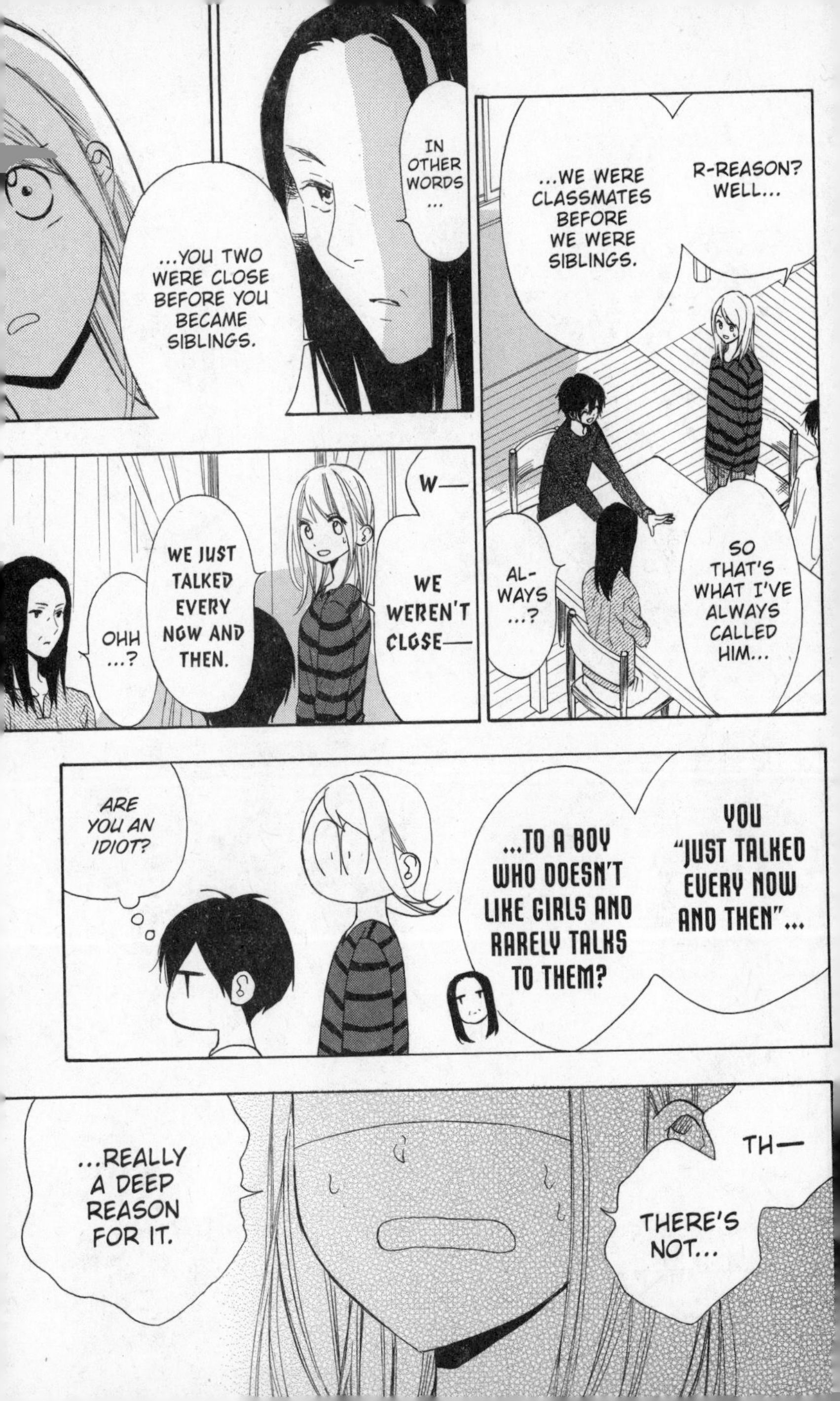
R-REASON? WELL...
...WE WERE CLASSMATES BEFORE WE WERE SIBLINGS.
SO THAT'S WHAT I'VE ALWAYS CALLED HIM...
AL-WAYS...?
IN OTHER WORDS...
...YOU TWO WERE CLOSE BEFORE YOU BECAME SIBLINGS.
W—
WE WEREN'T CLOSE—
WE JUST TALKED EVERY NOW AND THEN.
OHH...?
YOU "JUST TALKED EVERY NOW AND THEN"...
...TO A BOY WHO DOESN'T LIKE GIRLS AND RARELY TALKS TO THEM?
ARE YOU AN IDIOT?
TH—
THERE'S NOT...
...REALLY A DEEP REASON FOR IT.

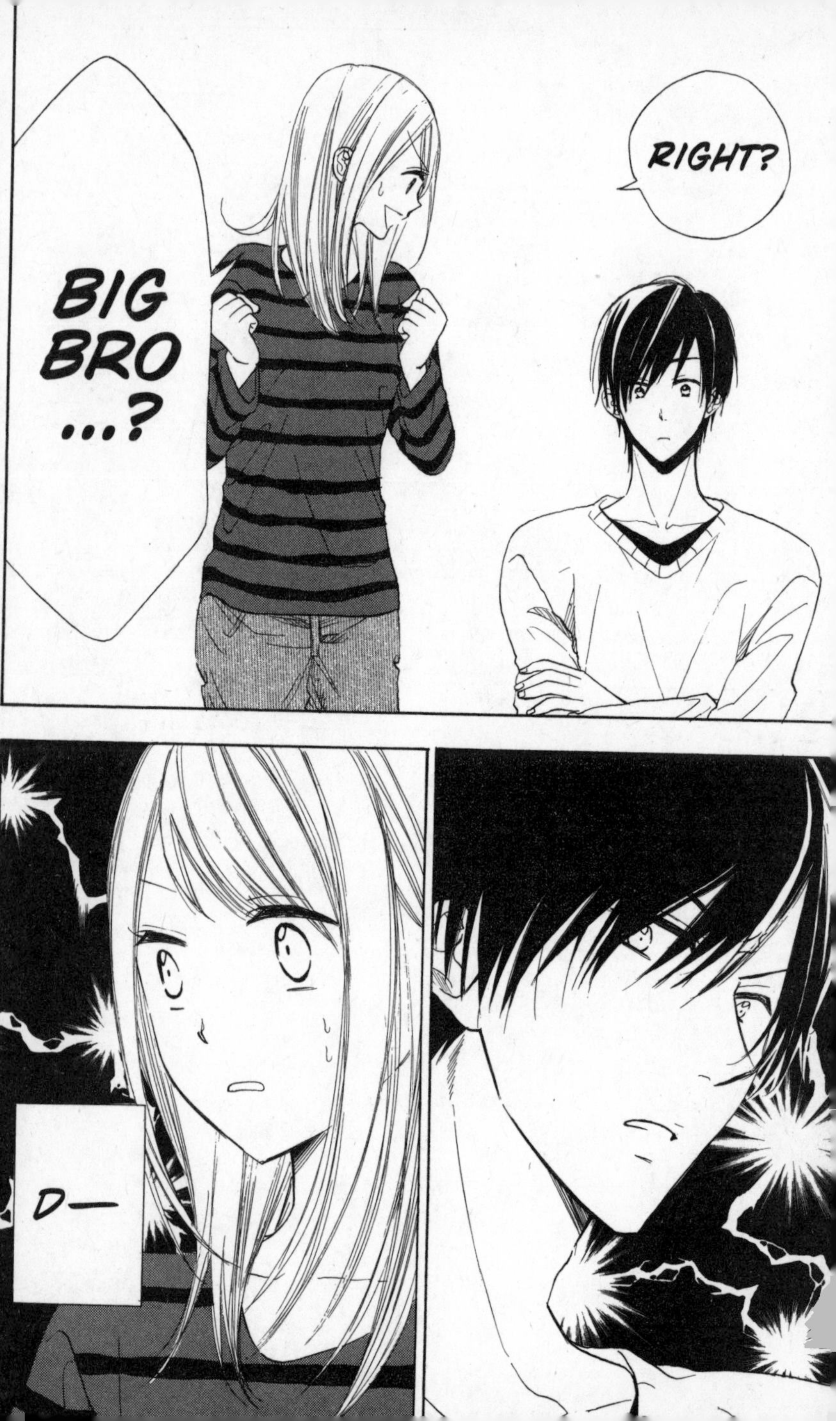
RIGHT?
BIG BRO ...?
D—

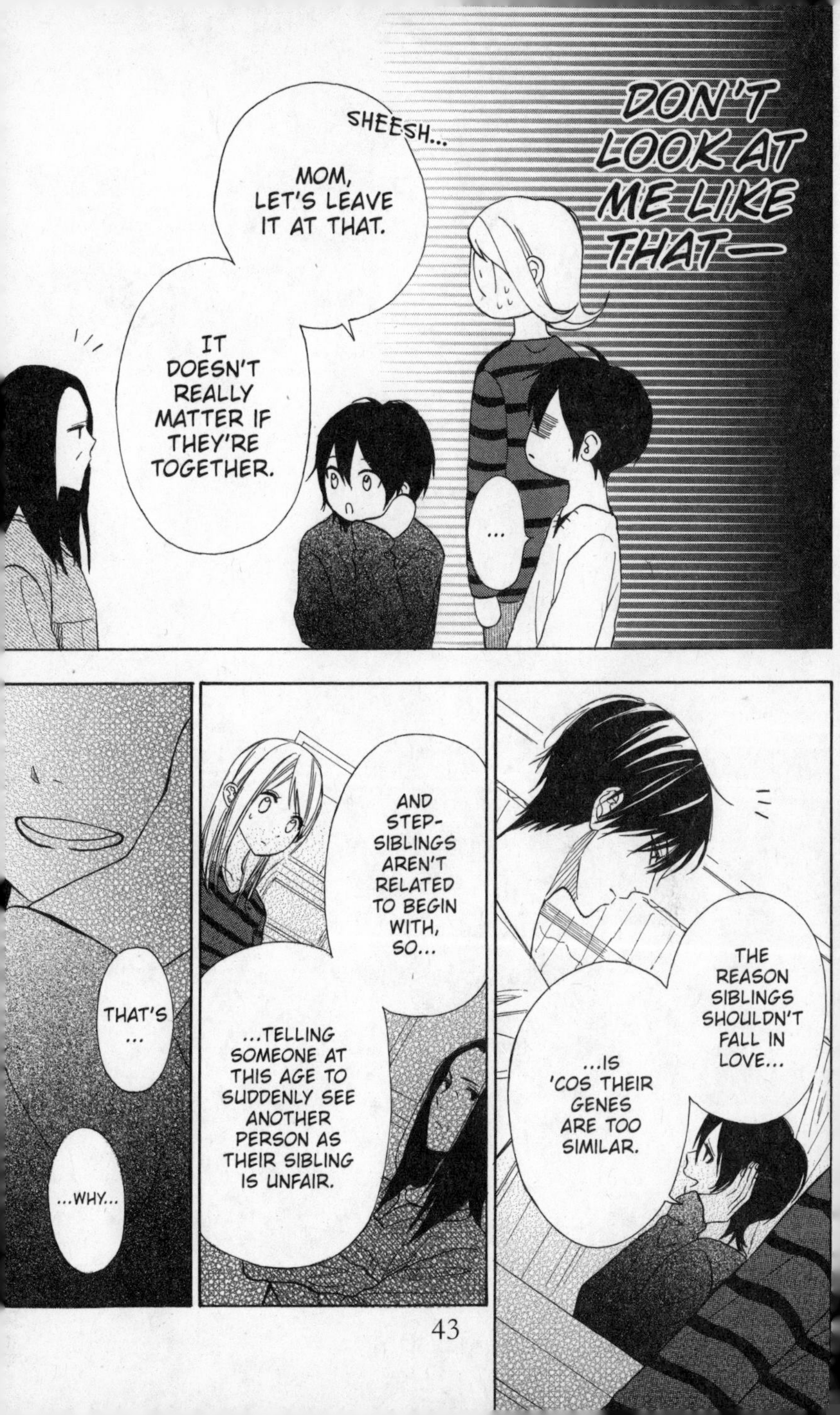
DON'T LOOK AT ME LIKE THAT—
SHEESH...
MOM, LET'S LEAVE IT AT THAT.
IT DOESN'T REALLY MATTER IF THEY'RE TOGETHER.
...
THE REASON SIBLINGS SHOULDN'T FALL IN LOVE...
...IS 'COS THEIR GENES ARE TOO SIMILAR.
AND STEP-SIBLINGS AREN'T RELATED TO BEGIN WITH, SO...
...TELLING SOMEONE AT THIS AGE TO SUDDENLY SEE ANOTHER PERSON AS THEIR SIBLING IS UNFAIR.
THAT'S...
...WHY...

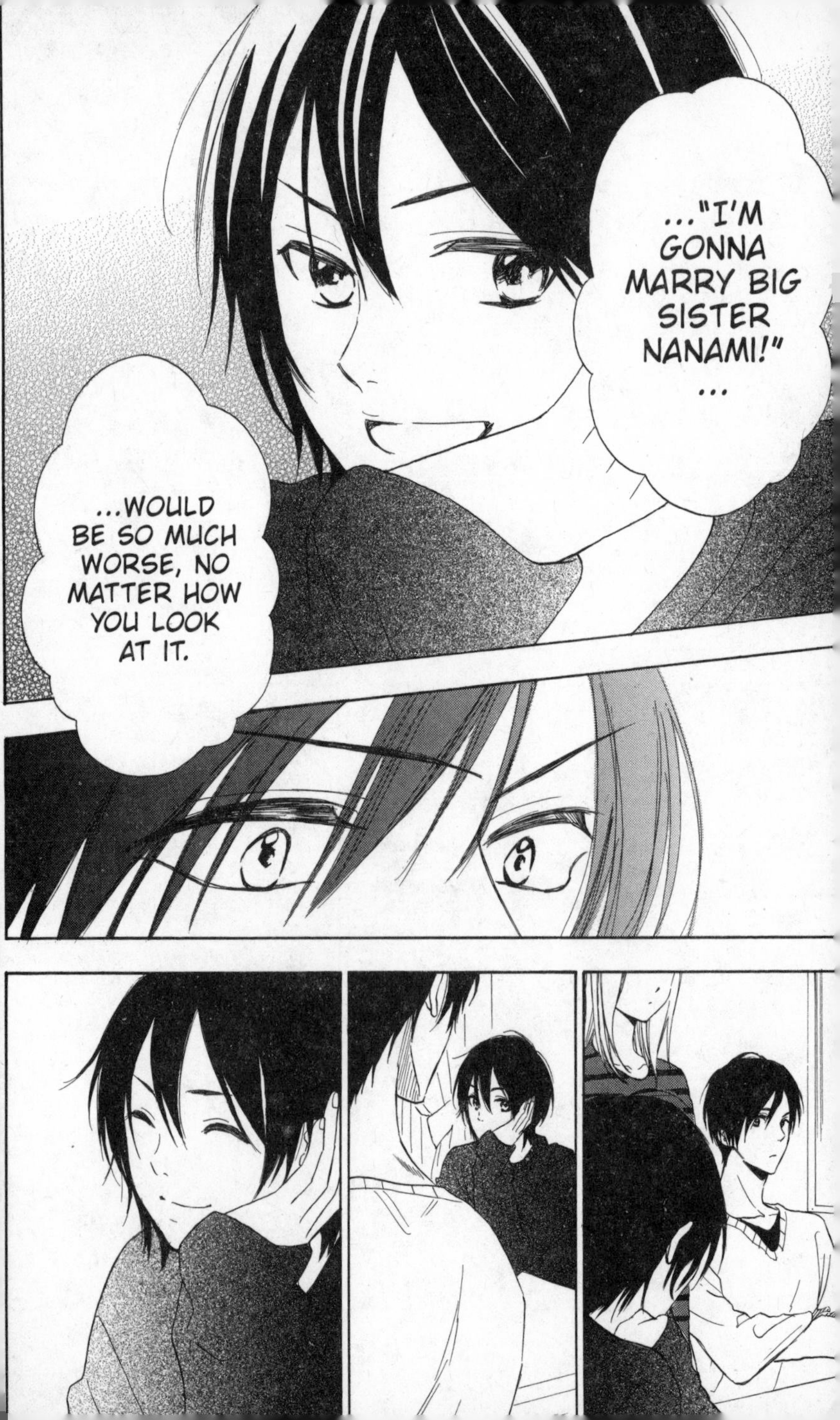
..."I'M GONNA MARRY BIG SISTER NANAMI!" ...
...WOULD BE SO MUCH WORSE, NO MATTER HOW YOU LOOK AT IT.

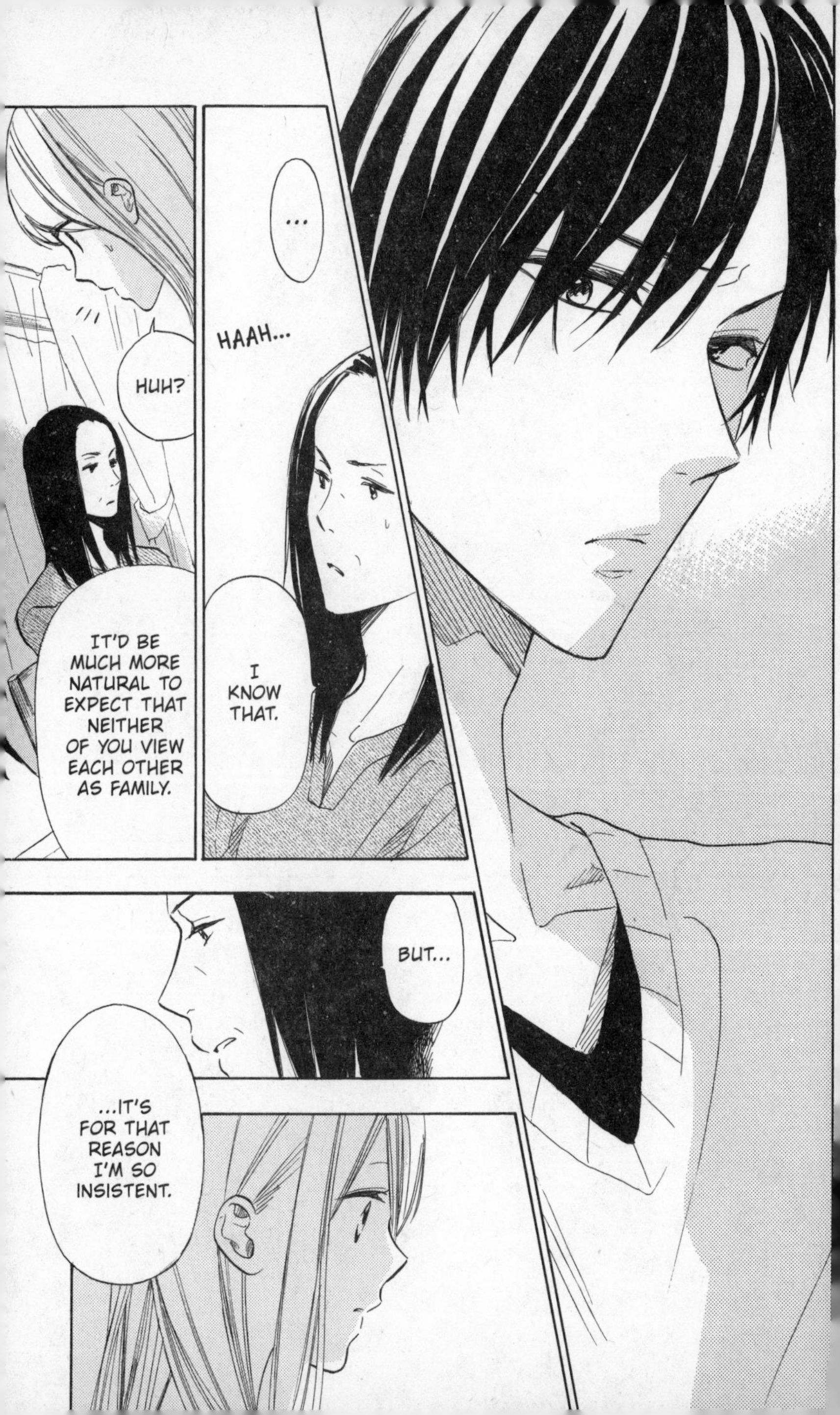
...
HAAH...
I KNOW THAT.
HUH?
IT'D BE MUCH MORE NATURAL TO EXPECT THAT NEITHER OF YOU VIEW EACH OTHER AS FAMILY.
BUT...
...IT'S FOR THAT REASON I'M SO INSISTENT.

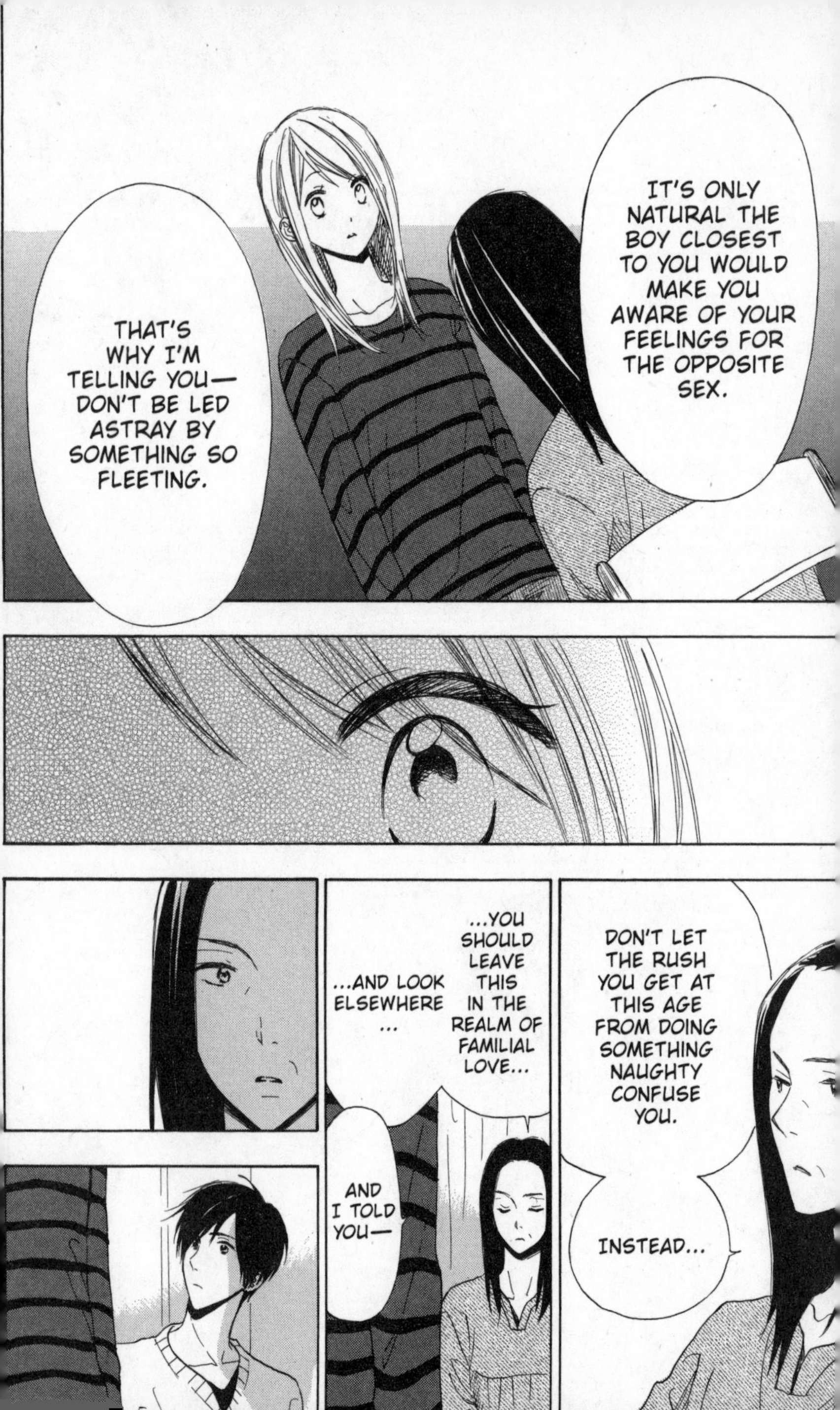
IT'S ONLY NATURAL THE BOY CLOSEST TO YOU WOULD MAKE YOU AWARE OF YOUR FEELINGS FOR THE OPPOSITE SEX.
THAT'S WHY I'M TELLING YOU—DON'T BE LED ASTRAY BY SOMETHING SO FLEETING.
DON'T LET THE RUSH YOU GET AT THIS AGE FROM DOING SOMETHING NAUGHTY CONFUSE YOU.
INSTEAD...
...YOU SHOULD LEAVE THIS IN THE REALM OF FAMILIAL LOVE...
...AND LOOK ELSEWHERE...
AND I TOLD YOU—

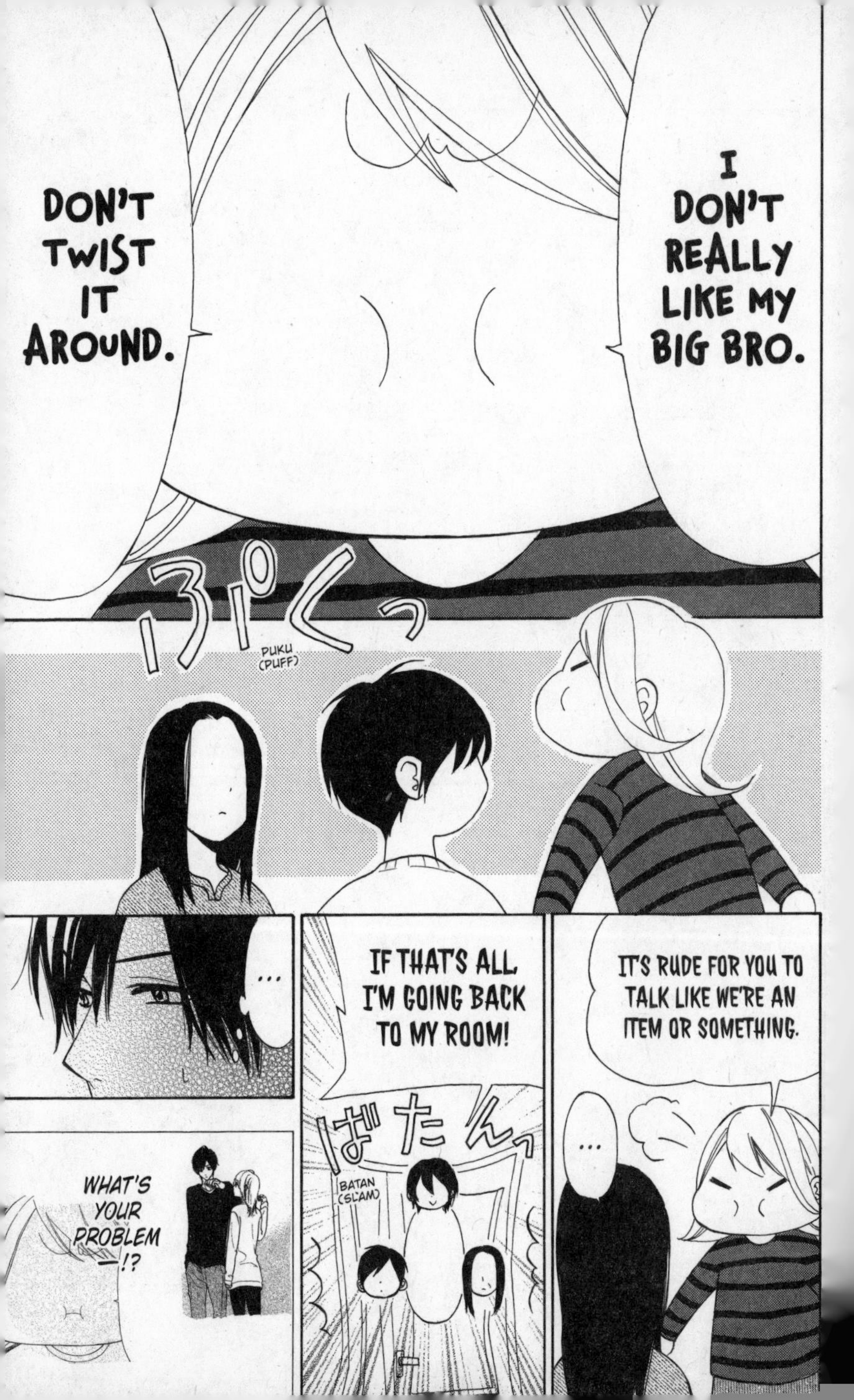

I DON'T REALLY LIKE MY BIG BRO.
DON'T TWIST IT AROUND.
ぷくっ
PUKU (PUFF)
IT'S RUDE FOR YOU TO TALK LIKE WE'RE AN ITEM OR SOMETHING.
...
IF THAT'S ALL, I'M GOING BACK TO MY ROOM!
ばたんっ
BATAN (SLAM)
...
WHAT'S YOUR PROBLEM—!?

GATA
(CLATTER)

MY...I SUPPOSE IT WAS A LITTLE SOON TO SPEAK WITH HER ABOUT THAT.

GACHA
(KACHAK)

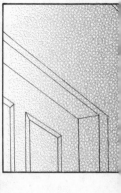

BIKU
(FREEZE)

HEY...

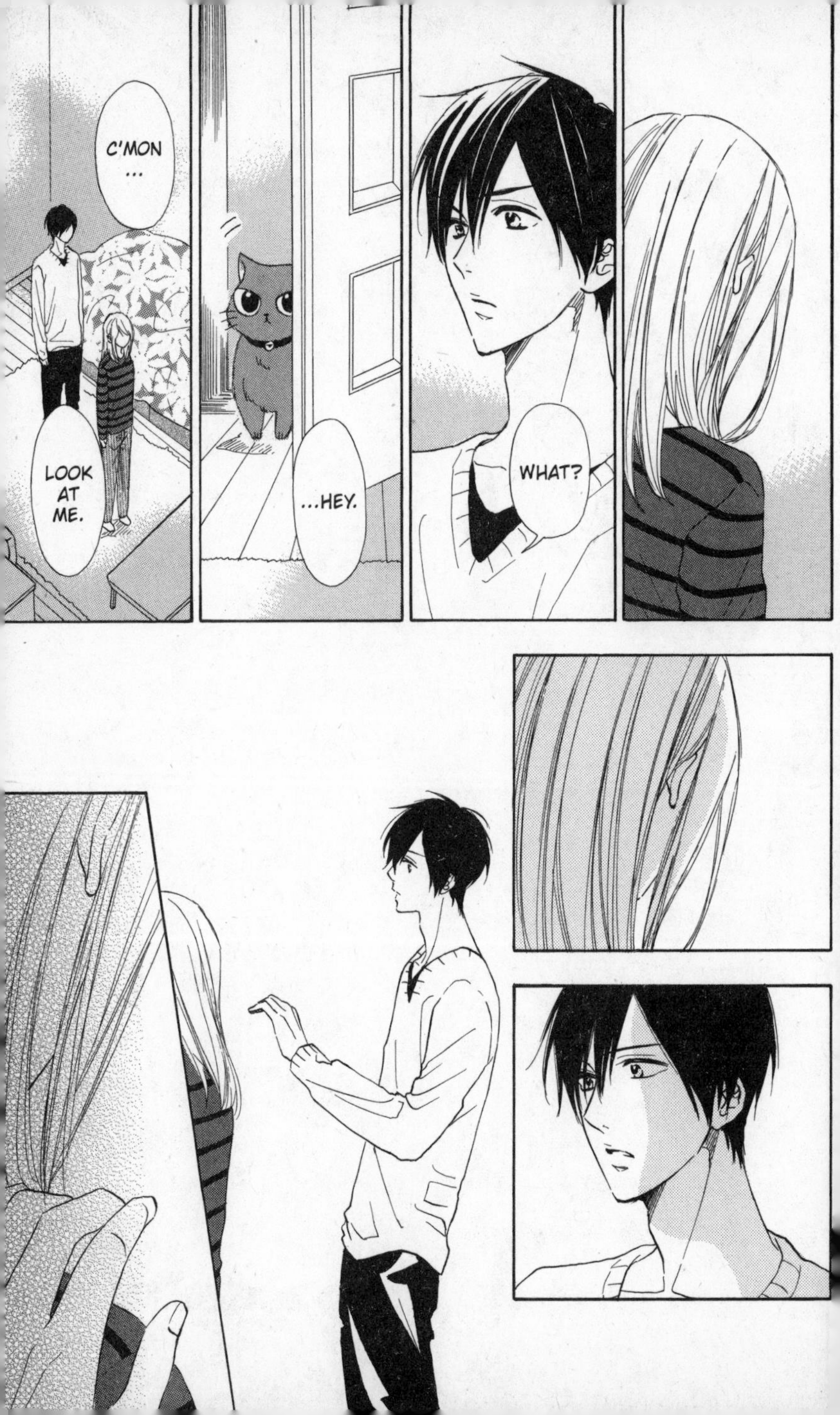
WHAT?
...HEY.
C'MON ...
LOOK AT ME.

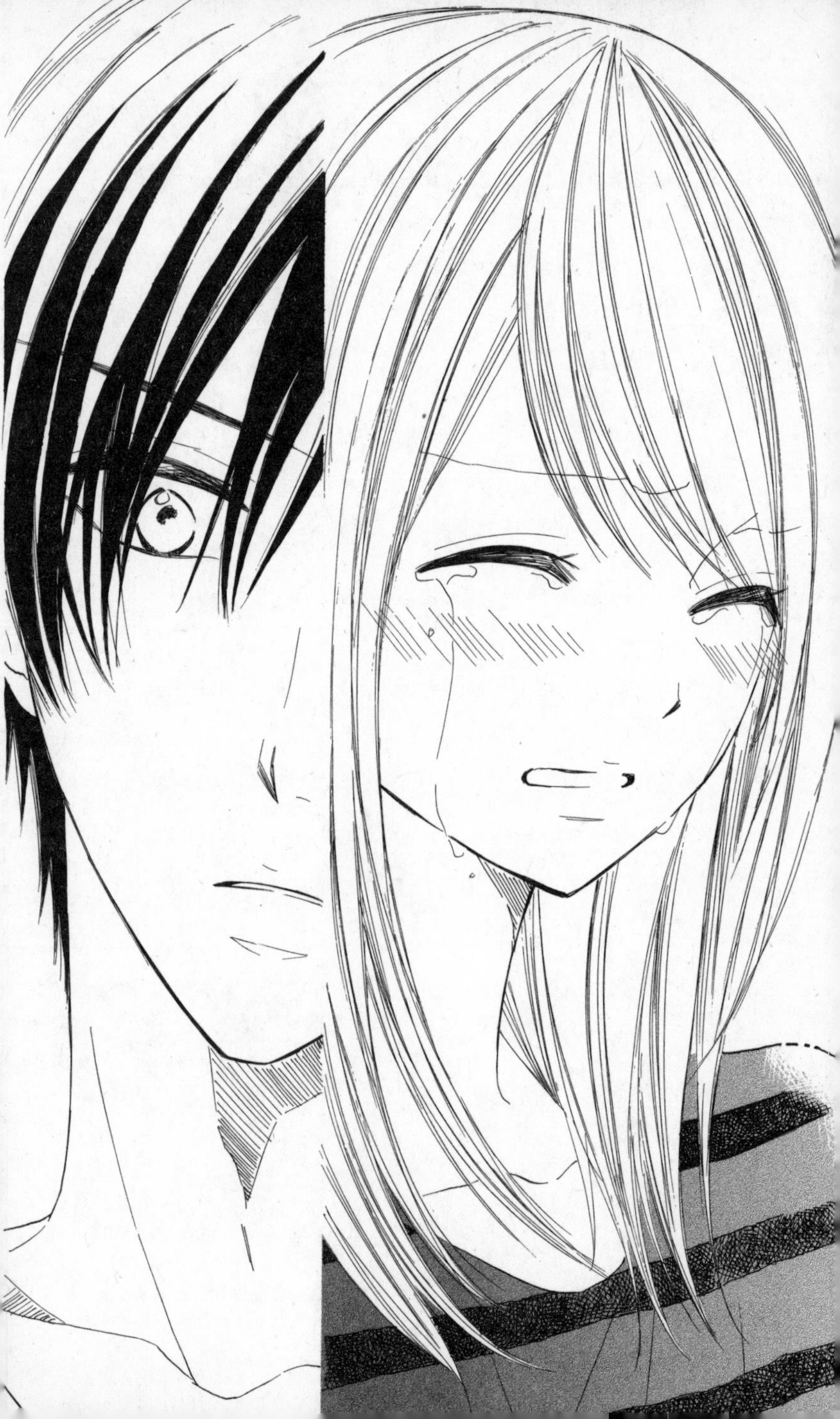

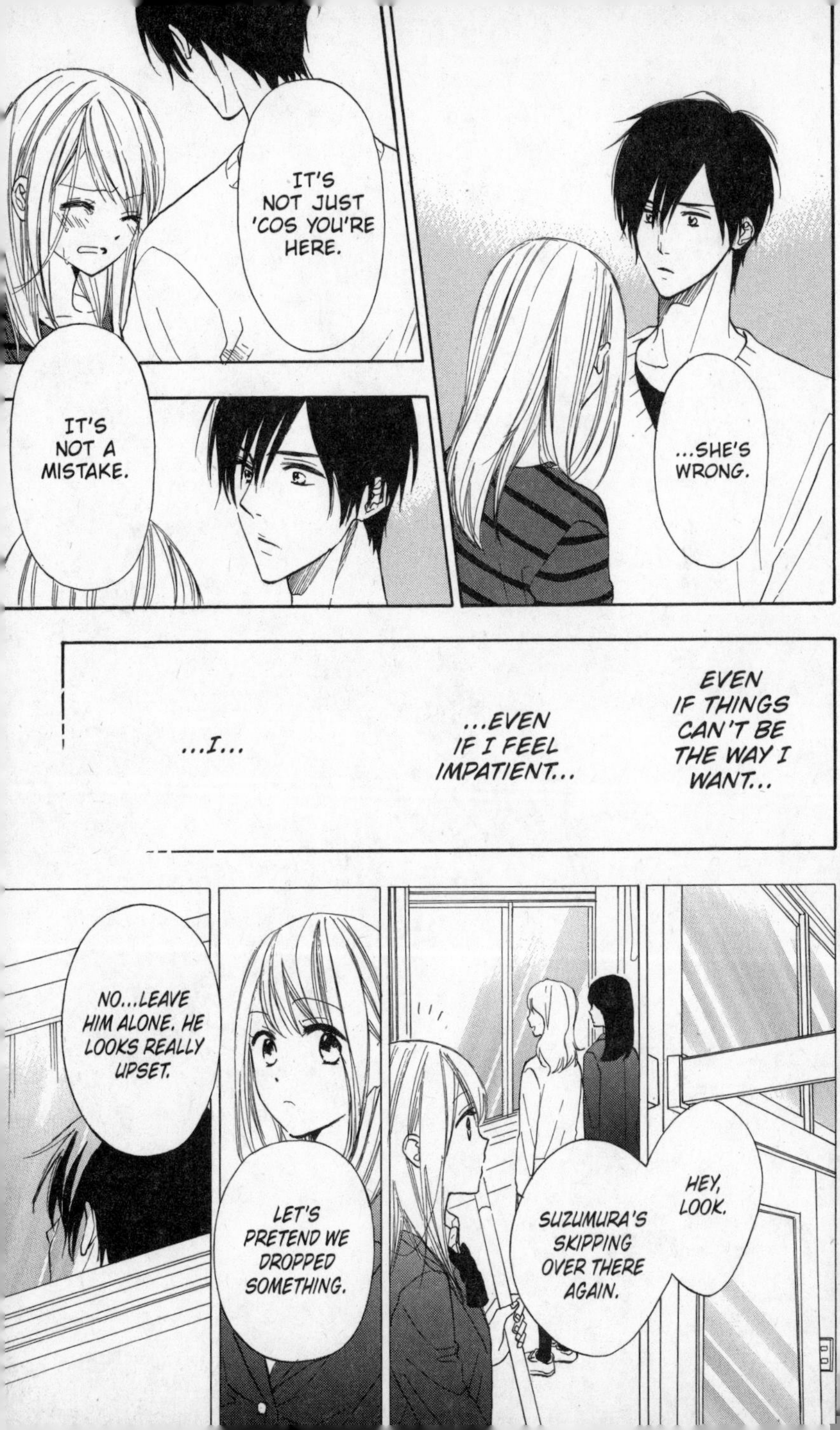
...SHE'S WRONG.
IT'S NOT JUST 'COS YOU'RE HERE.
IT'S NOT A MISTAKE.
EVEN IF THINGS CAN'T BE THE WAY I WANT...
...EVEN IF I FEEL IMPATIENT...
...I...
HEY, LOOK.
SUZUMURA'S SKIPPING OVER THERE AGAIN.
LET'S PRETEND WE DROPPED SOMETHING.
NO...LEAVE HIM ALONE. HE LOOKS REALLY UPSET.

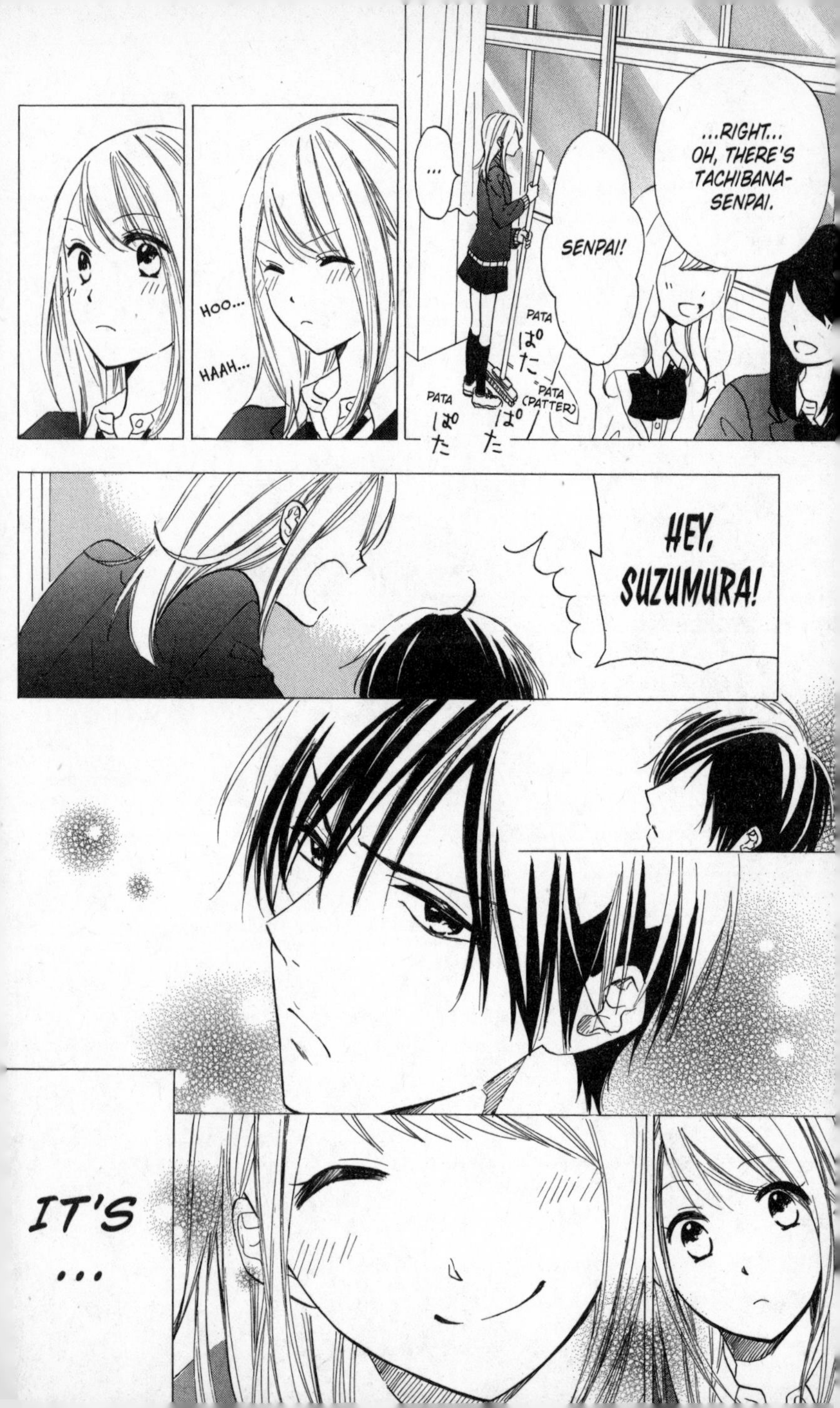
...RIGHT... OH, THERE'S TACHIBANA-SENPAI.
SENPAI!
...
PATA ぱた
PATA (PATTER)
PATA ぱた
ぱた
ぱた
HOO...
HAAH...
HEY, SUZUMURA!
IT'S ...

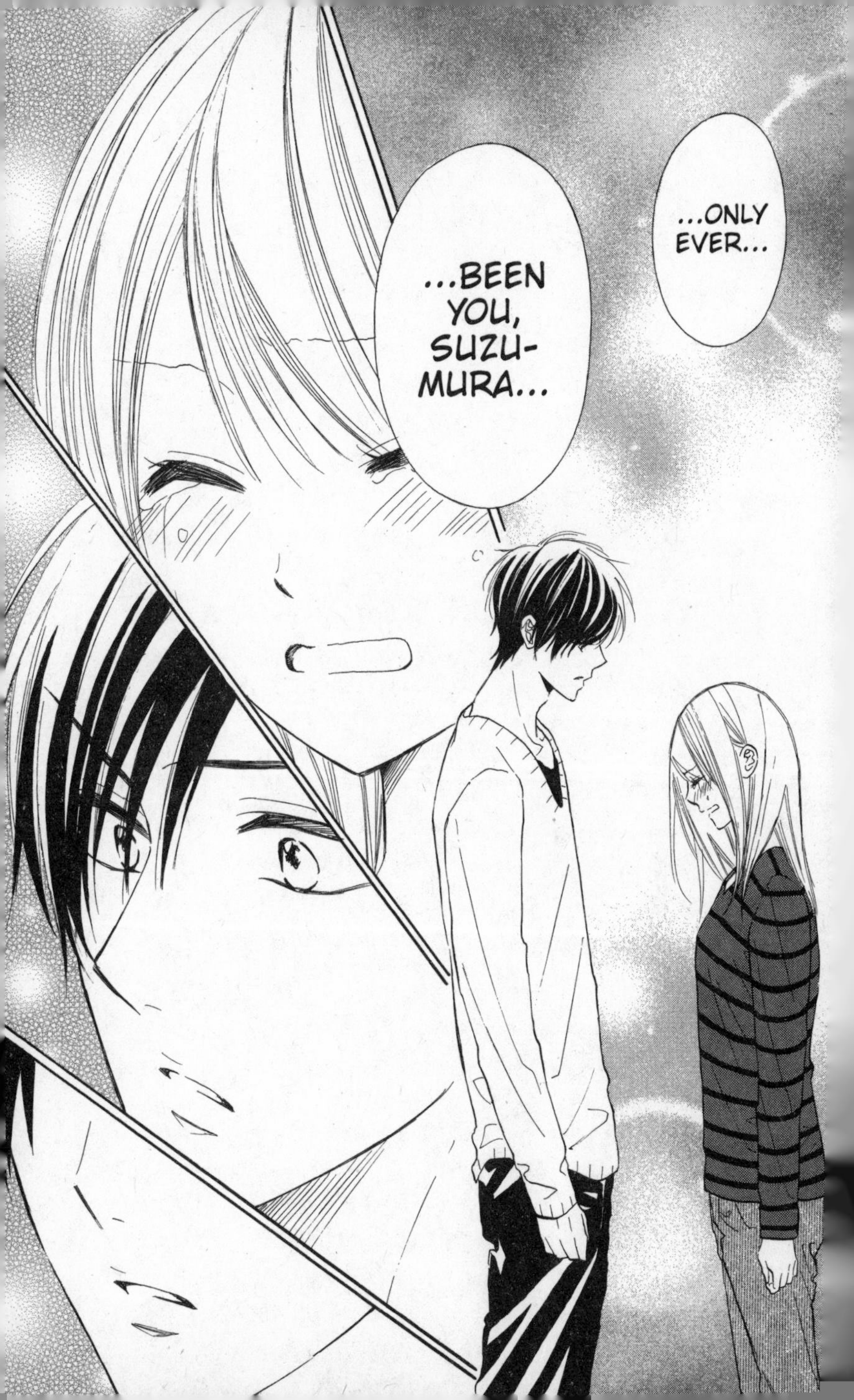
...ONLY EVER...
...BEEN YOU, SUZU-MURA...

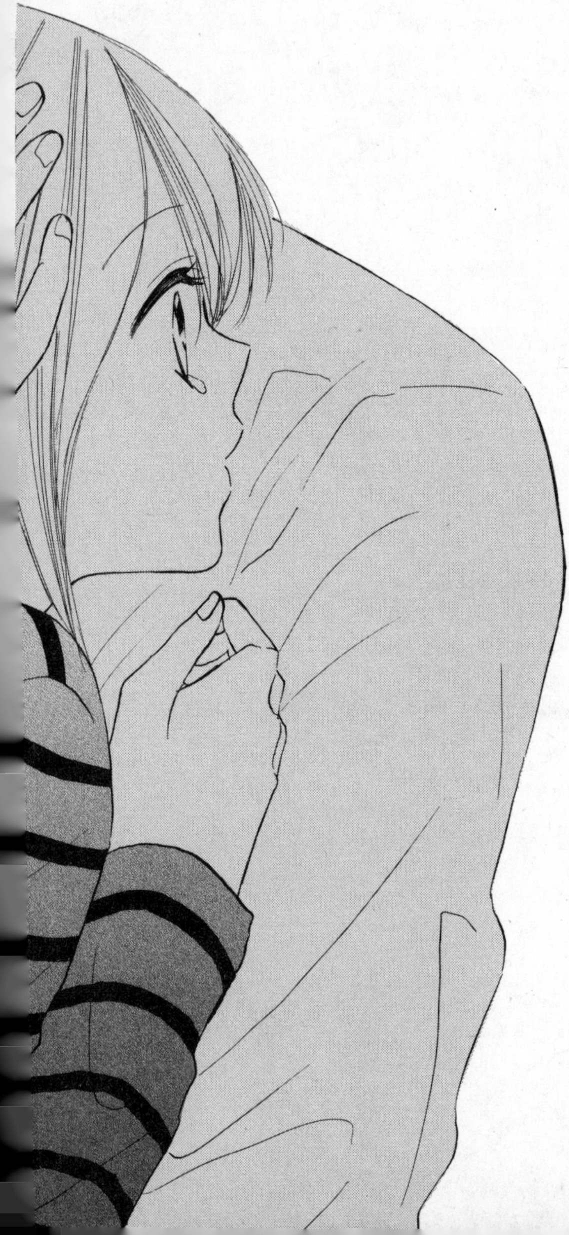

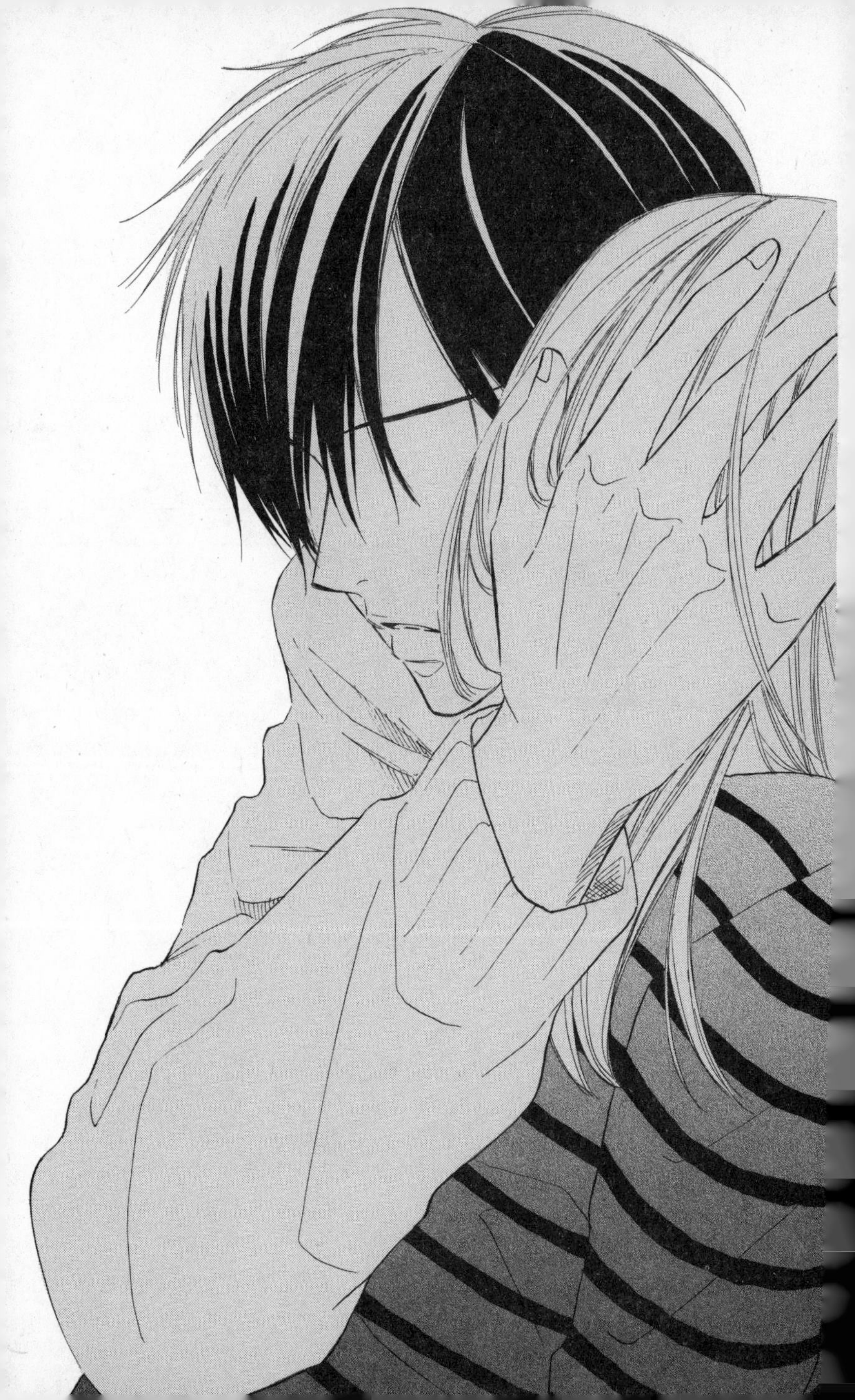

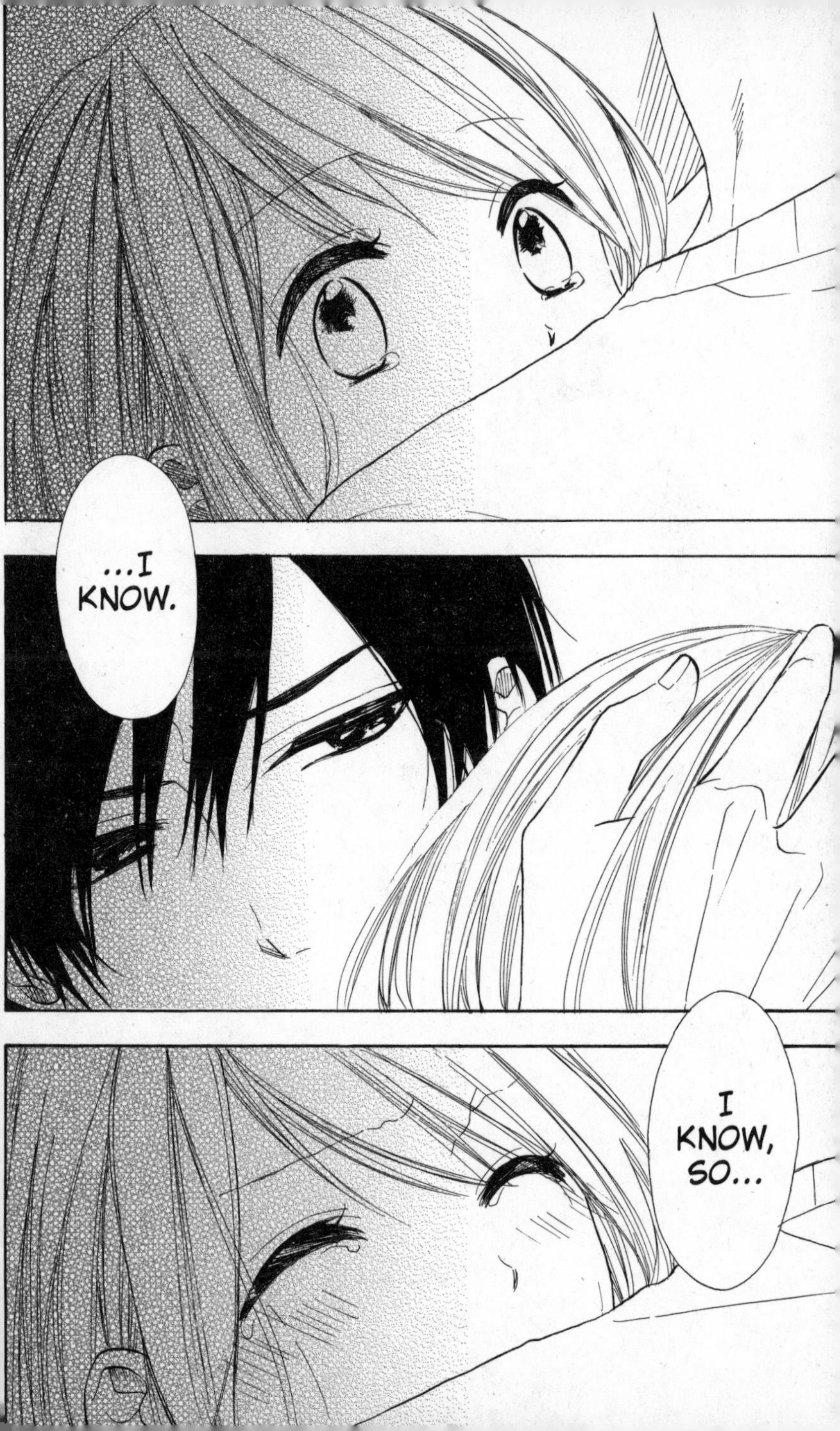
...I KNOW.
I KNOW, SO...

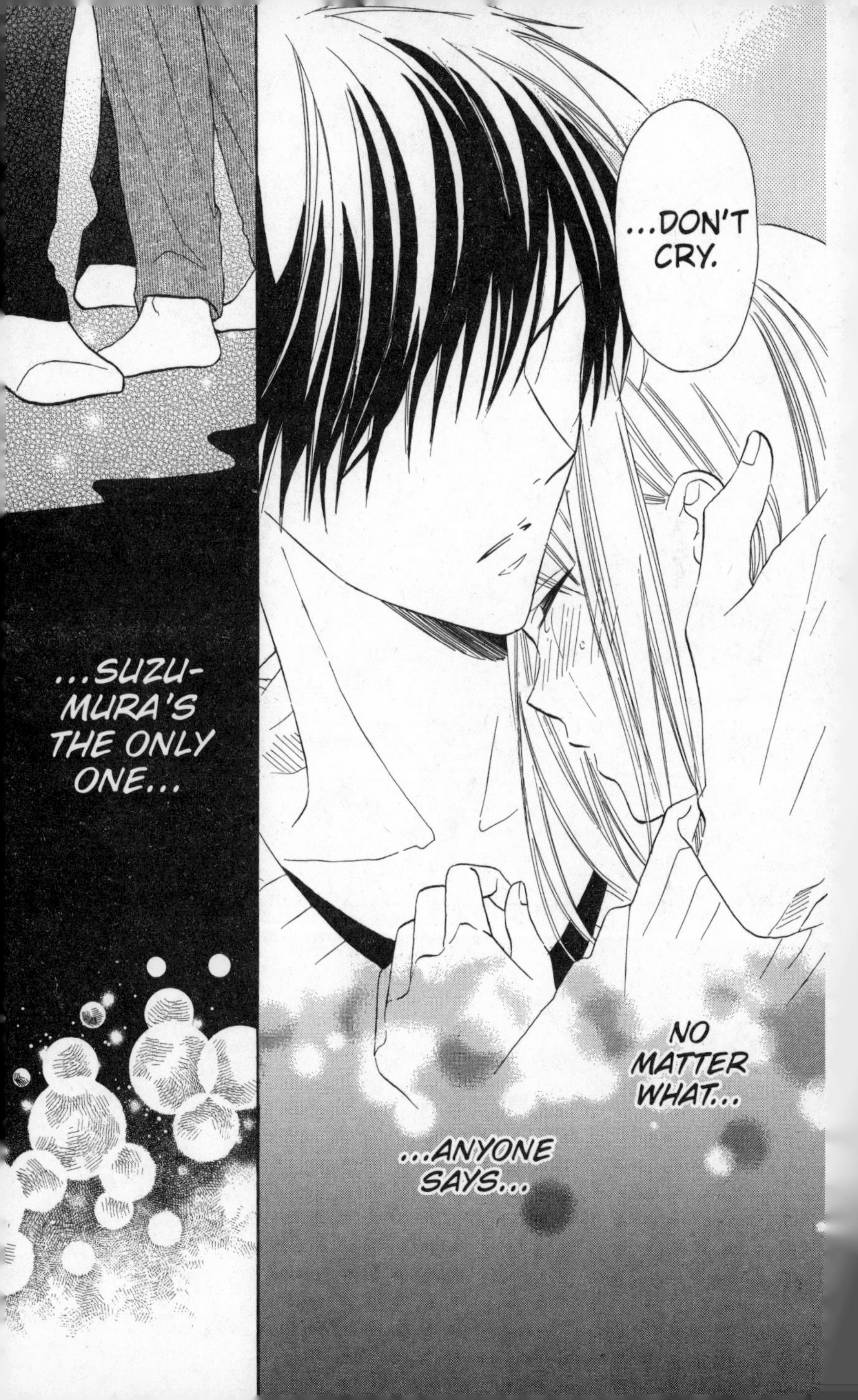
...DON'T CRY.
NO MATTER WHAT...
...ANYONE SAYS...
...SUZU-MURA'S THE ONLY ONE...

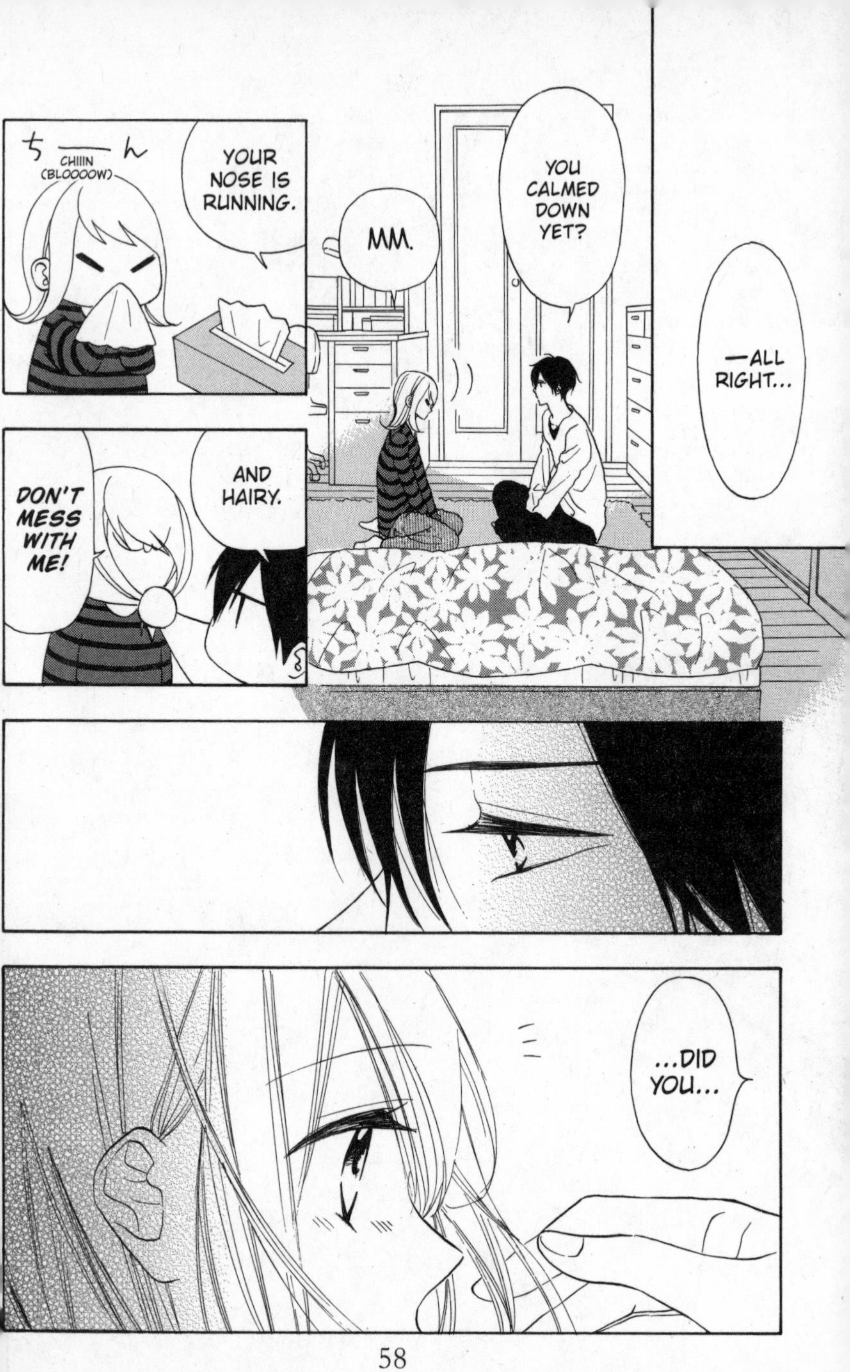
—ALL RIGHT...
YOU CALMED DOWN YET?
MM.
YOUR NOSE IS RUNNING.
ちーん
CHIIIN (BLOOOOW)
AND HAIRY.
DON'T MESS WITH ME!
...DID YOU...

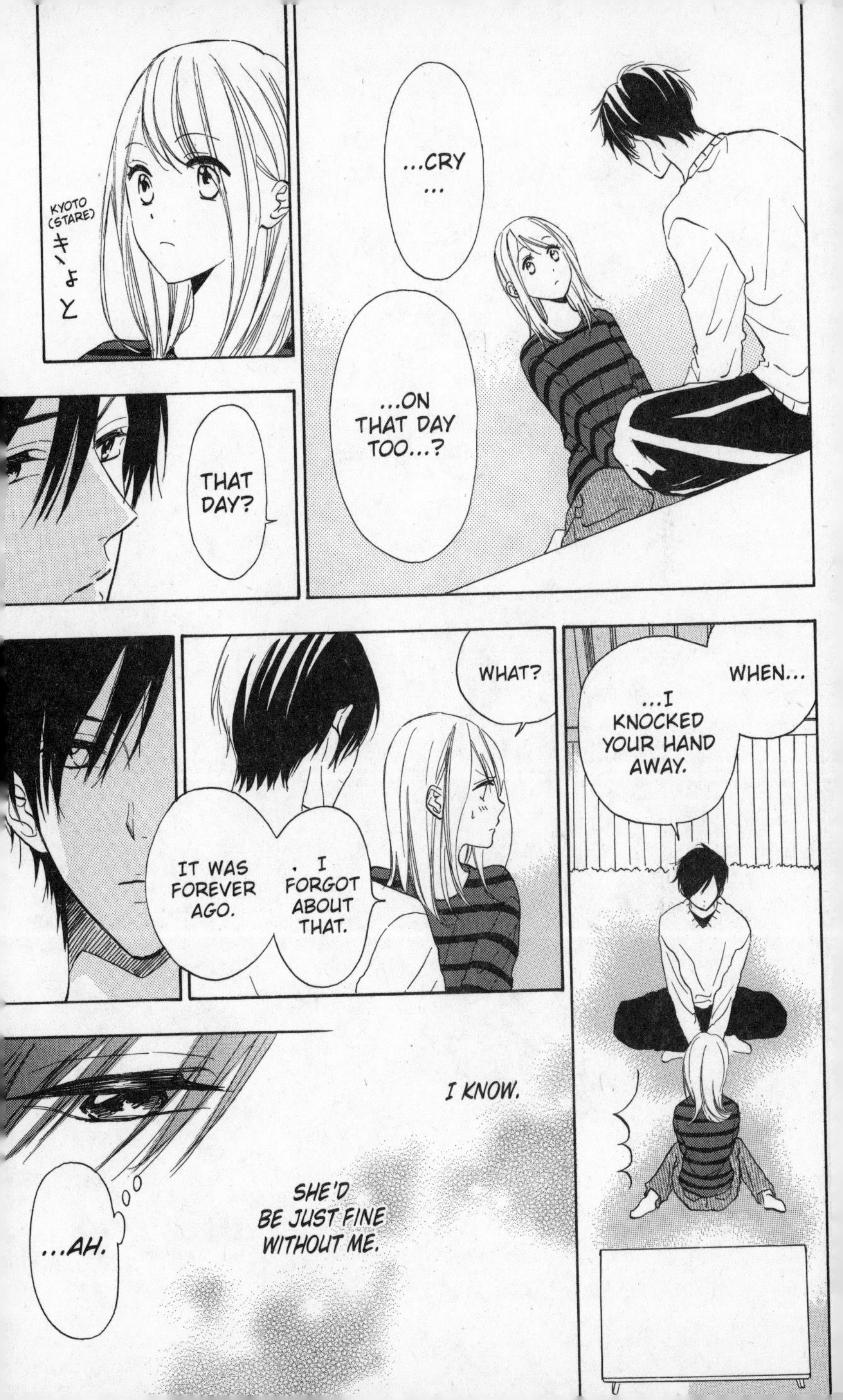
...CRY ...
...ON THAT DAY TOO...?
KYOTO (STARE)
キょと
THAT DAY?
WHEN...
...I KNOCKED YOUR HAND AWAY.
WHAT?
I FORGOT ABOUT THAT.
IT WAS FOREVER AGO.
I KNOW.
SHE'D BE JUST FINE WITHOUT ME.
...AH.

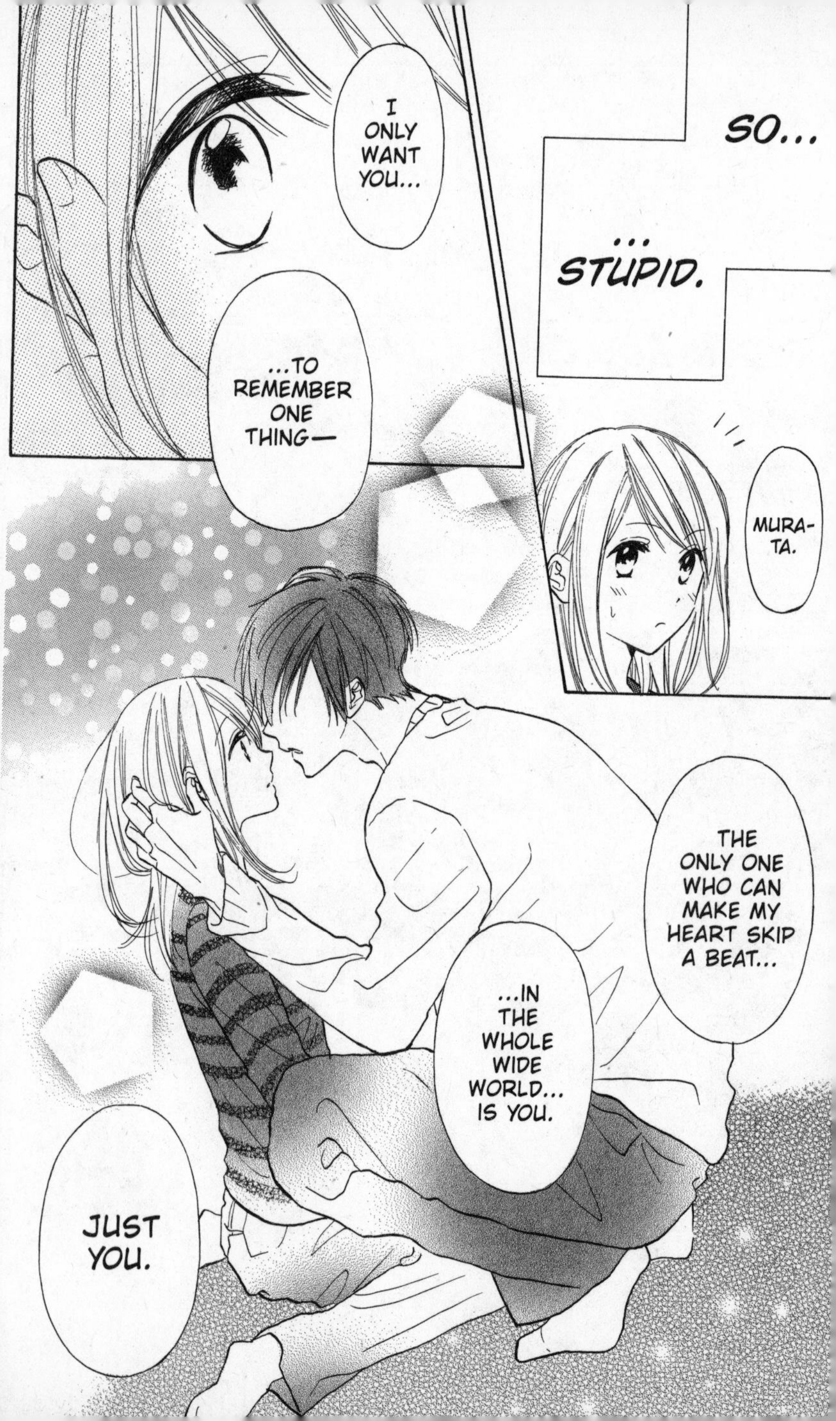
SO...
... STUPID.
I ONLY WANT YOU...
...TO REMEMBER ONE THING—
MURA-TA.
THE ONLY ONE WHO CAN MAKE MY HEART SKIP A BEAT...
...IN THE WHOLE WIDE WORLD... IS YOU.
JUST YOU.

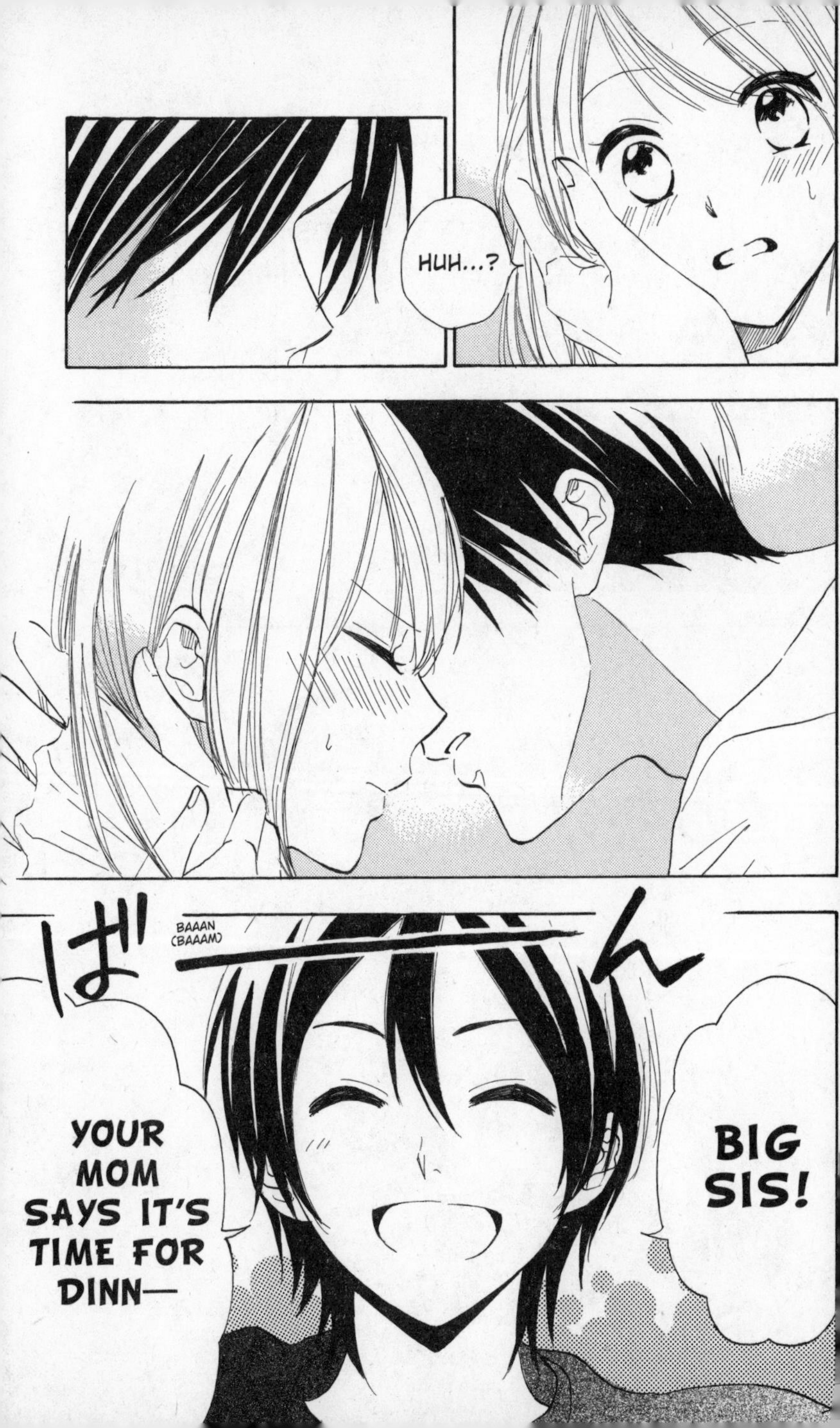
HUH...?
ばーーん
BAAAN (BAAAM)
BIG SIS!
YOUR MOM SAYS IT'S TIME FOR DINN—

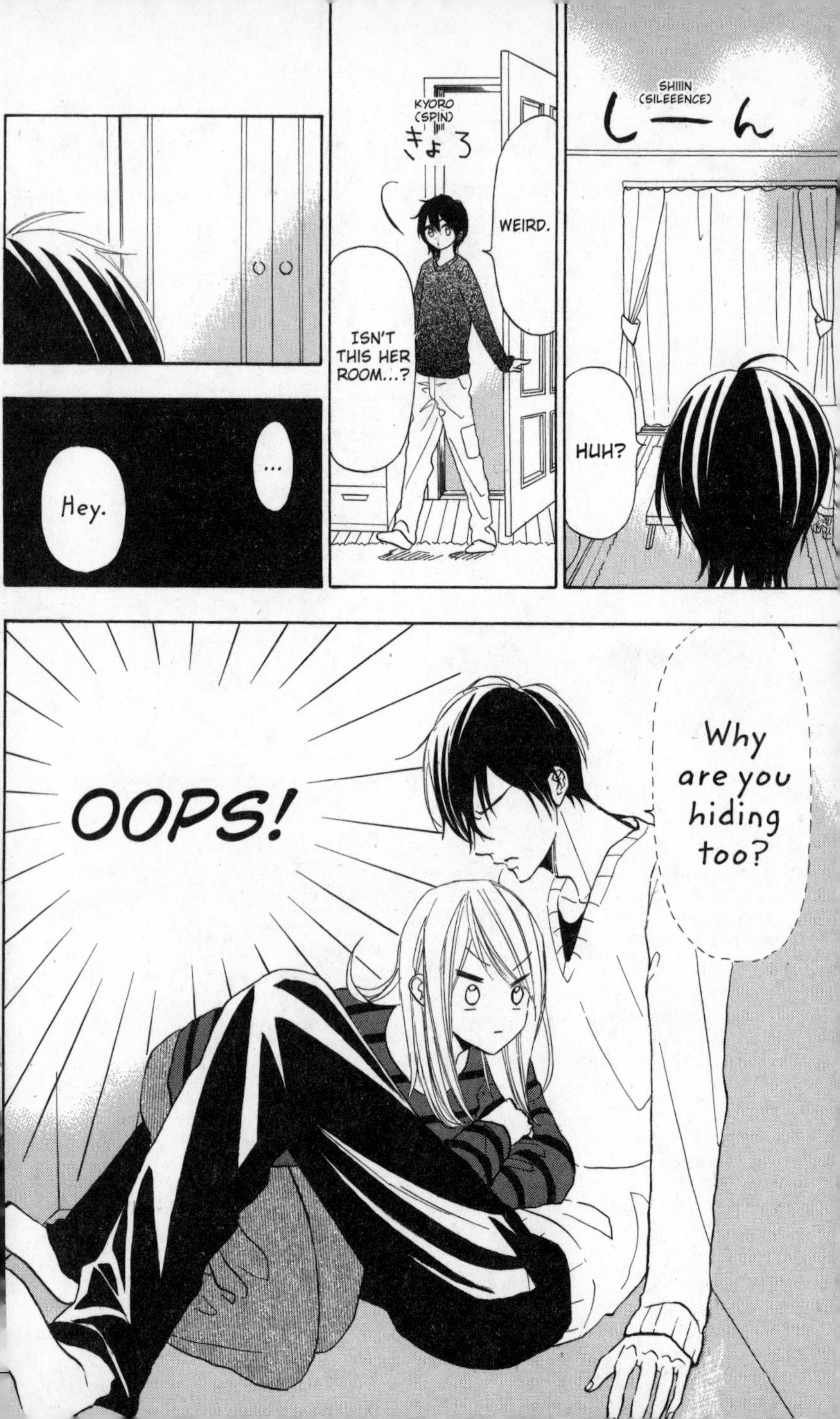
SHIIIN (SILEEENCE)
しーん
HUH?
KYORO (SPIN)
きょろ
WEIRD.
ISN'T THIS HER ROOM...?
...
Hey.
Why are you hiding too?
OOPS!

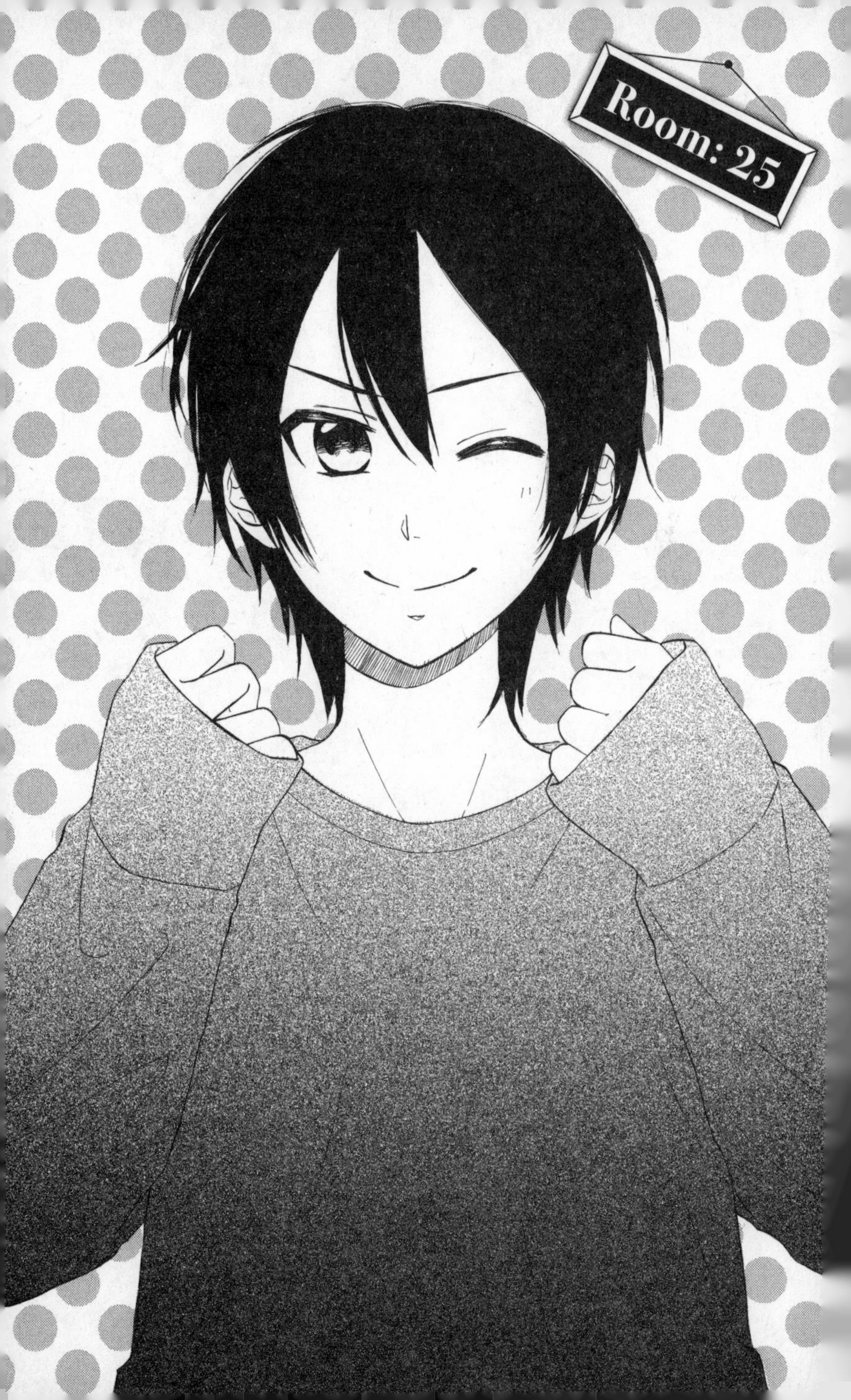
Room: 25

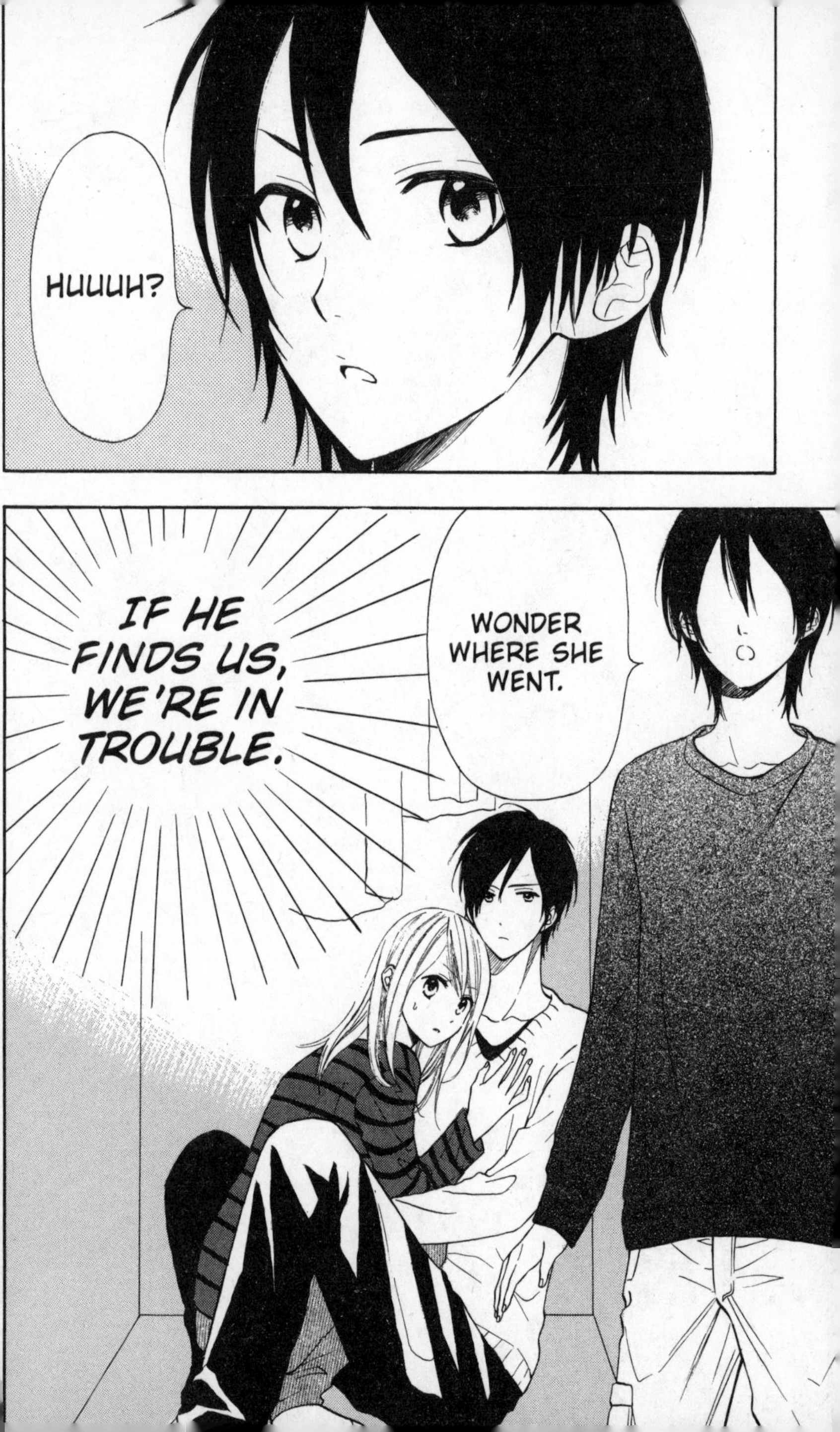
HUUUH?
WONDER WHERE SHE WENT.
IF HE FINDS US, WE'RE IN TROUBLE.

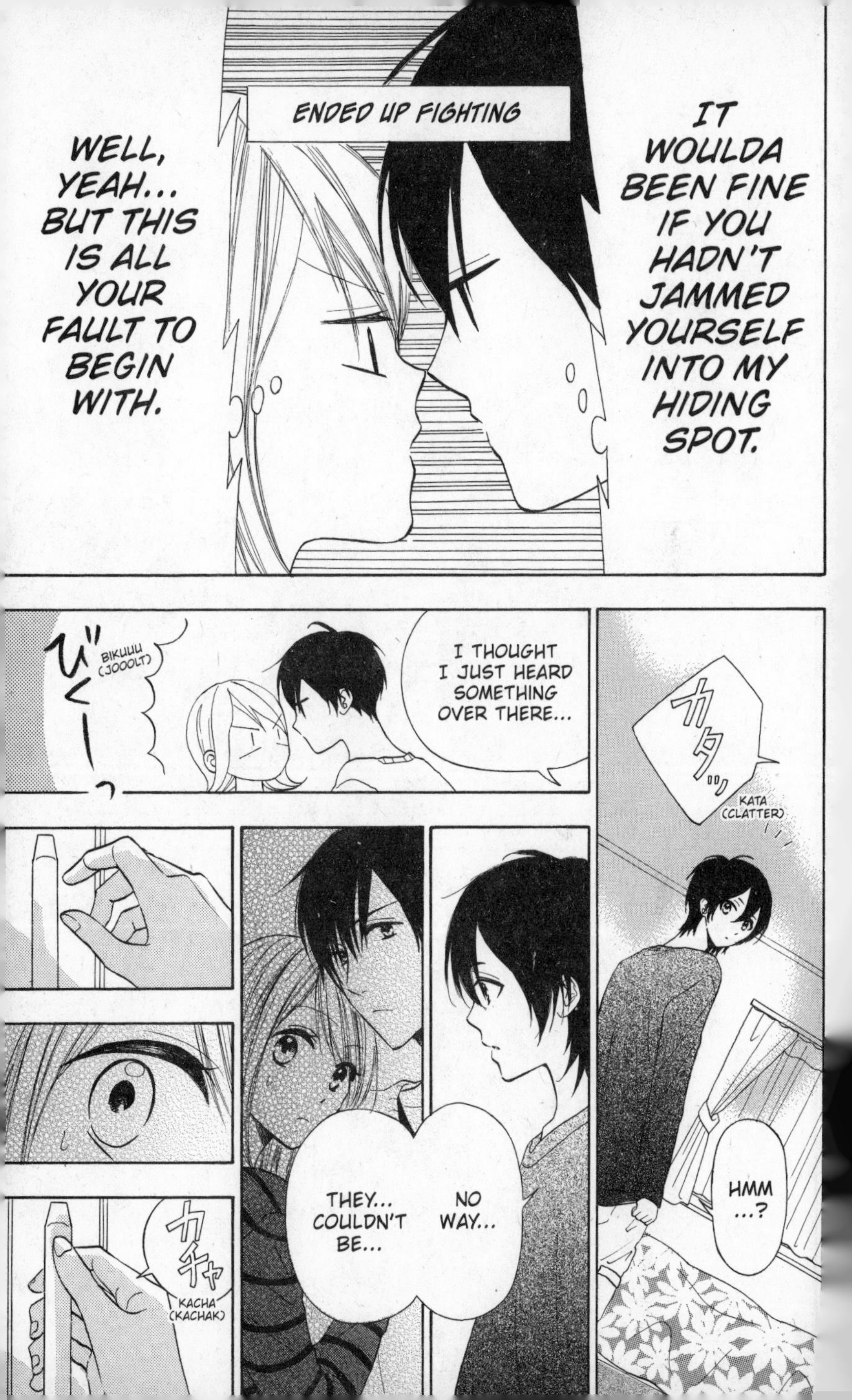
ENDED UP FIGHTING
IT WOULDA BEEN FINE IF YOU HADN'T JAMMED YOURSELF INTO MY HIDING SPOT.
WELL, YEAH... BUT THIS IS ALL YOUR FAULT TO BEGIN WITH.
カタッ
KATA (CLATTER)
HMM ...?
I THOUGHT I JUST HEARD SOMETHING OVER THERE...
びくーっ
BIKUUU (JOOOLT)
NO WAY...
THEY... COULDN'T BE...
カチャ
KACHA (KACHAK)

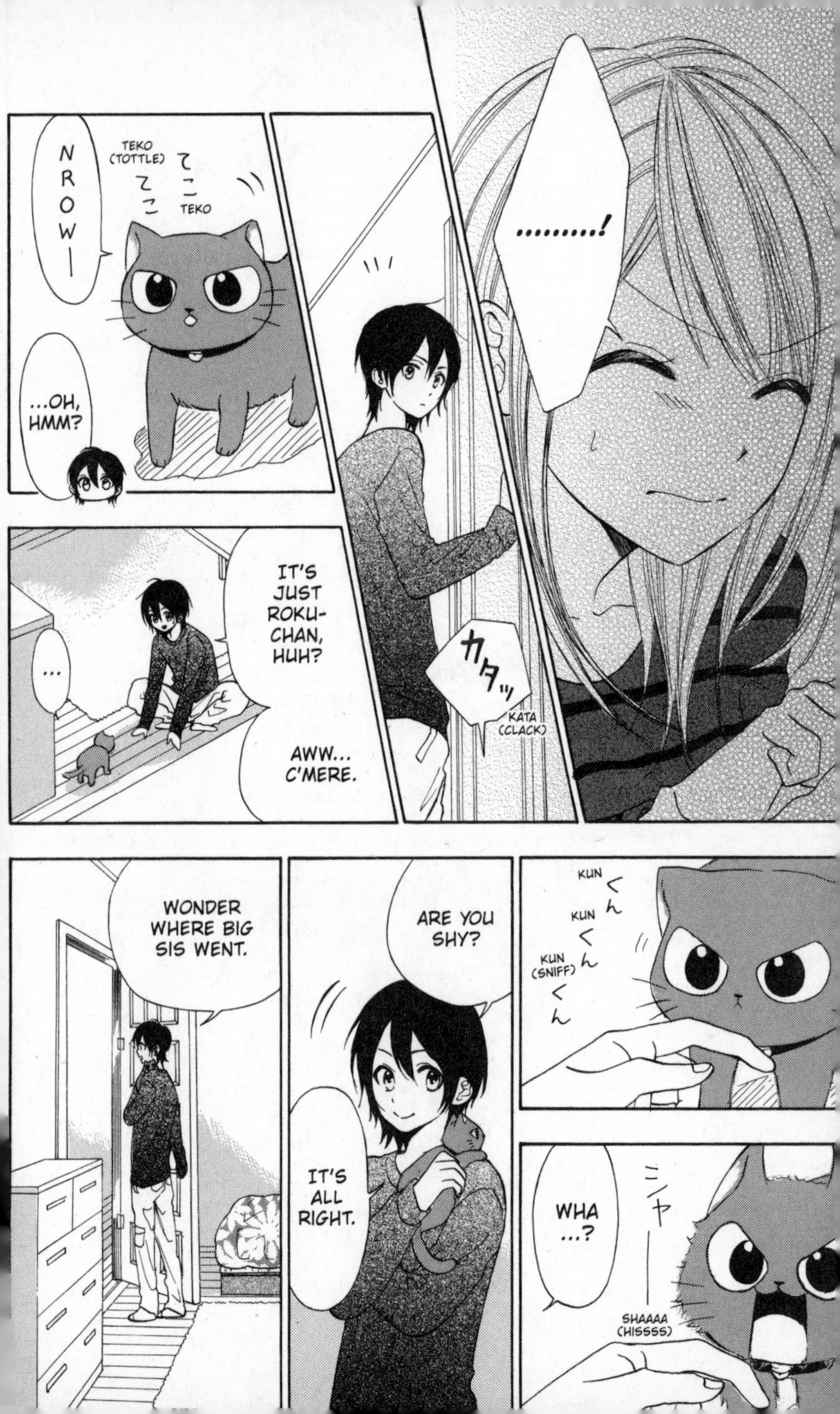
..........!
カタッ
KATA (CLACK)
てこ てこ
TEKO (TOTTLE) TEKO
NROW!
...OH, HMM?
IT'S JUST ROKU-CHAN, HUH?
...
AWW... C'MERE.
くん くん くん
KUN KUN KUN (SNIFF)
シャー
SHAAAA (HISSSS)
WHA ...?
ARE YOU SHY?
IT'S ALL RIGHT.
WONDER WHERE BIG SIS WENT.

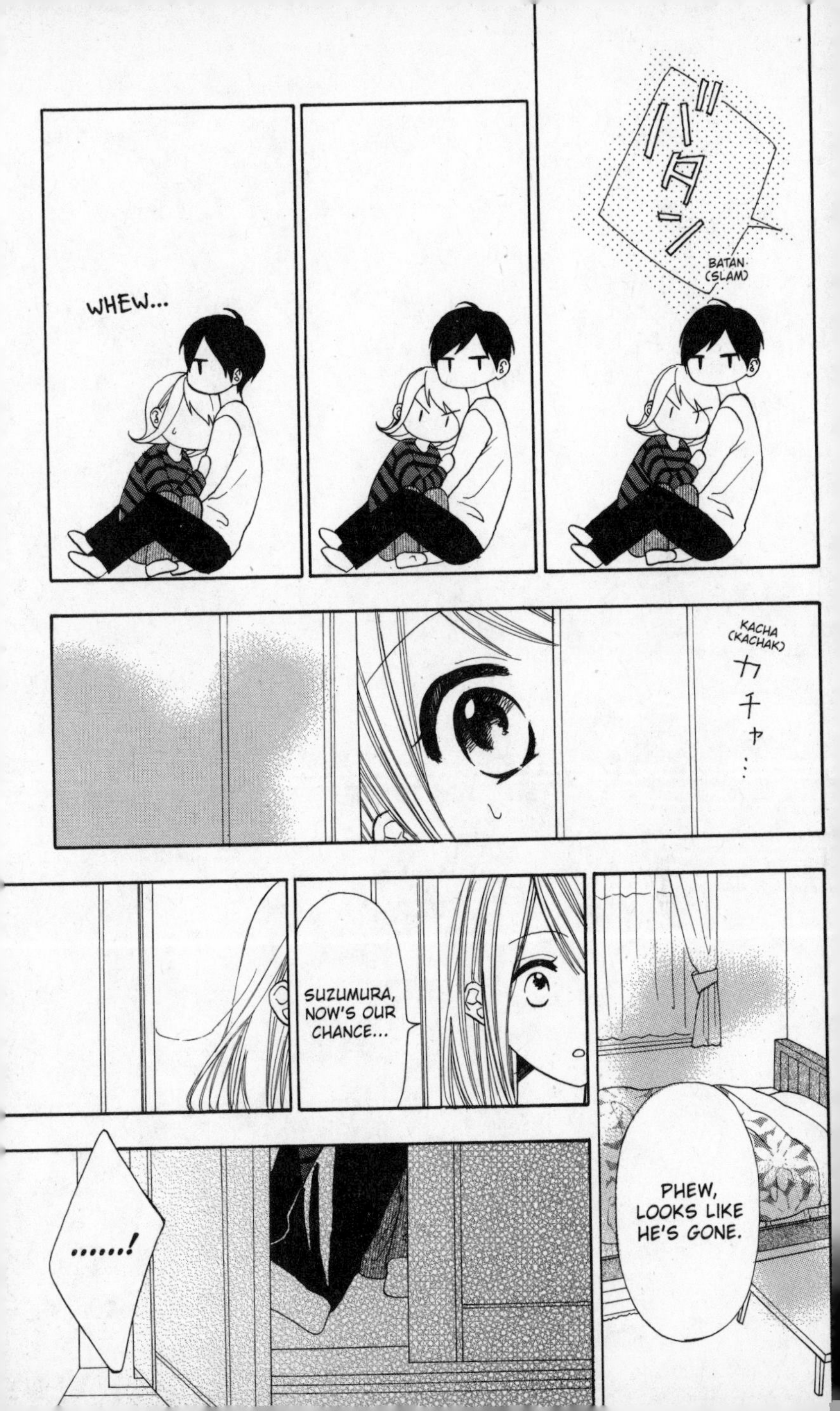
バターン
BATAN (SLAM)
WHEW...
KACHA (KACHAK)
カチャ…
PHEW, LOOKS LIKE HE'S GONE.
SUZUMURA, NOW'S OUR CHANCE...
......!

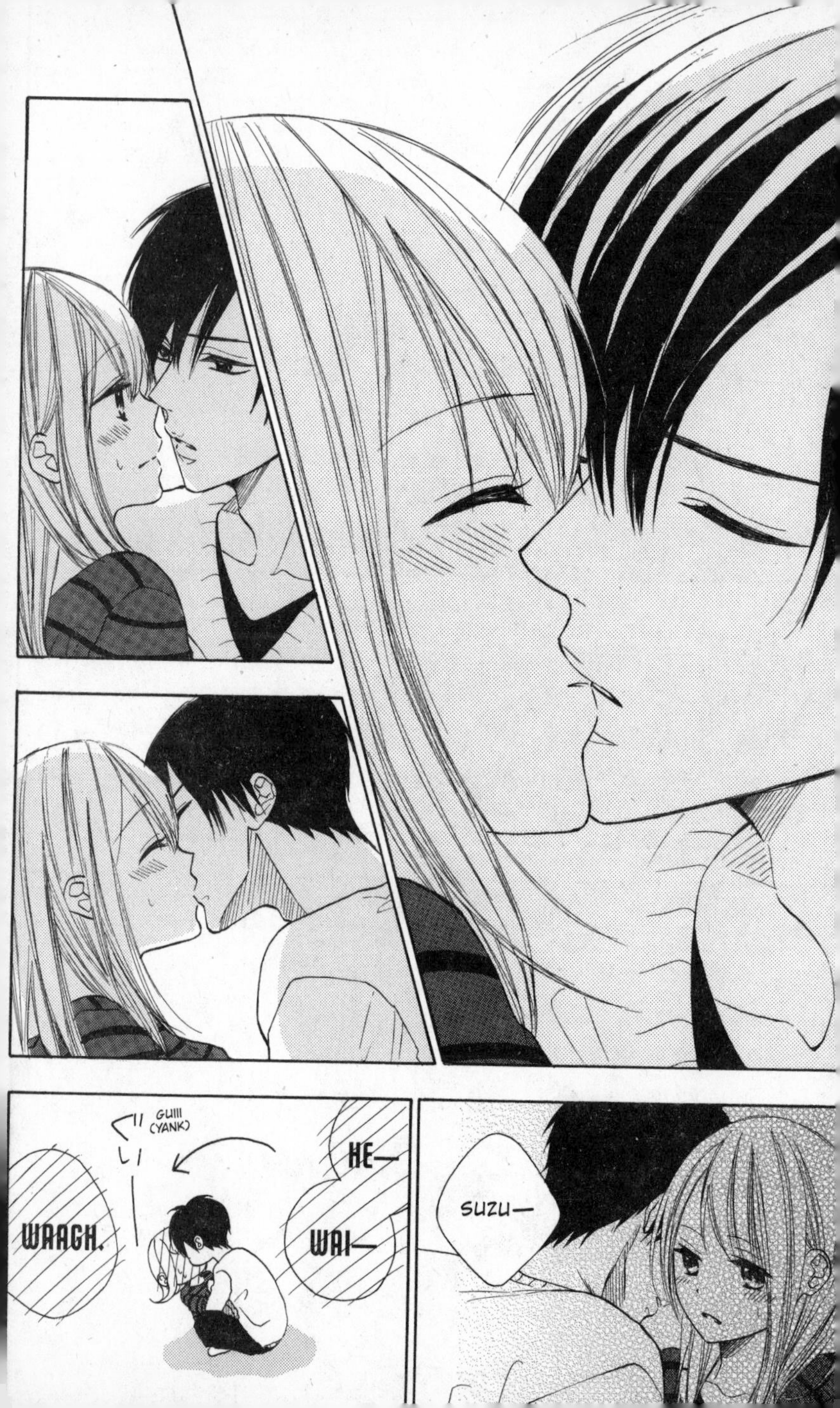
SUZU—
HE—
WAI—
GUIII
(YANK)
WRAGH.

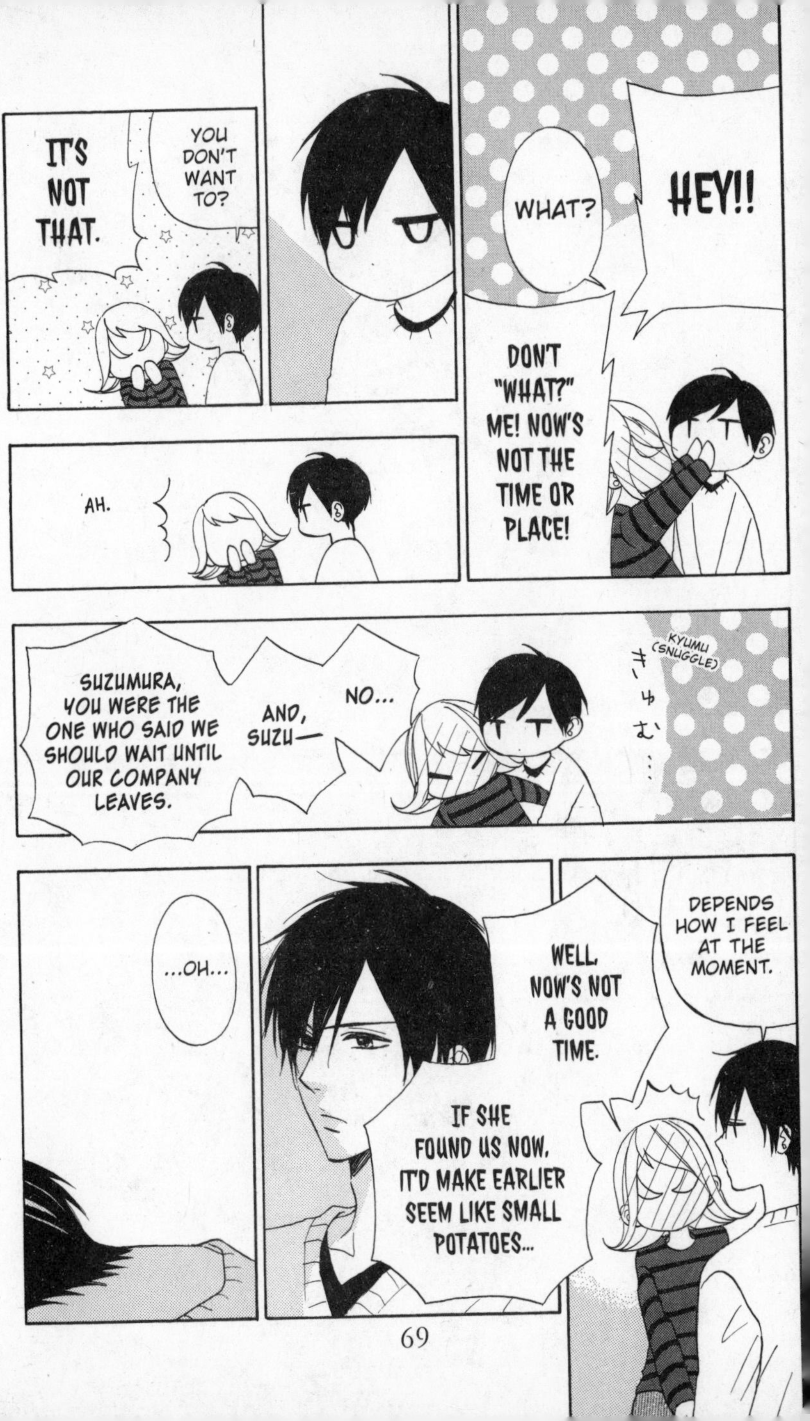
HEY!!
WHAT?
DON'T "WHAT?" ME! NOW'S NOT THE TIME OR PLACE!
YOU DON'T WANT TO?
IT'S NOT THAT.
AH.
KYUMU (SNUGGLE)
きゅむ…
NO...
AND, SUZU—
SUZUMURA, YOU WERE THE ONE WHO SAID WE SHOULD WAIT UNTIL OUR COMPANY LEAVES.
DEPENDS HOW I FEEL AT THE MOMENT.
WELL, NOW'S NOT A GOOD TIME.
IF SHE FOUND US NOW, IT'D MAKE EARLIER SEEM LIKE SMALL POTATOES...
...OH...

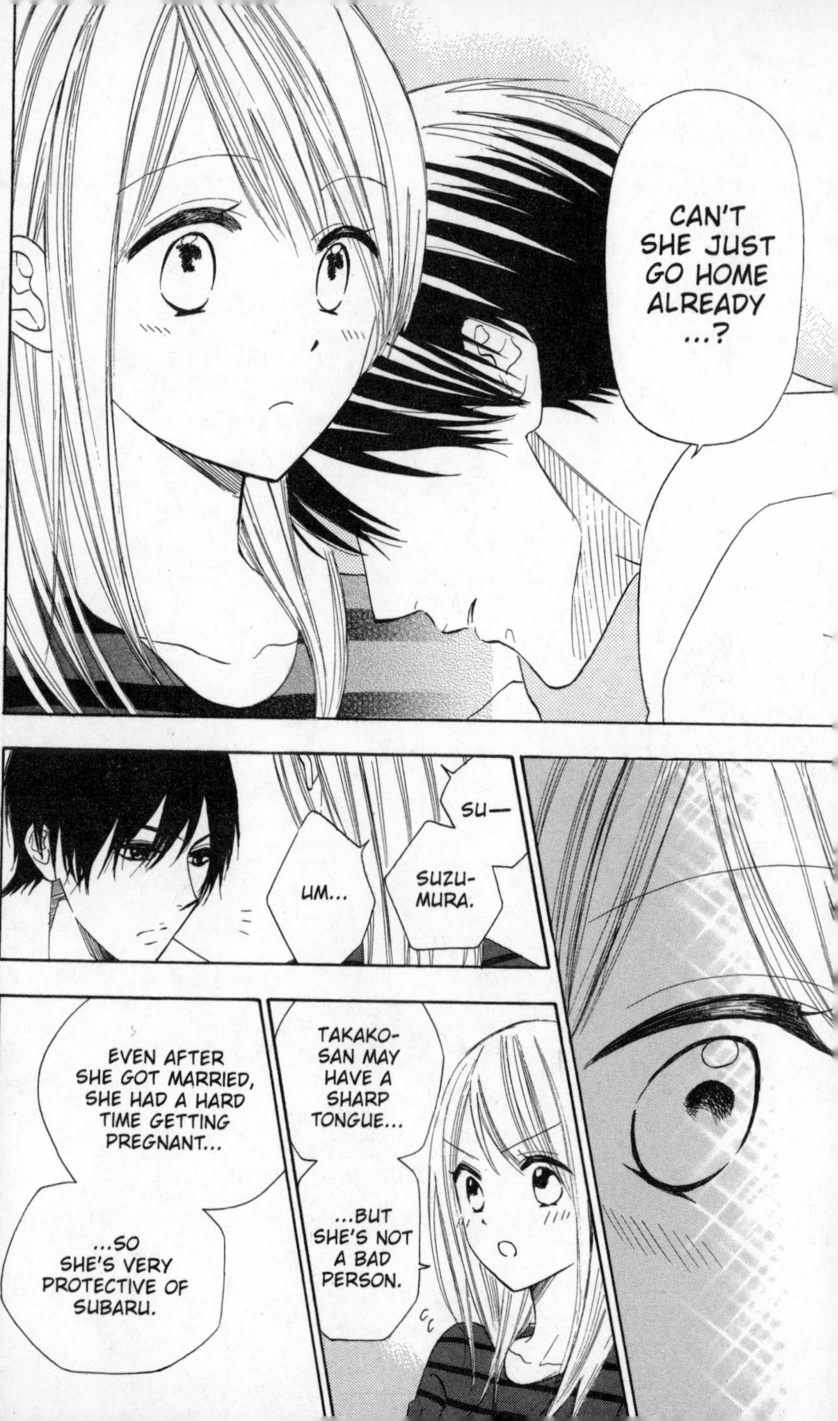
CAN'T SHE JUST GO HOME ALREADY ...?
SU—
SUZU-MURA.
UM...
TAKAKO-SAN MAY HAVE A SHARP TONGUE...
...BUT SHE'S NOT A BAD PERSON.
EVEN AFTER SHE GOT MARRIED, SHE HAD A HARD TIME GETTING PREGNANT...
...SO SHE'S VERY PROTECTIVE OF SUBARU.

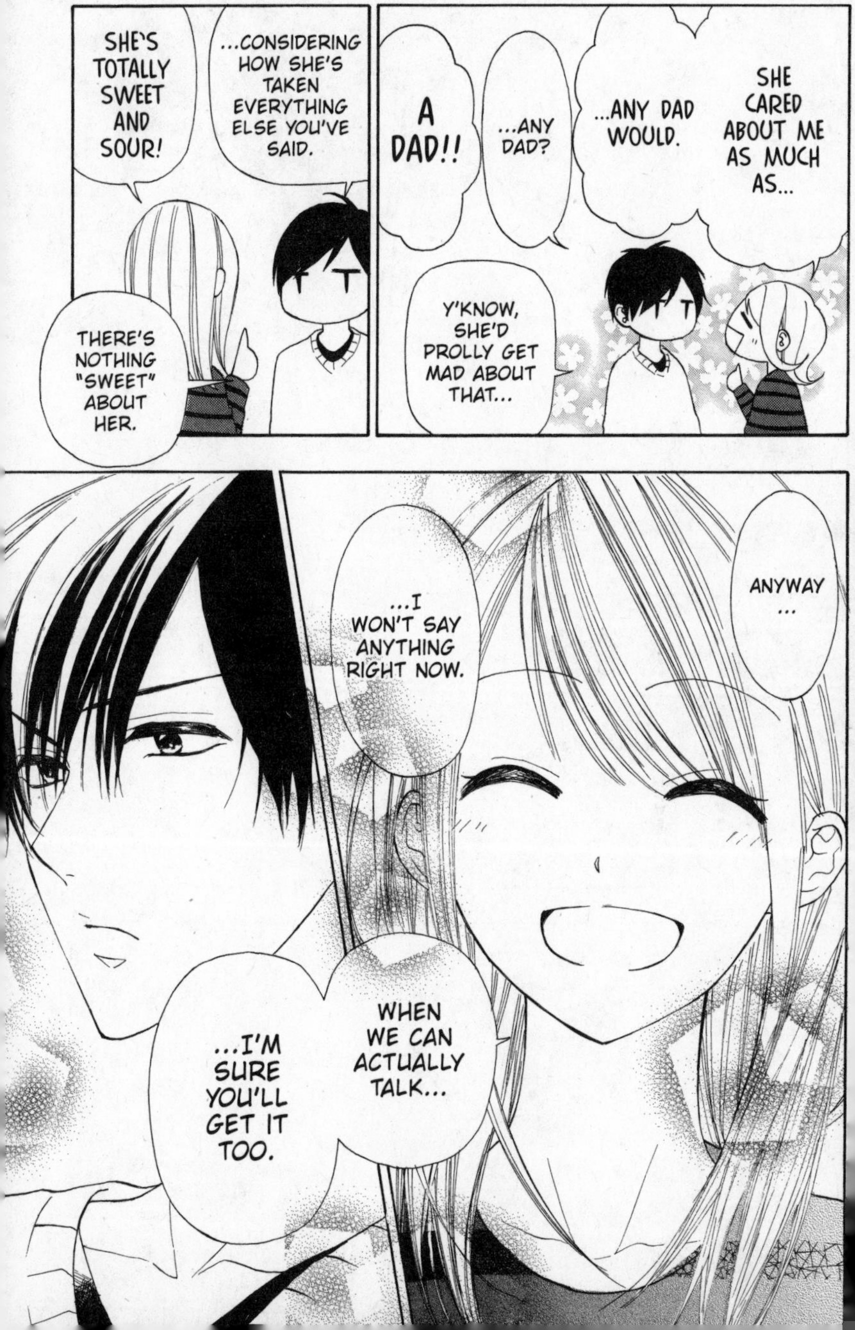
SHE CARED ABOUT ME AS MUCH AS...
...ANY DAD WOULD.
...ANY DAD?
A DAD!!
Y'KNOW, SHE'D PROLLY GET MAD ABOUT THAT...
...CONSIDERING HOW SHE'S TAKEN EVERYTHING ELSE YOU'VE SAID.
SHE'S TOTALLY SWEET AND SOUR!
THERE'S NOTHING "SWEET" ABOUT HER.
ANYWAY...
...I WON'T SAY ANYTHING RIGHT NOW.
WHEN WE CAN ACTUALLY TALK...
...I'M SURE YOU'LL GET IT TOO.

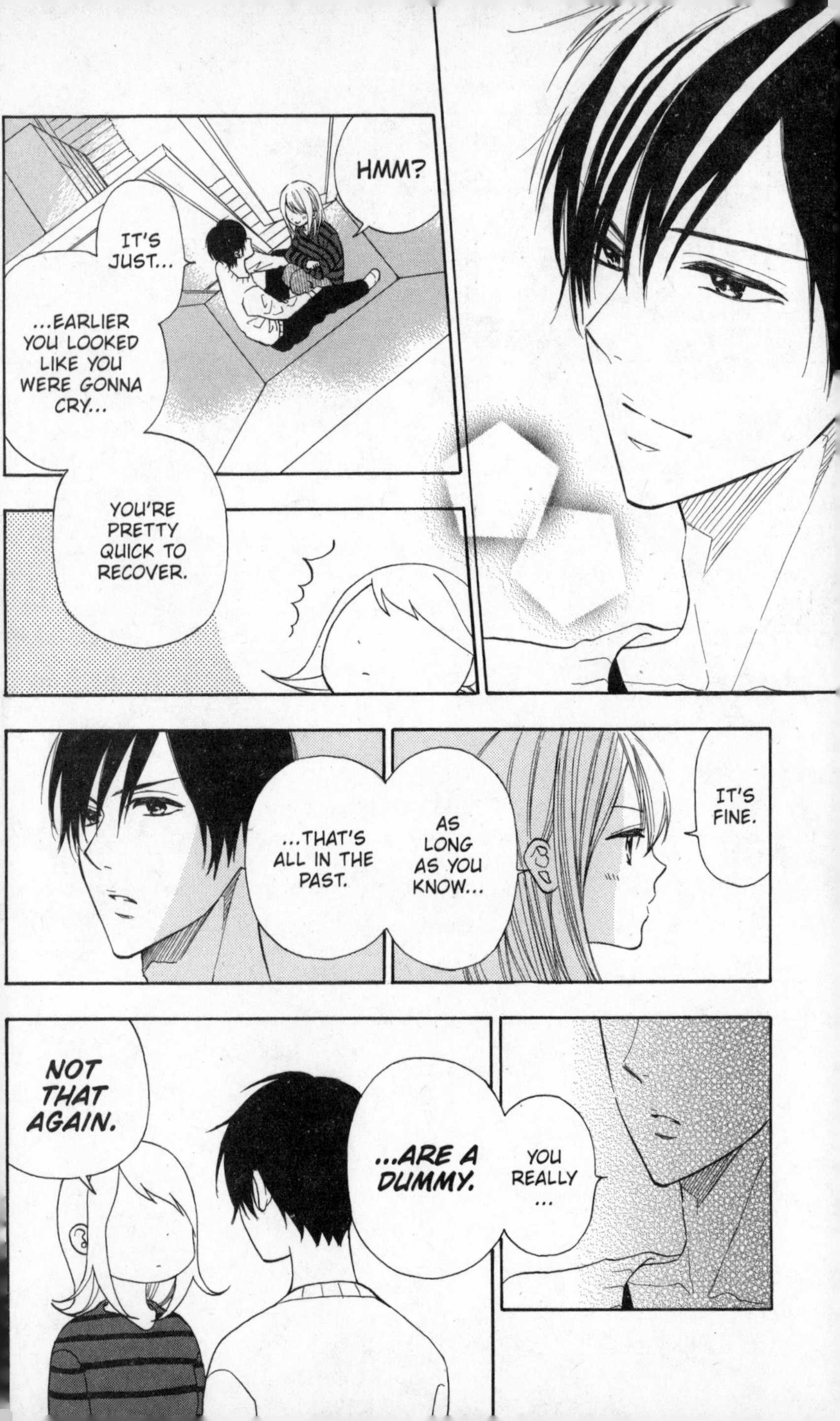
HMM?
IT'S JUST...
...EARLIER YOU LOOKED LIKE YOU WERE GONNA CRY...
YOU'RE PRETTY QUICK TO RECOVER.
IT'S FINE.
AS LONG AS YOU KNOW...
...THAT'S ALL IN THE PAST.
YOU REALLY ...
...ARE A DUMMY.
NOT THAT AGAIN.

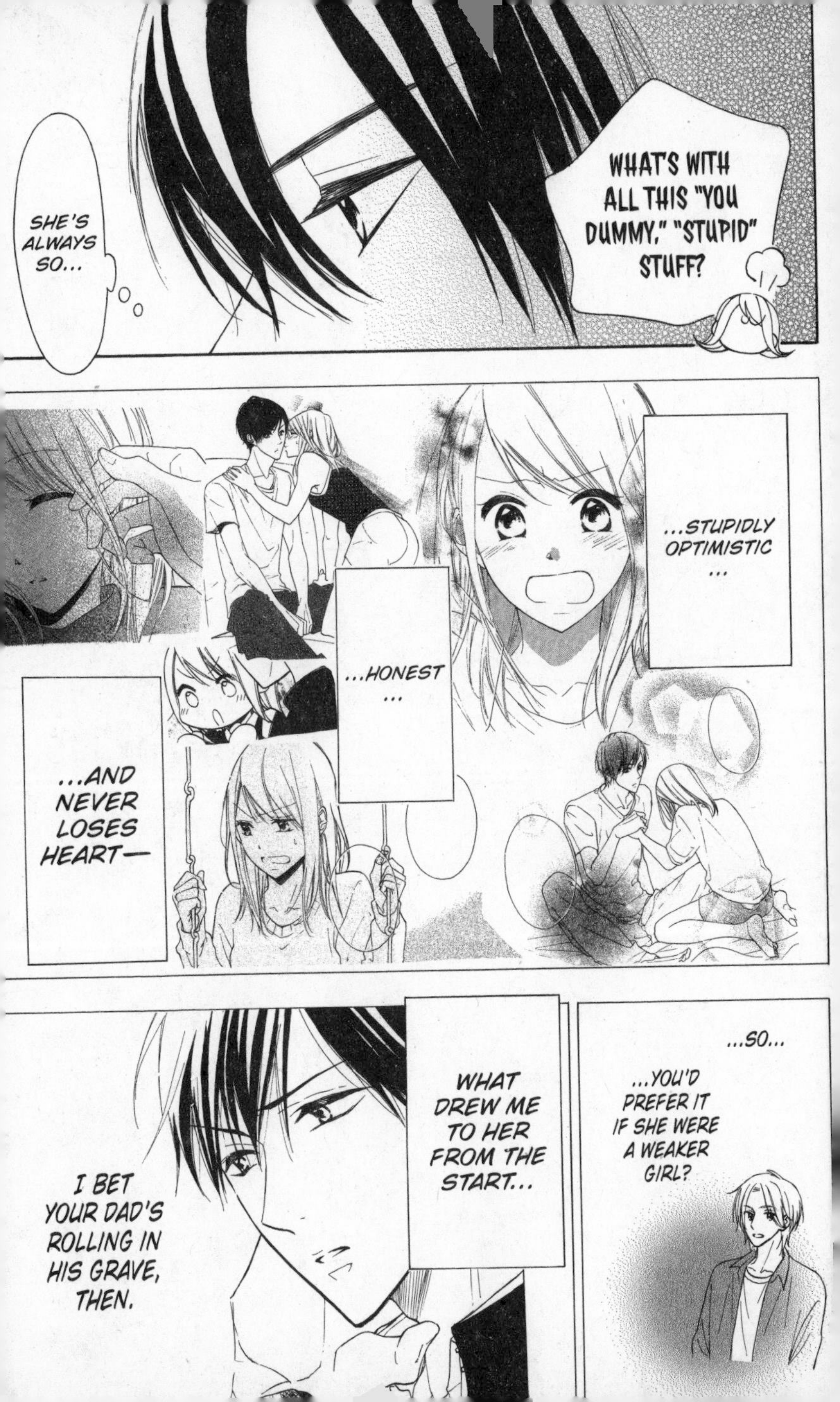
WHAT'S WITH ALL THIS "YOU DUMMY," "STUPID" STUFF?
SHE'S ALWAYS SO...
...STUPIDLY OPTIMISTIC ...
...HONEST ...
...AND NEVER LOSES HEART—
...SO...
...YOU'D PREFER IT IF SHE WERE A WEAKER GIRL?
WHAT DREW ME TO HER FROM THE START...
I BET YOUR DAD'S ROLLING IN HIS GRAVE, THEN.

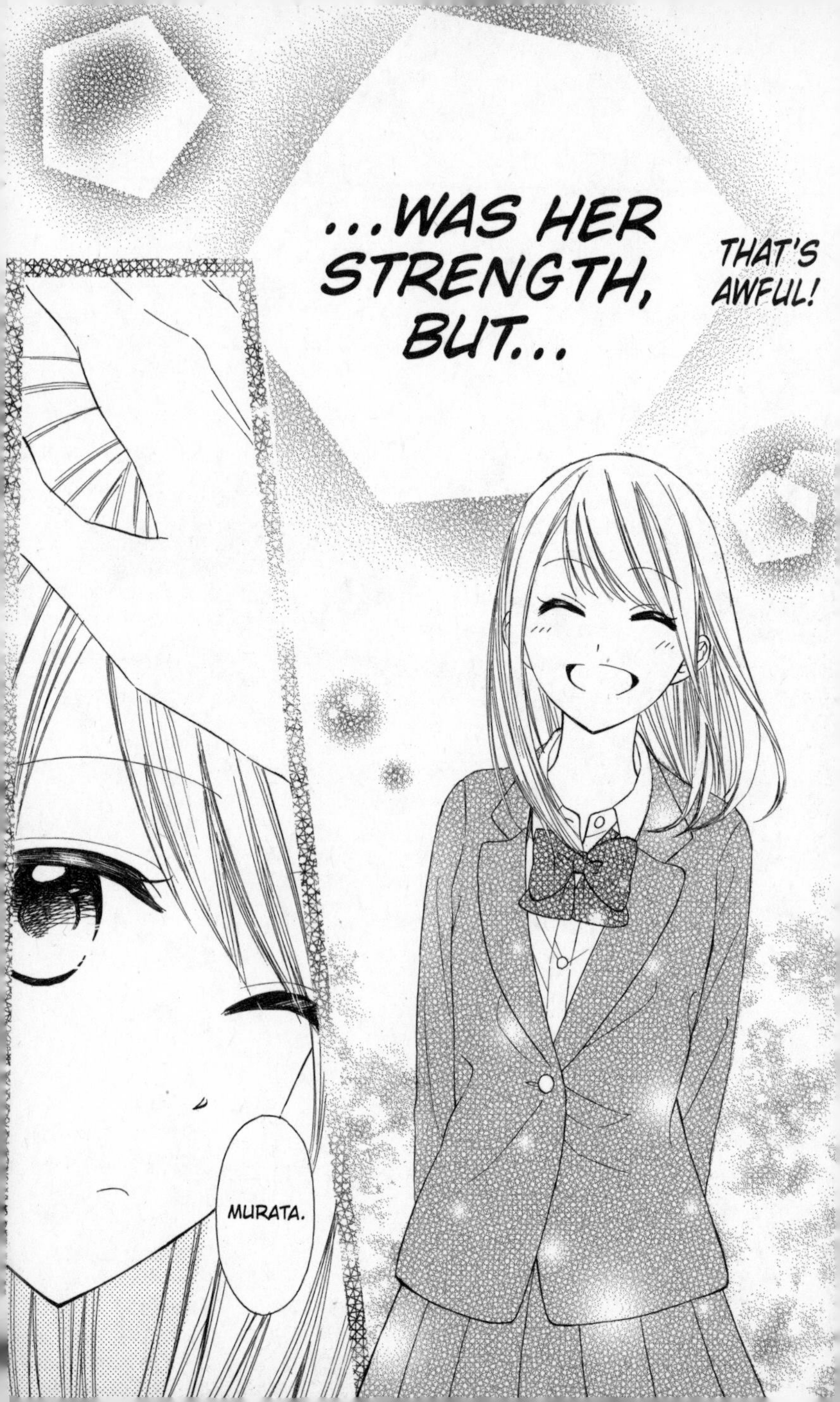
THAT'S AWFUL!
...WAS HER STRENGTH, BUT...
MURATA.

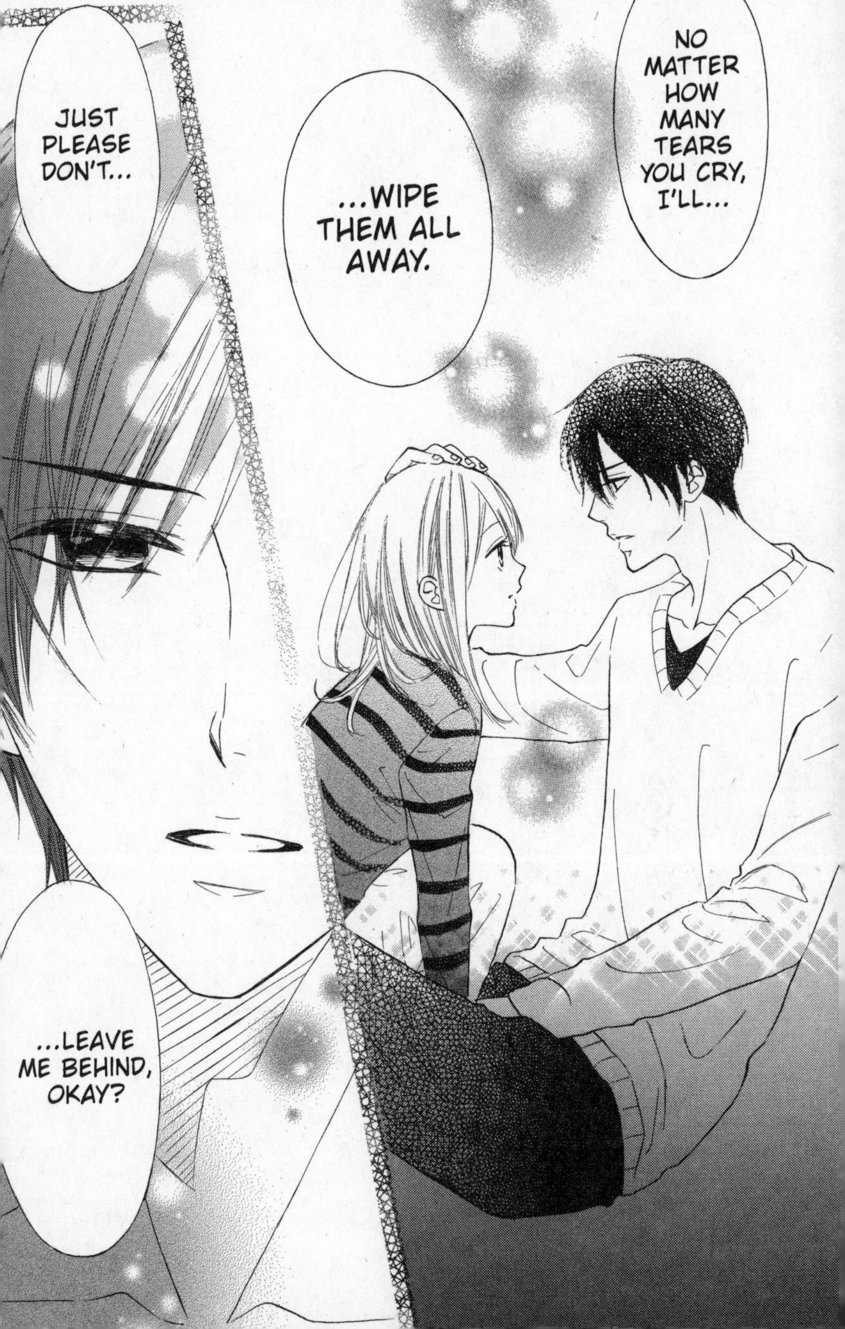
NO MATTER HOW MANY TEARS YOU CRY, I'LL...
...WIPE THEM ALL AWAY.
JUST PLEASE DON'T...
...LEAVE ME BEHIND, OKAY?

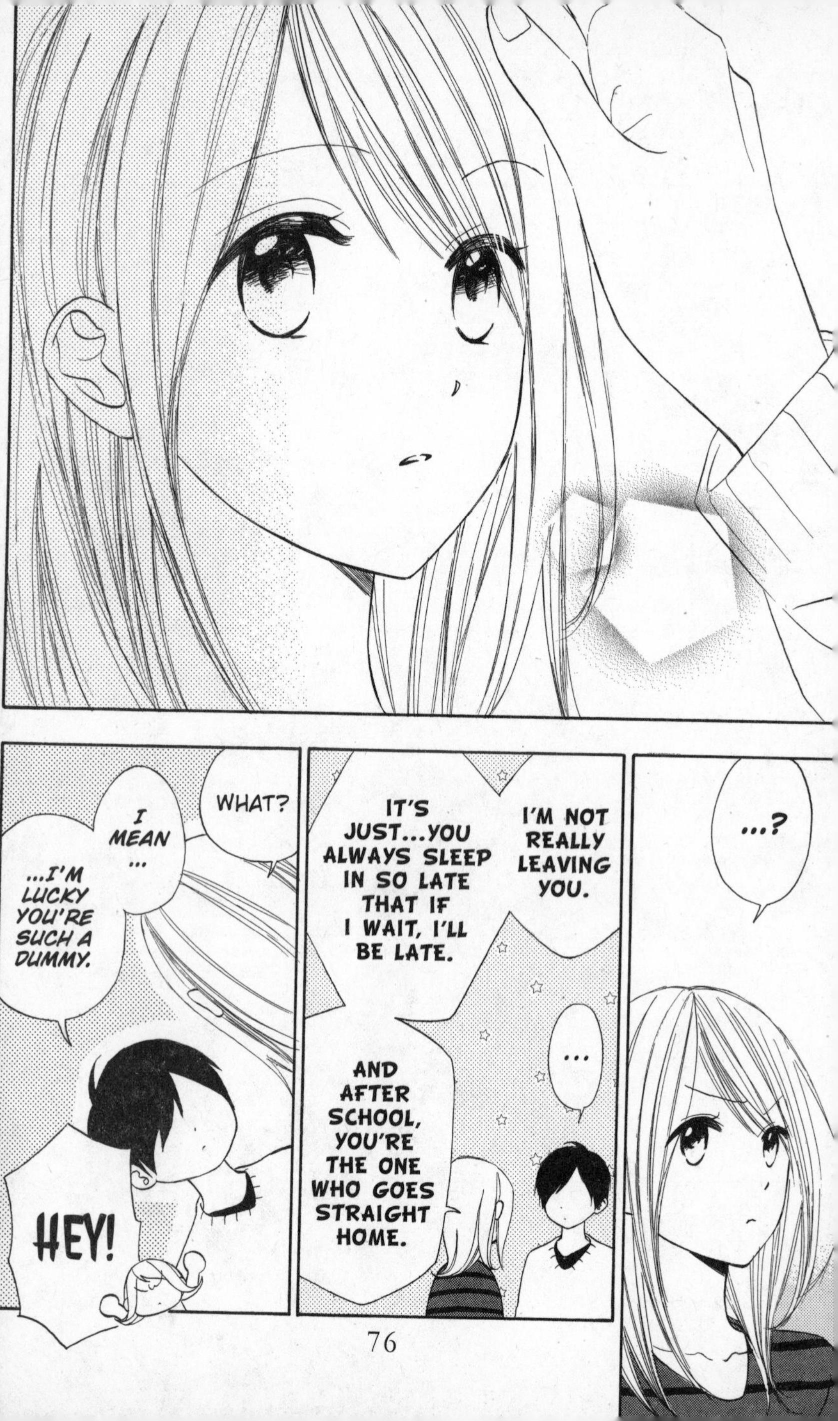

...?
I'M NOT REALLY LEAVING YOU.
IT'S JUST...YOU ALWAYS SLEEP IN SO LATE THAT IF I WAIT, I'LL BE LATE.
...
AND AFTER SCHOOL, YOU'RE THE ONE WHO GOES STRAIGHT HOME.
WHAT?
I MEAN ...
...I'M LUCKY YOU'RE SUCH A DUMMY.
HEY!

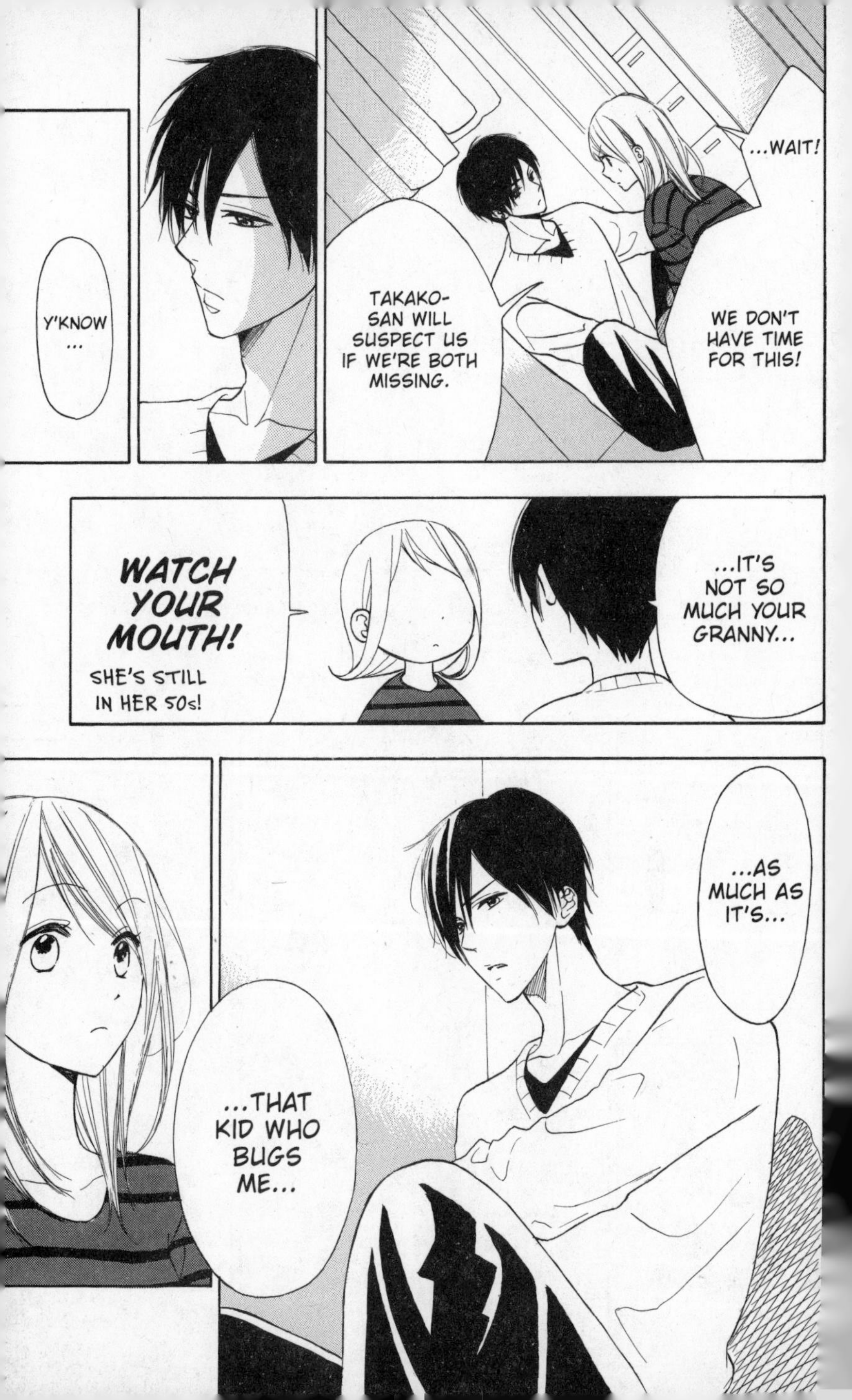
...WAIT!
WE DON'T HAVE TIME FOR THIS!
TAKAKO-SAN WILL SUSPECT US IF WE'RE BOTH MISSING.
Y'KNOW ...
...IT'S NOT SO MUCH YOUR GRANNY...
WATCH YOUR MOUTH!
SHE'S STILL IN HER 50s!
...AS MUCH AS IT'S...
...THAT KID WHO BUGS ME...

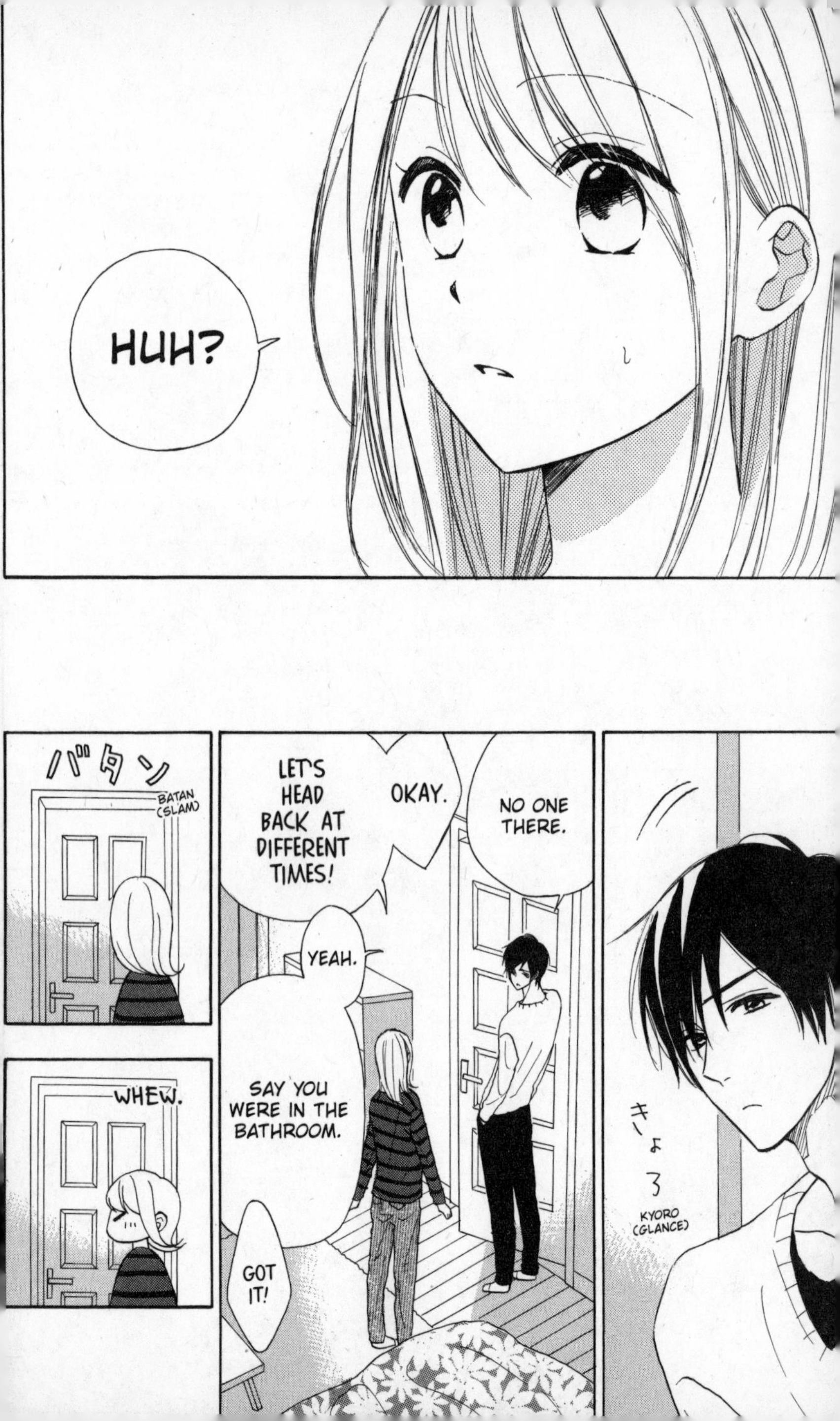
HUH?
きょろ
KYORO (GLANCE)
NO ONE THERE.
OKAY.
LET'S HEAD BACK AT DIFFERENT TIMES!
YEAH.
SAY YOU WERE IN THE BATHROOM.
GOT IT!
バタン
BATAN (SLAM)
WHEW.

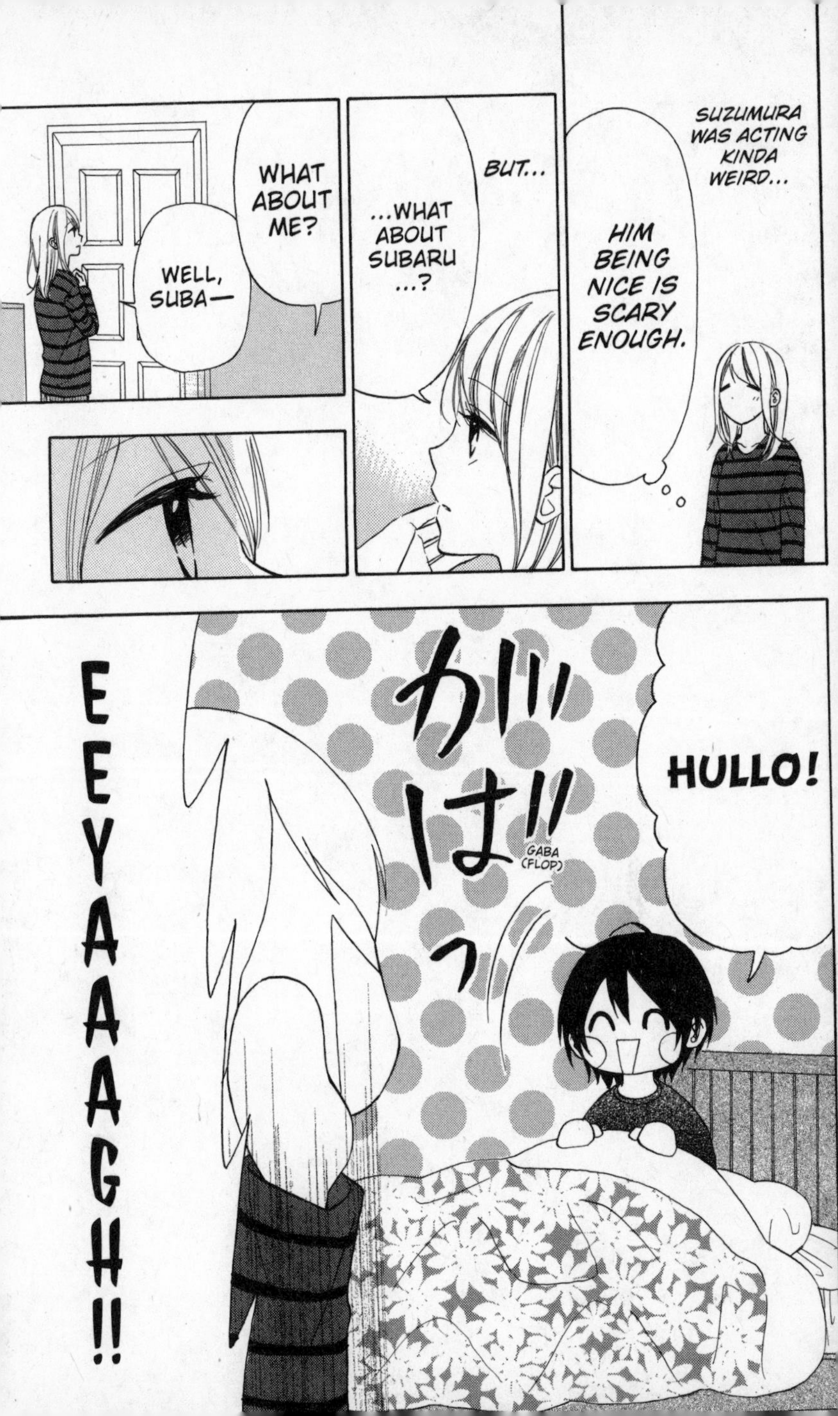
SUZUMURA WAS ACTING KINDA WEIRD...
HIM BEING NICE IS SCARY ENOUGH.
BUT...
...WHAT ABOUT SUBARU ...?
WHAT ABOUT ME?
WELL, SUBA—
HULLO!
がばっ
GABA (FLOP)
EEYAAAAGH!!

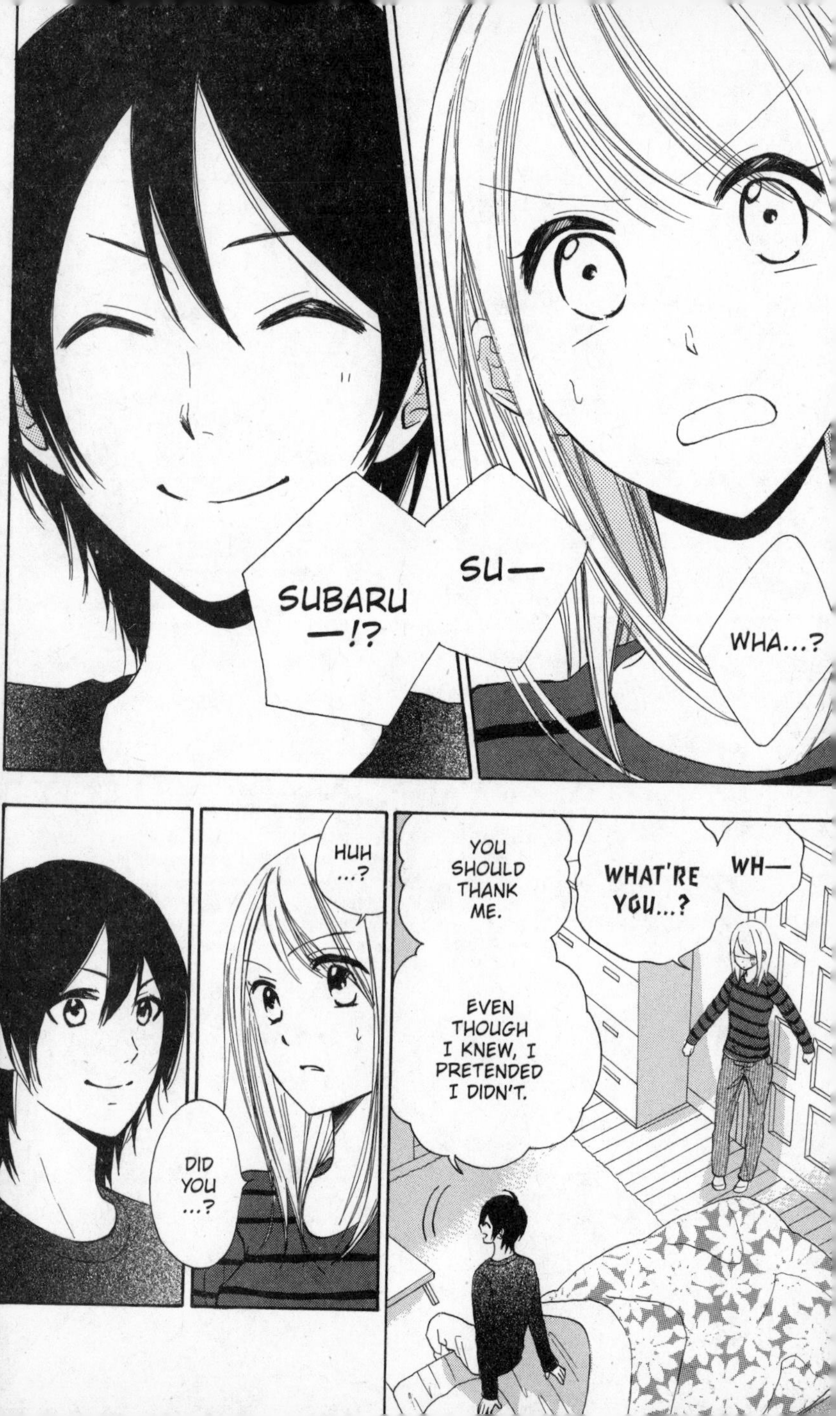
WHA...?
SU—
SUBARU—!?
WH—
WHAT'RE YOU...?
YOU SHOULD THANK ME.
EVEN THOUGH I KNEW, I PRETENDED I DIDN'T.
HUH...?
DID YOU...?

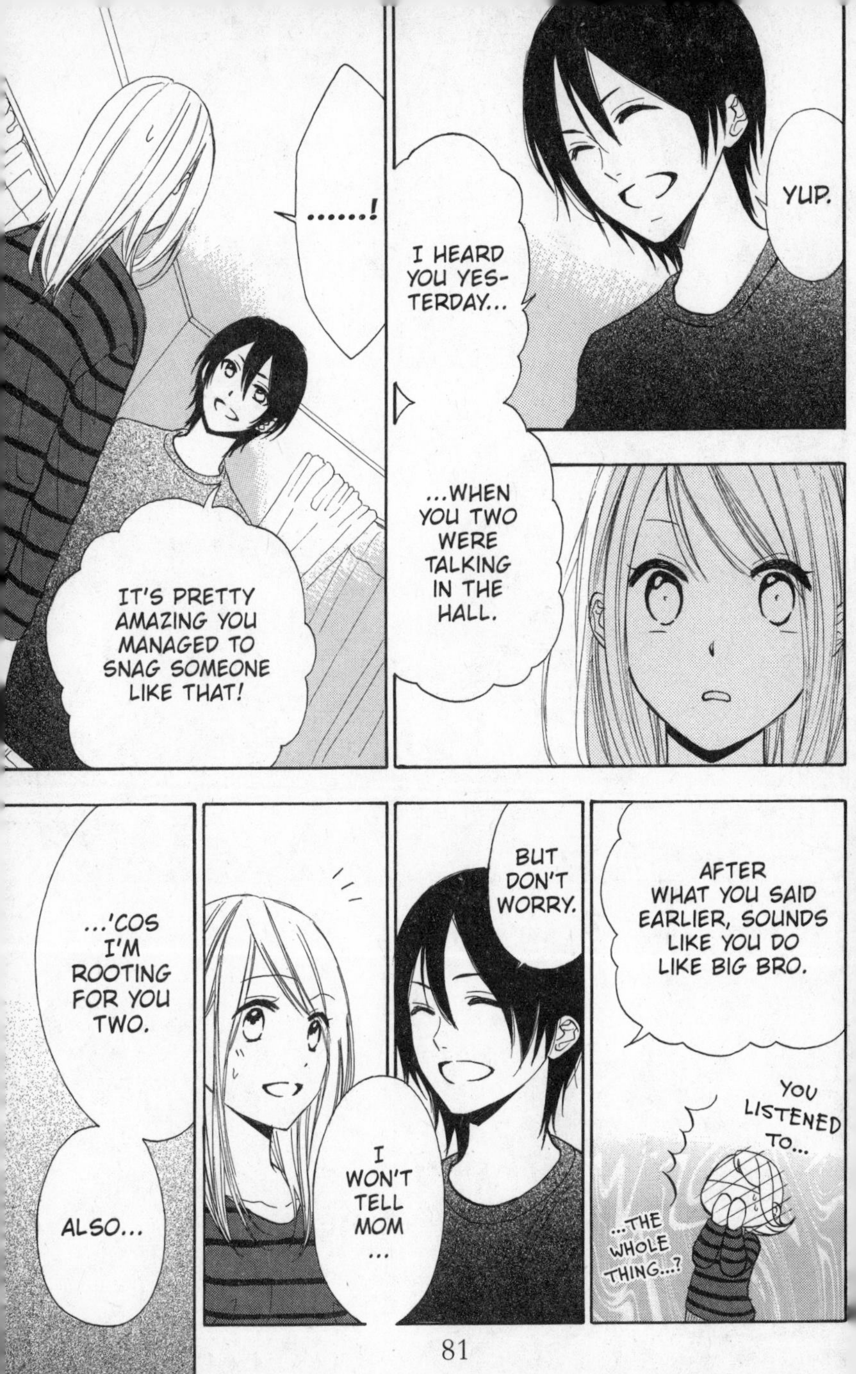
YUP.
I HEARD YOU YESTERDAY...
...WHEN YOU TWO WERE TALKING IN THE HALL.
......!
IT'S PRETTY AMAZING YOU MANAGED TO SNAG SOMEONE LIKE THAT!
AFTER WHAT YOU SAID EARLIER, SOUNDS LIKE YOU DO LIKE BIG BRO.
YOU LISTENED TO...
...THE WHOLE THING...?
BUT DON'T WORRY.
I WON'T TELL MOM...
...'COS I'M ROOTING FOR YOU TWO.
ALSO...

IF YOU MARRIED BIG BRO...

...IT'D BE BETTER FOR ME TOO.

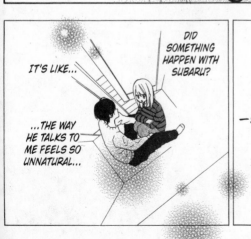

DID SOMETHING HAPPEN WITH SUBARU?

IT'S LIKE...

...THE WAY HE TALKS TO ME FEELS SO UNNATURAL...

—SUBARU?

—...

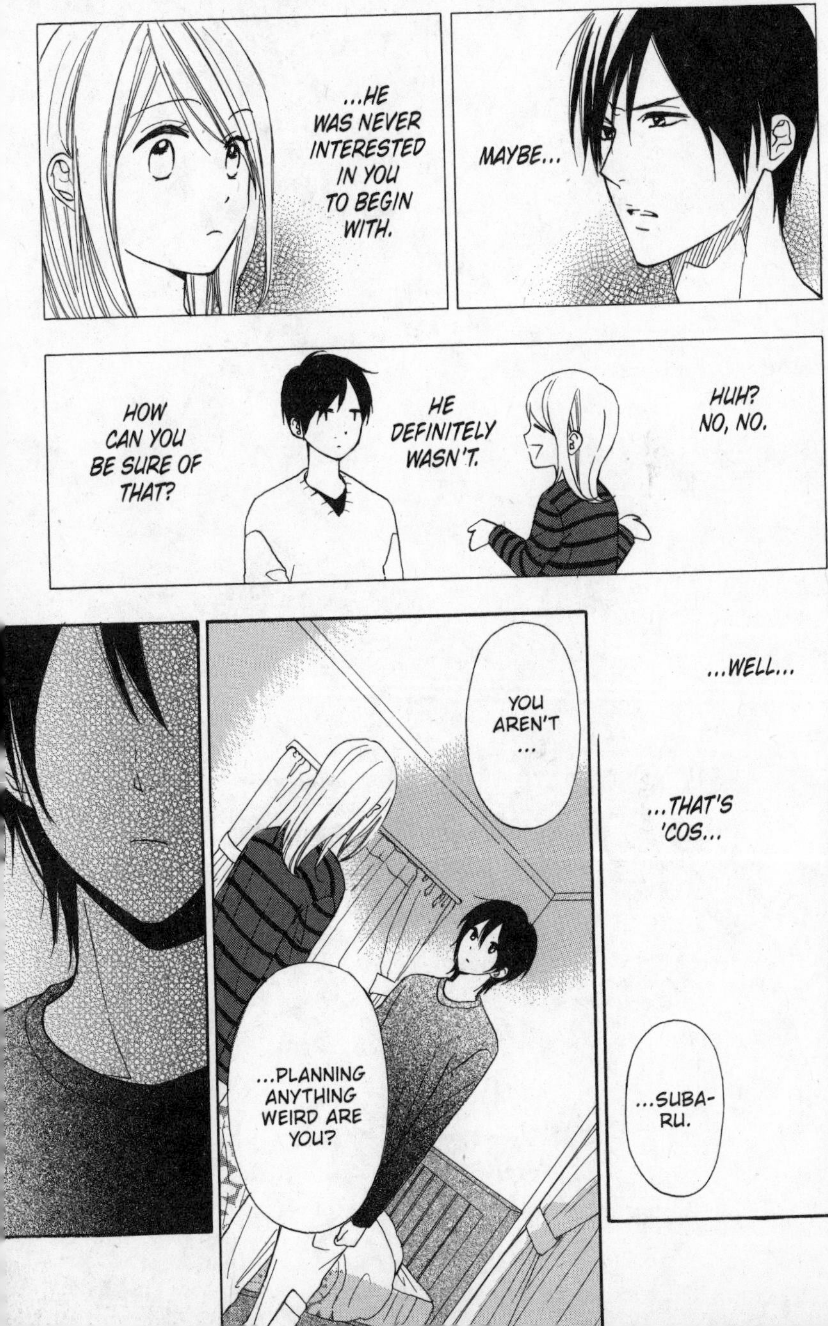
MAYBE...
...HE WAS NEVER INTERESTED IN YOU TO BEGIN WITH.
HUH? NO, NO.
HE DEFINITELY WASN'T.
HOW CAN YOU BE SURE OF THAT?
...WELL...
...THAT'S 'COS...
...SUBARU.
YOU AREN'T ...
...PLANNING ANYTHING WEIRD ARE YOU?

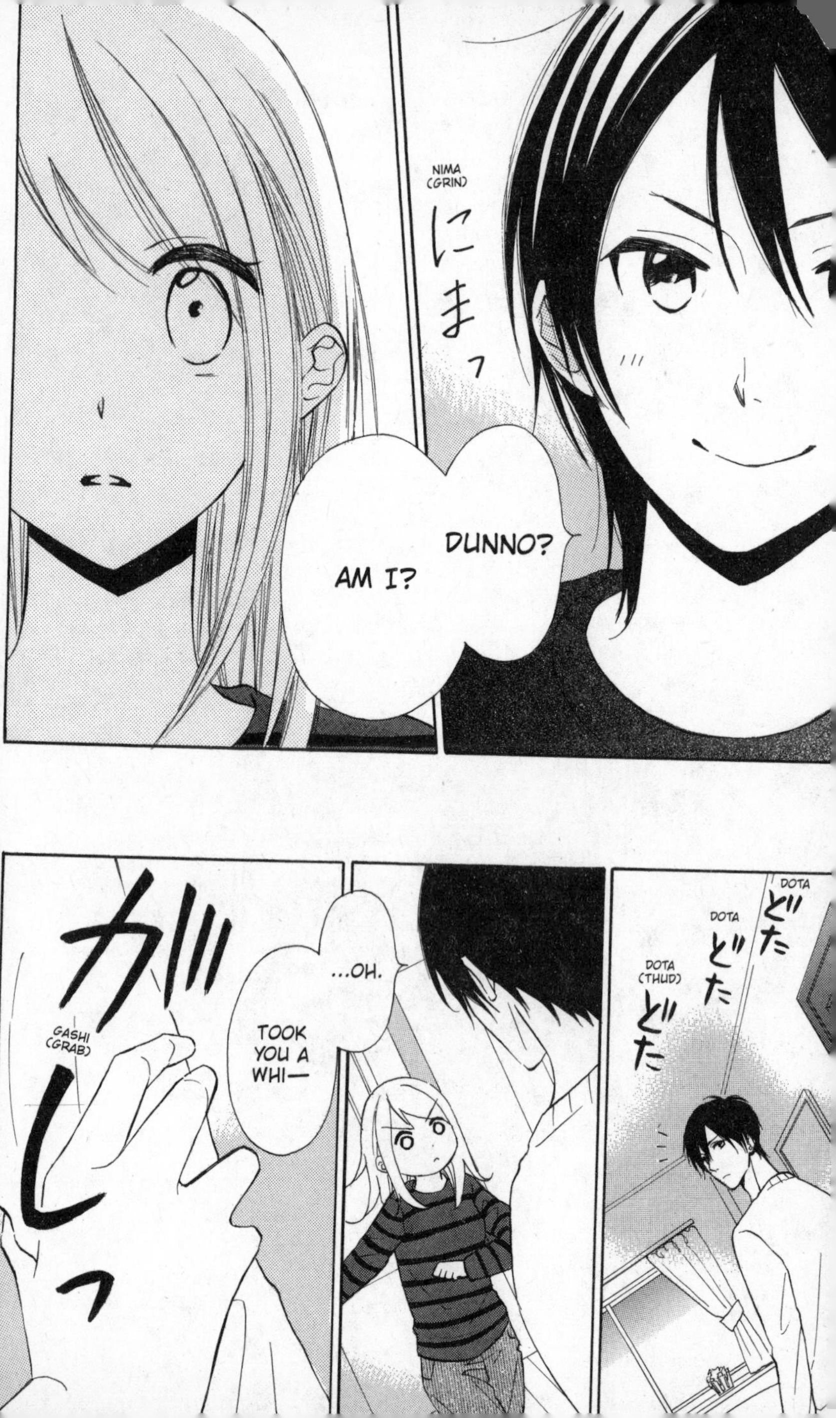
NIMA (GRIN)
にまっ
DUNNO?
AM I?
DOTA
どた
DOTA
どた
DOTA (THUD)
どた
...OH.
TOOK YOU A WHI—
GASHI (GRAB)
ガしっ

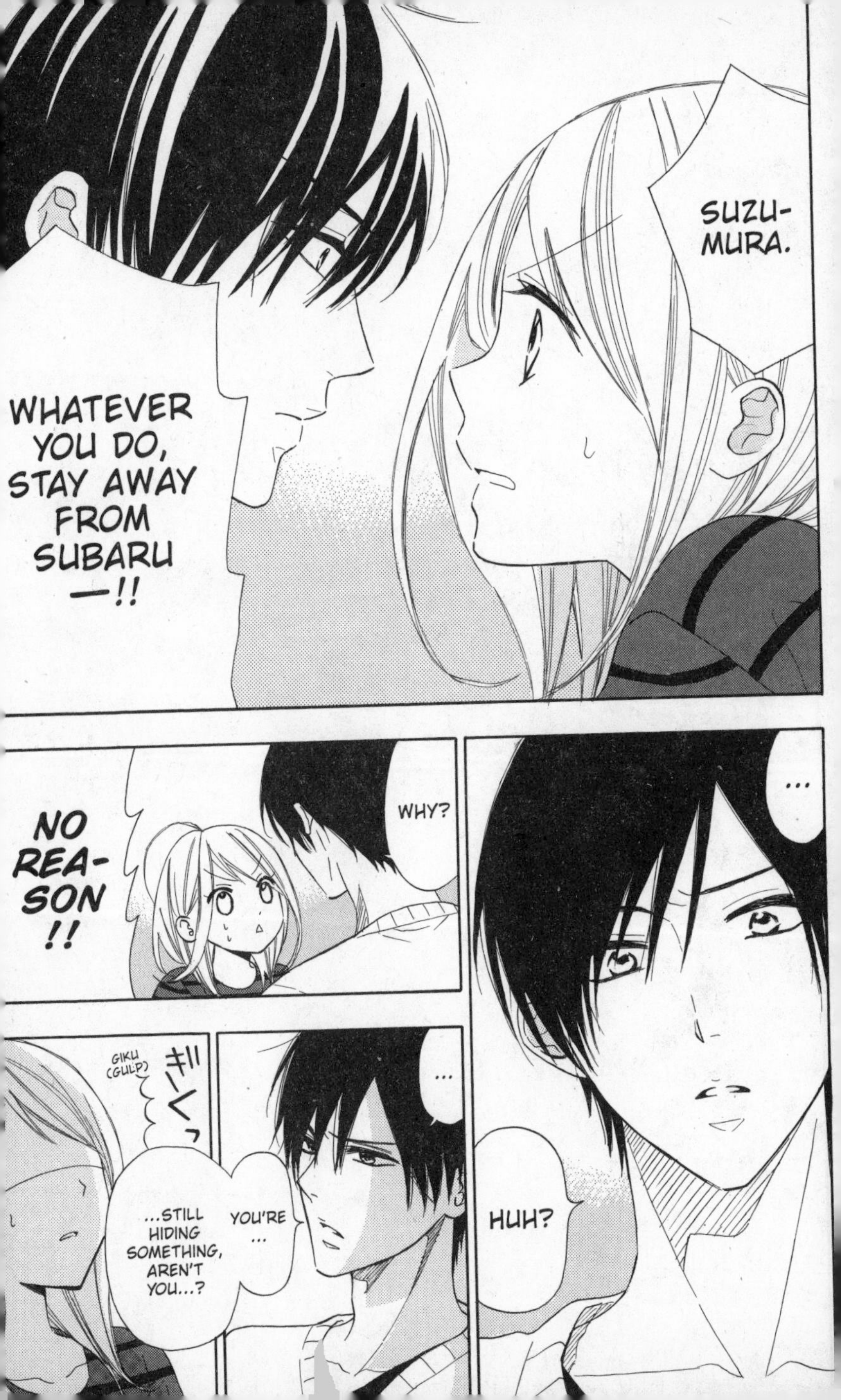
SUZU-MURA.
WHATEVER YOU DO, STAY AWAY FROM SUBARU—!!
...
HUH?
WHY?
NO REA-SON!!
...
YOU'RE ...
ギくっ
GIKU (GULP)
...STILL HIDING SOMETHING, AREN'T YOU...?

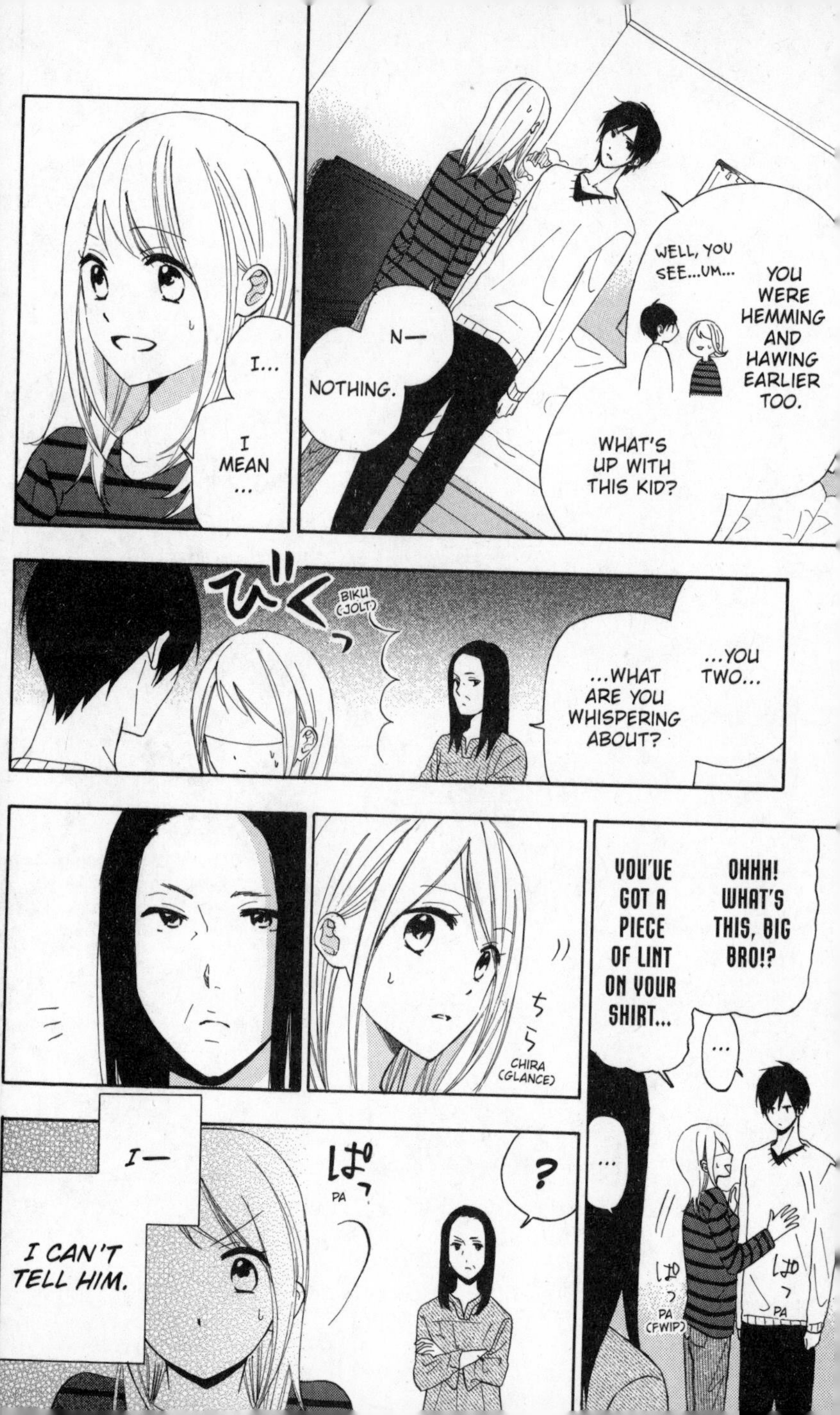
YOU WERE HEMMING AND HAWING EARLIER TOO.
WELL, YOU SEE...UM...
WHAT'S UP WITH THIS KID?
N—
NOTHING.
I...
I MEAN ...
...YOU TWO...
...WHAT ARE YOU WHISPERING ABOUT?
びくっ
BIKU (JOLT)
OHHH! WHAT'S THIS, BIG BRO!?
YOU'VE GOT A PIECE OF LINT ON YOUR SHIRT...
...
...
ぱっ
PA
ぱっ
PA (FWIP)
ちら
CHIRA (GLANCE)
?
ぱっ
PA
I—
I CAN'T TELL HIM.

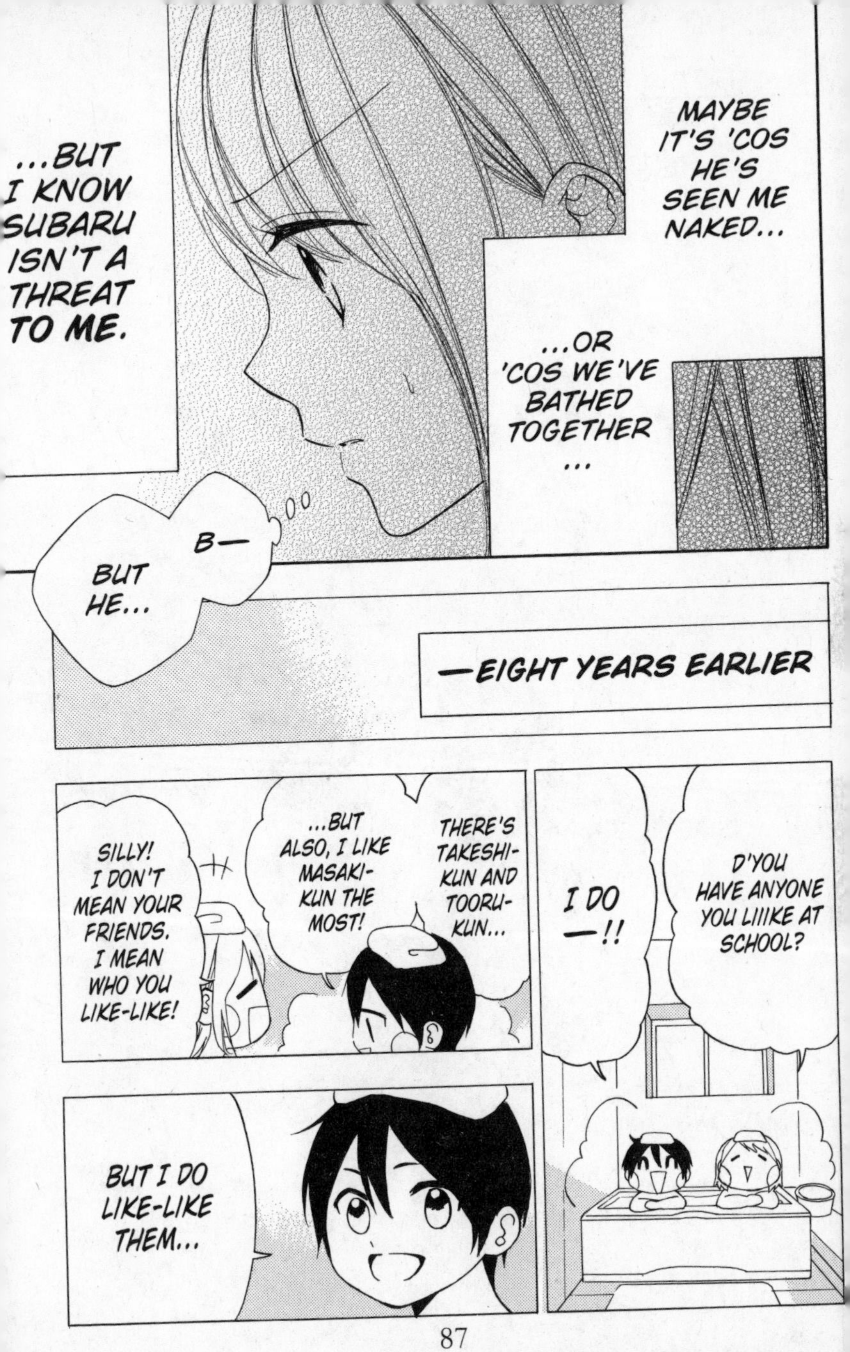

MAYBE IT'S 'COS HE'S SEEN ME NAKED...
...OR 'COS WE'VE BATHED TOGETHER...
...BUT I KNOW SUBARU ISN'T A THREAT TO ME.
B— BUT HE...
—EIGHT YEARS EARLIER
D'YOU HAVE ANYONE YOU LIIIKE AT SCHOOL?
I DO—!!
THERE'S TAKESHI-KUN AND TOORU-KUN...
...BUT ALSO, I LIKE MASAKI-KUN THE MOST!
SILLY! I DON'T MEAN YOUR FRIENDS. I MEAN WHO YOU LIKE-LIKE!
BUT I DO LIKE-LIKE THEM...

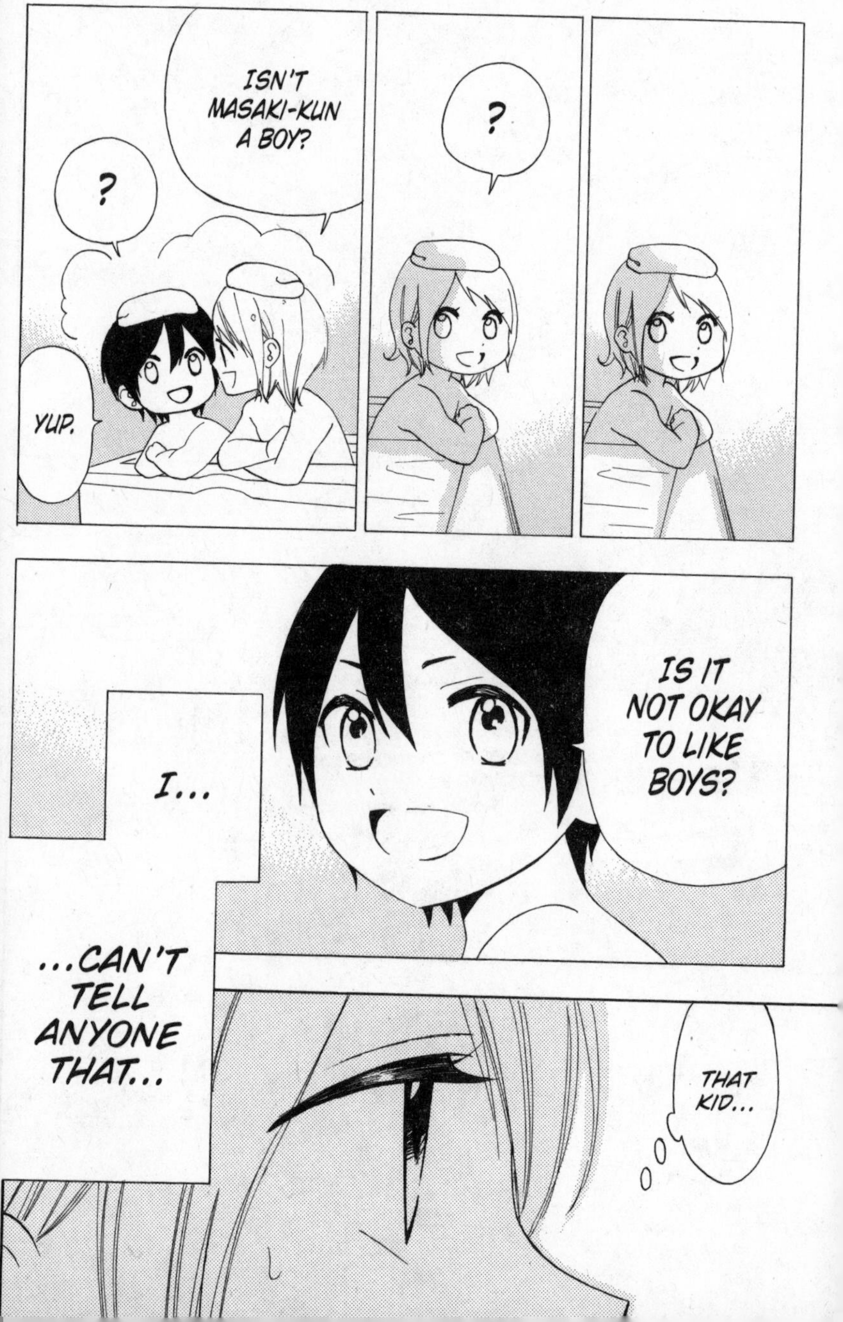
?
ISN'T MASAKI-KUN A BOY?
?
YUP.
IS IT NOT OKAY TO LIKE BOYS?
I...
...CAN'T TELL ANYONE THAT...
THAT KID...

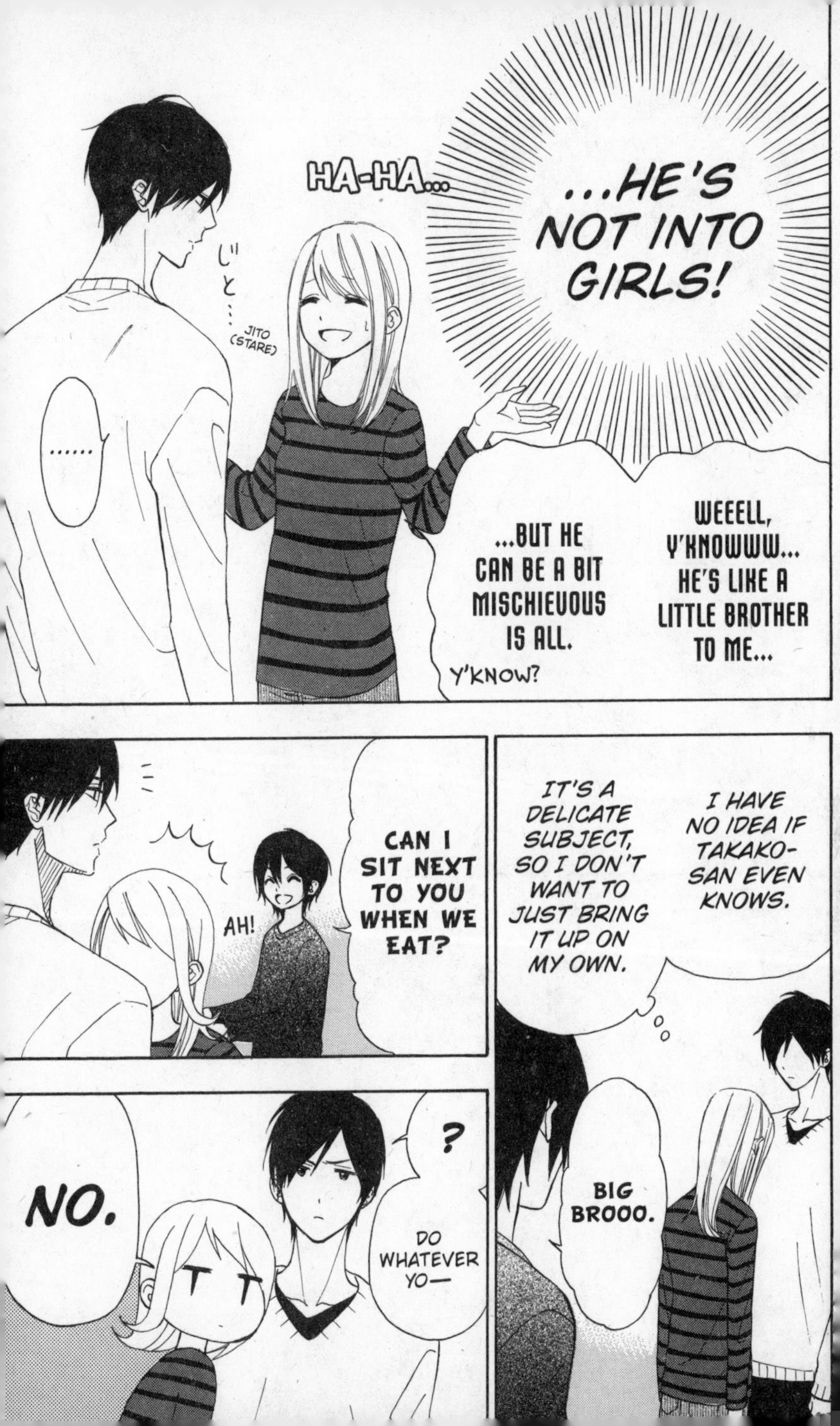
...HE'S NOT INTO GIRLS!
HA-HA...
じと…
JITO (STARE)
WEEELL, Y'KNOWWW... HE'S LIKE A LITTLE BROTHER TO ME...
...BUT HE CAN BE A BIT MISCHIEVOUS IS ALL.
Y'KNOW?
......
I HAVE NO IDEA IF TAKAKO-SAN EVEN KNOWS.
IT'S A DELICATE SUBJECT, SO I DON'T WANT TO JUST BRING IT UP ON MY OWN.
BIG BROOO.
CAN I SIT NEXT TO YOU WHEN WE EAT?
AH!
?
DO WHATEVER YO—
NO.

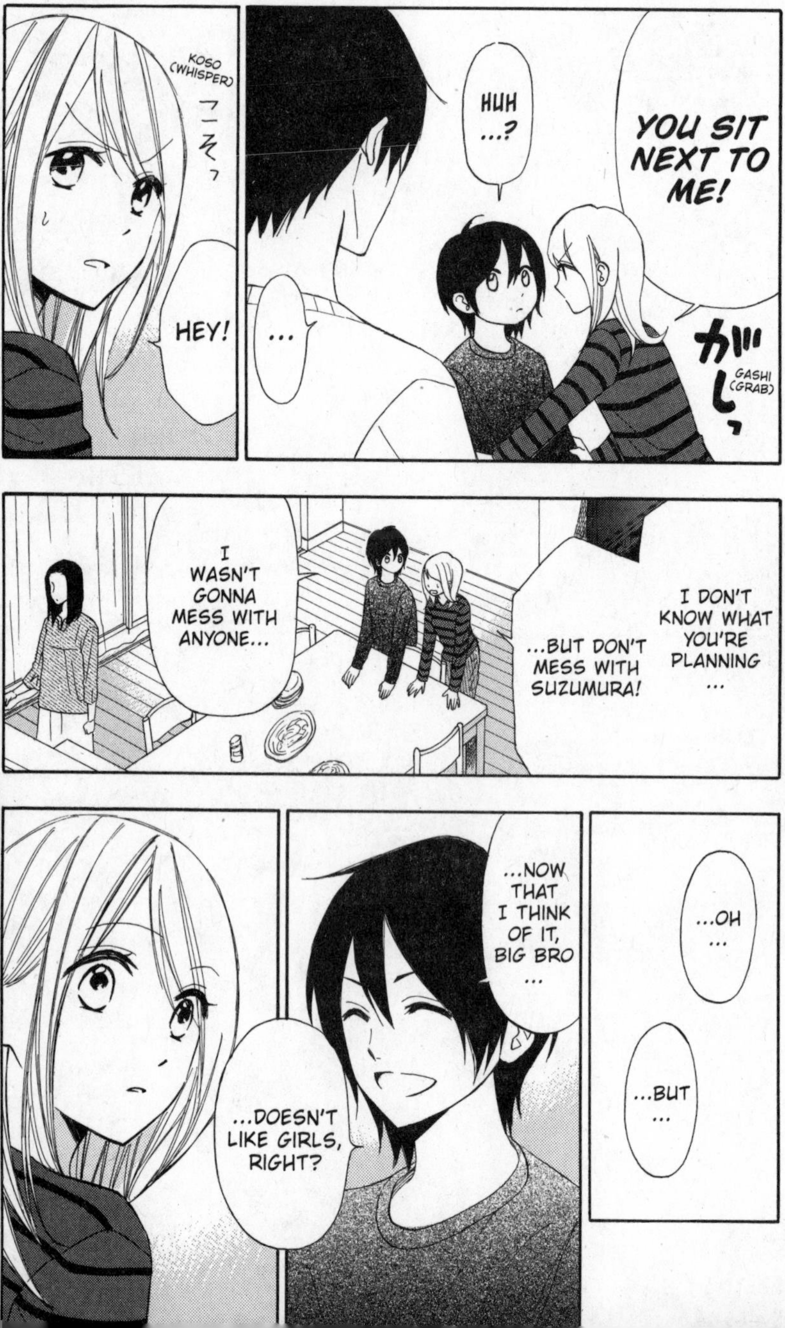
YOU SIT NEXT TO ME!
HUH ...?
...
がしっ
GASHI (GRAB)
こそっ
KOSO (WHISPER)
HEY!
I DON'T KNOW WHAT YOU'RE PLANNING ...
...BUT DON'T MESS WITH SUZUMURA!
I WASN'T GONNA MESS WITH ANYONE...
...OH ...
...BUT ...
...NOW THAT I THINK OF IT, BIG BRO ...
...DOESN'T LIKE GIRLS, RIGHT?

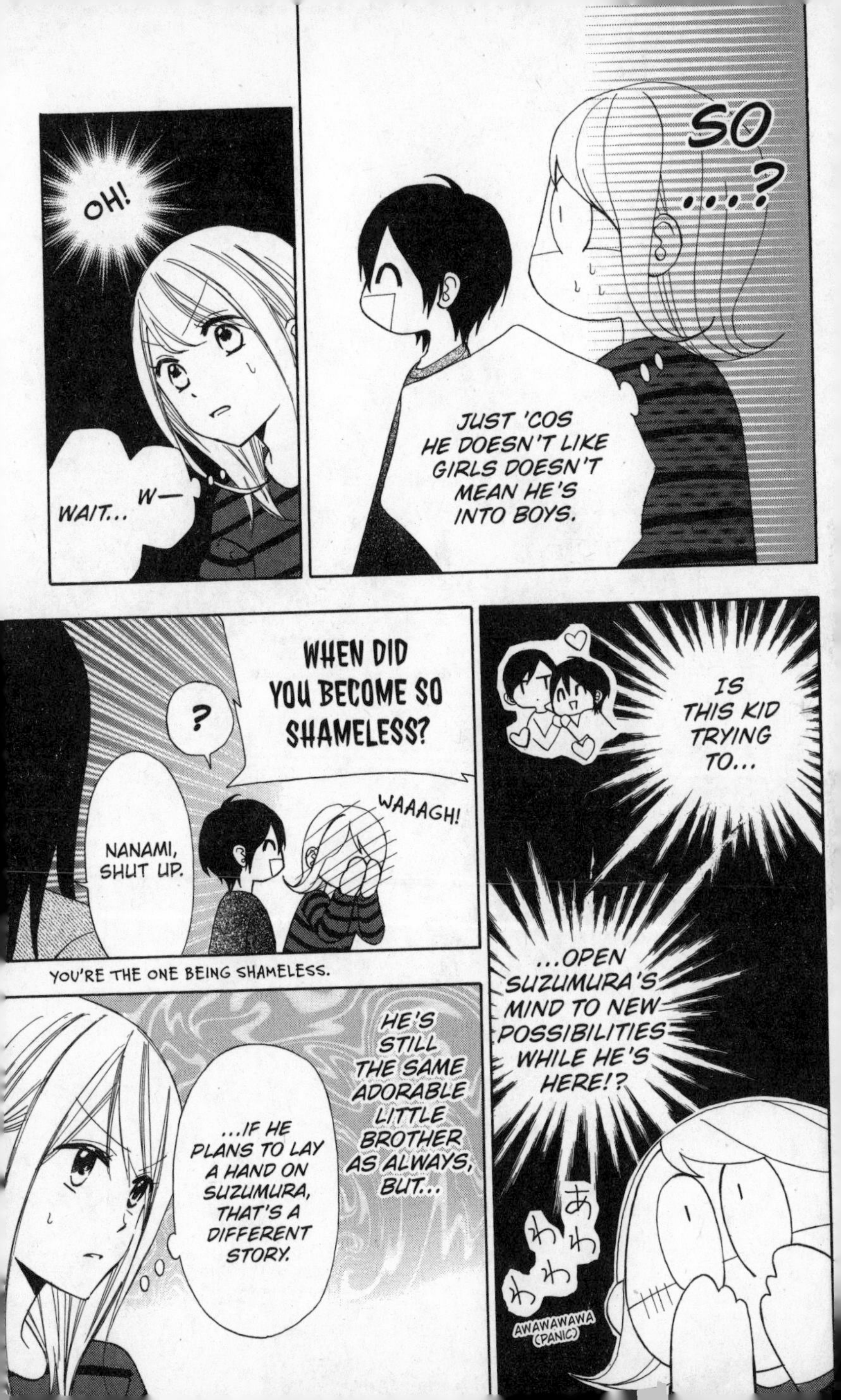
SO...?
JUST 'COS HE DOESN'T LIKE GIRLS DOESN'T MEAN HE'S INTO BOYS.
OH!
W— WAIT...
IS THIS KID TRYING TO...
...OPEN SUZUMURA'S MIND TO NEW POSSIBILITIES WHILE HE'S HERE!?
あわわわわ
AWAWAWAWA (PANIC)
WHEN DID YOU BECOME SO SHAMELESS?
?
WAAAGH!
NANAMI, SHUT UP.
YOU'RE THE ONE BEING SHAMELESS.
HE'S STILL THE SAME ADORABLE LITTLE BROTHER AS ALWAYS, BUT...
...IF HE PLANS TO LAY A HAND ON SUZUMURA, THAT'S A DIFFERENT STORY.

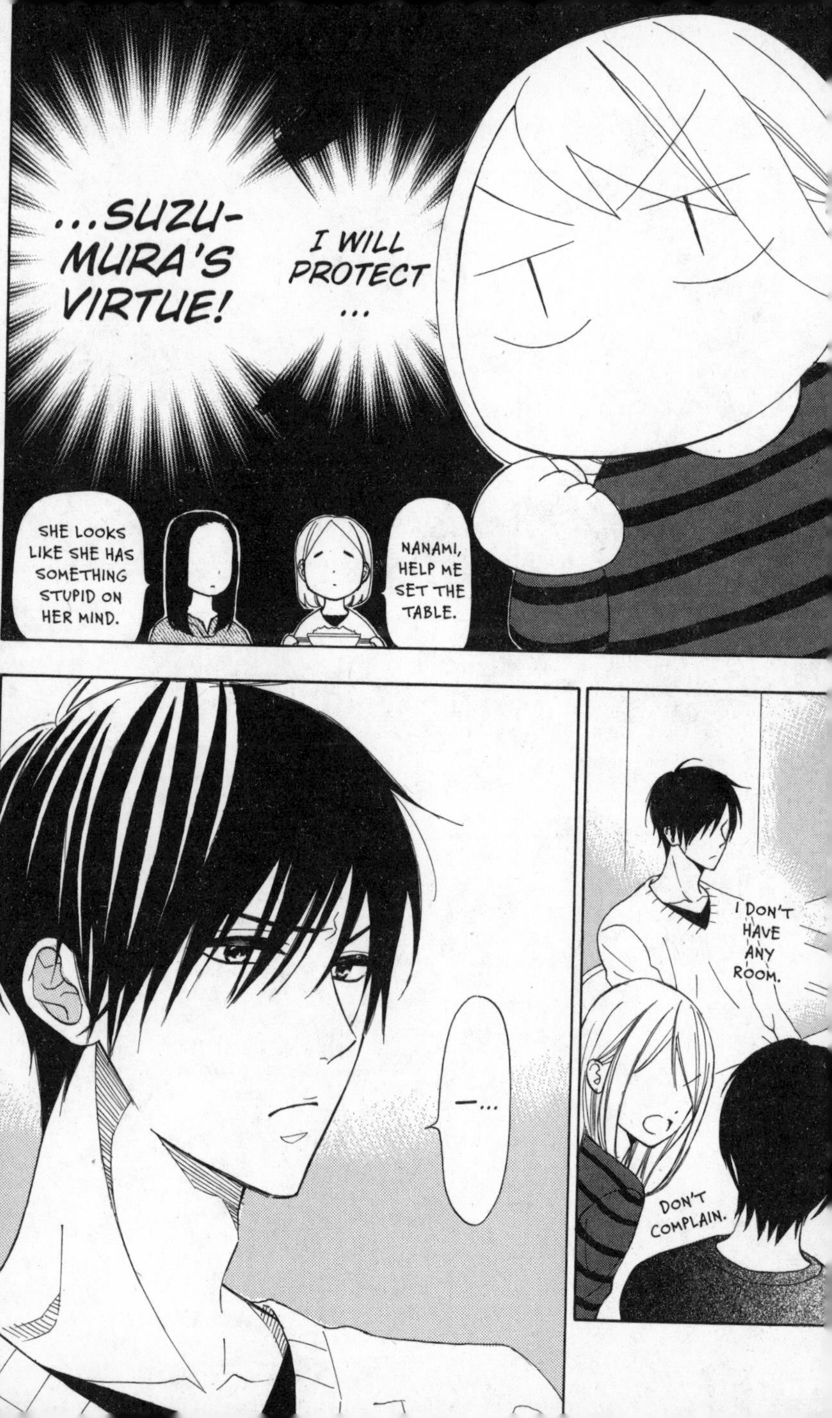
I WILL PROTECT ...
...SUZU-MURA'S VIRTUE!
NANAMI, HELP ME SET THE TABLE.
SHE LOOKS LIKE SHE HAS SOMETHING STUPID ON HER MIND.
I DON'T HAVE ANY ROOM.
DON'T COMPLAIN.
—...

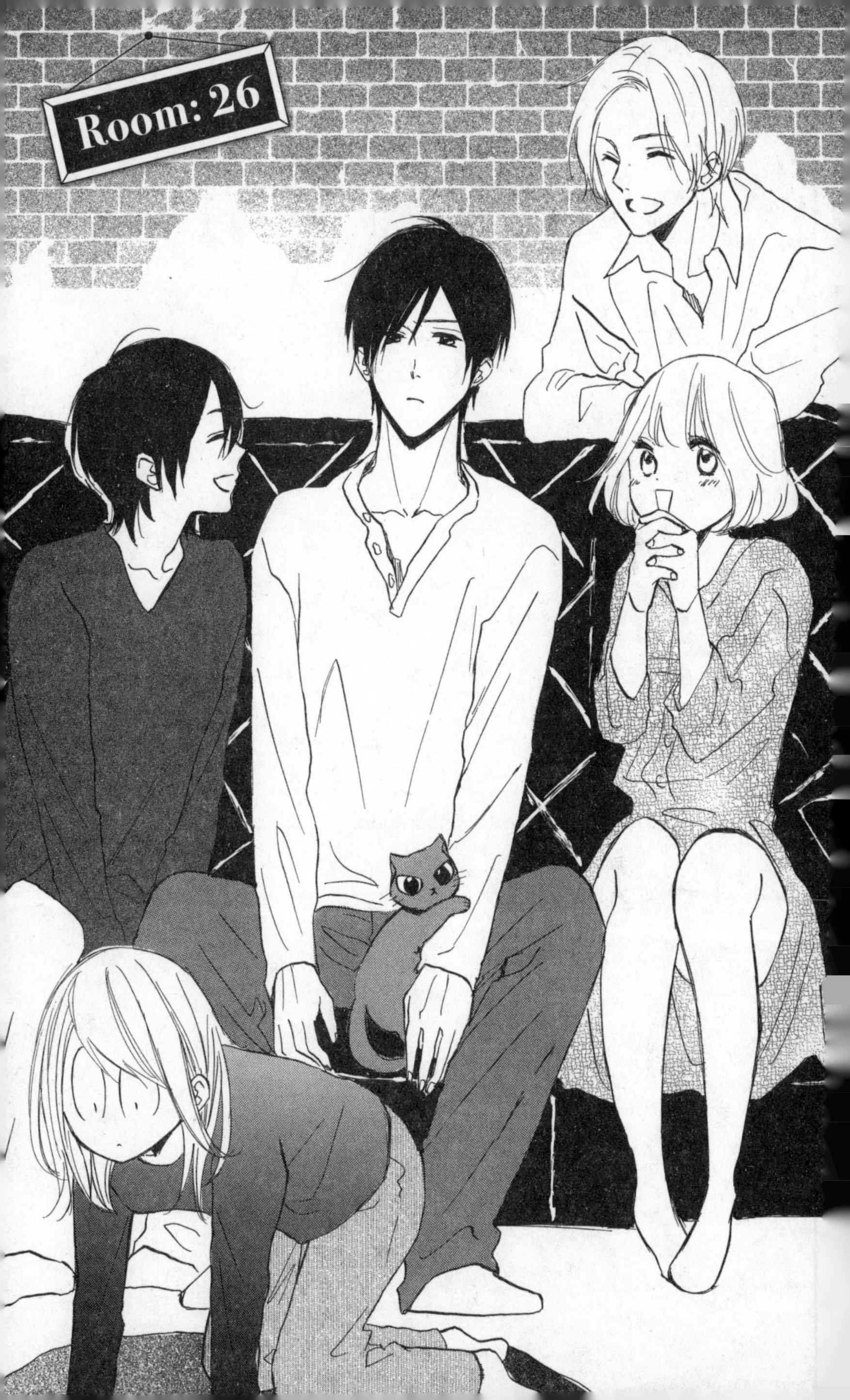
Room: 26

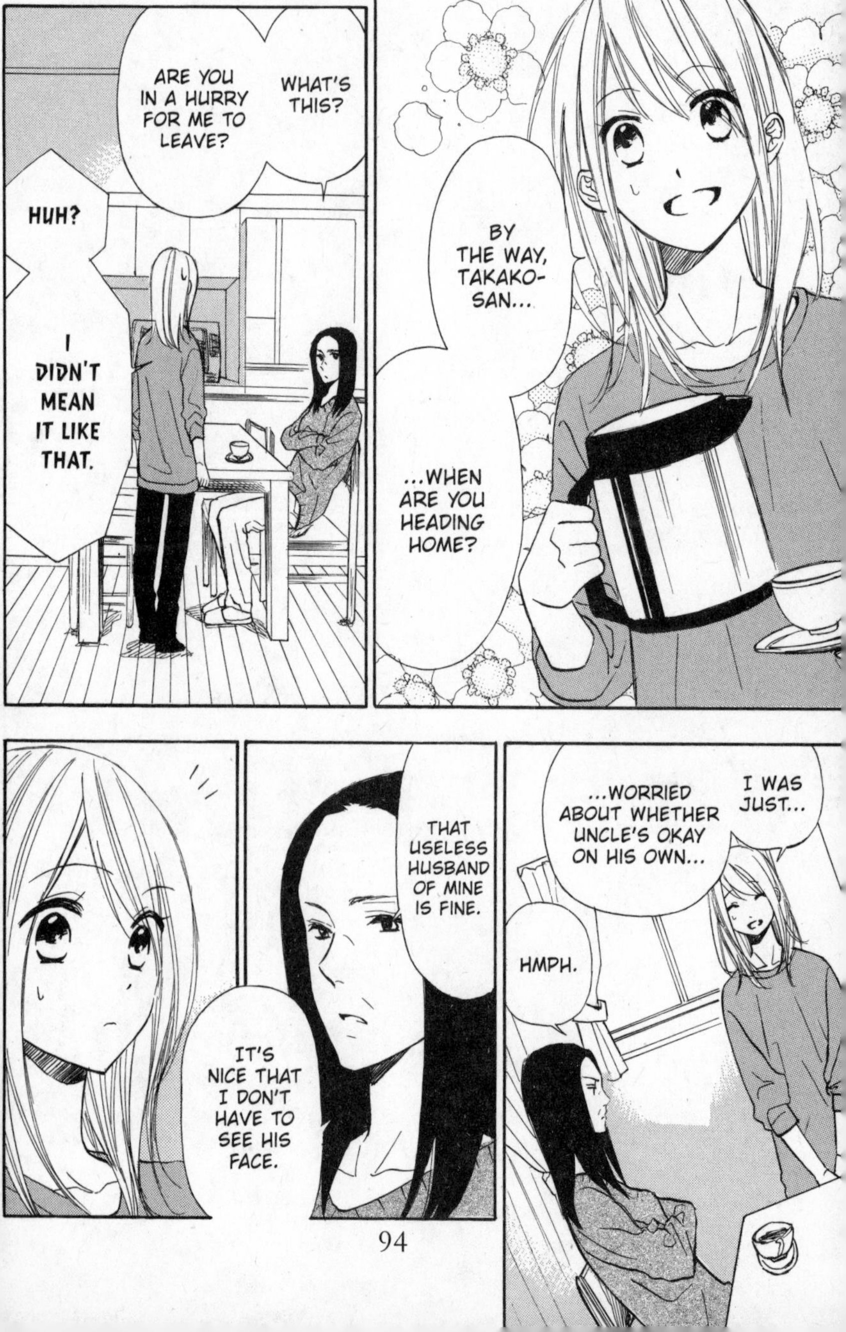
BY THE WAY, TAKAKO-SAN...
...WHEN ARE YOU HEADING HOME?
WHAT'S THIS?
ARE YOU IN A HURRY FOR ME TO LEAVE?
HUH?
I DIDN'T MEAN IT LIKE THAT.
I WAS JUST...
...WORRIED ABOUT WHETHER UNCLE'S OKAY ON HIS OWN...
HMPH.
THAT USELESS HUSBAND OF MINE IS FINE.
IT'S NICE THAT I DON'T HAVE TO SEE HIS FACE.

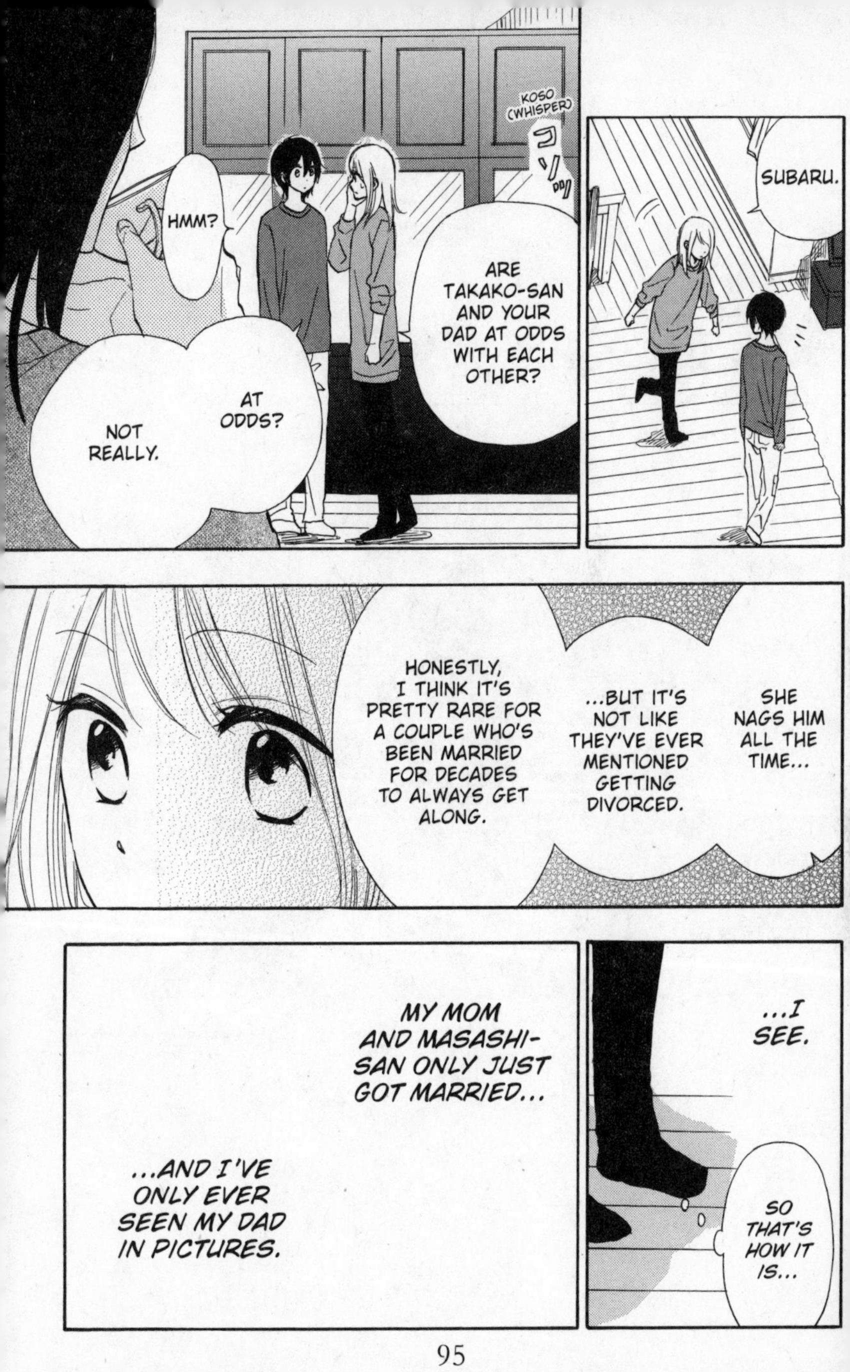
SUBARU.
KOSO (WHISPER)
ARE TAKAKO-SAN AND YOUR DAD AT ODDS WITH EACH OTHER?
HMM?
AT ODDS?
NOT REALLY.
SHE NAGS HIM ALL THE TIME...
...BUT IT'S NOT LIKE THEY'VE EVER MENTIONED GETTING DIVORCED.
HONESTLY, I THINK IT'S PRETTY RARE FOR A COUPLE WHO'S BEEN MARRIED FOR DECADES TO ALWAYS GET ALONG.
...I SEE.
SO THAT'S HOW IT IS...
MY MOM AND MASASHI-SAN ONLY JUST GOT MARRIED...
...AND I'VE ONLY EVER SEEN MY DAD IN PICTURES.

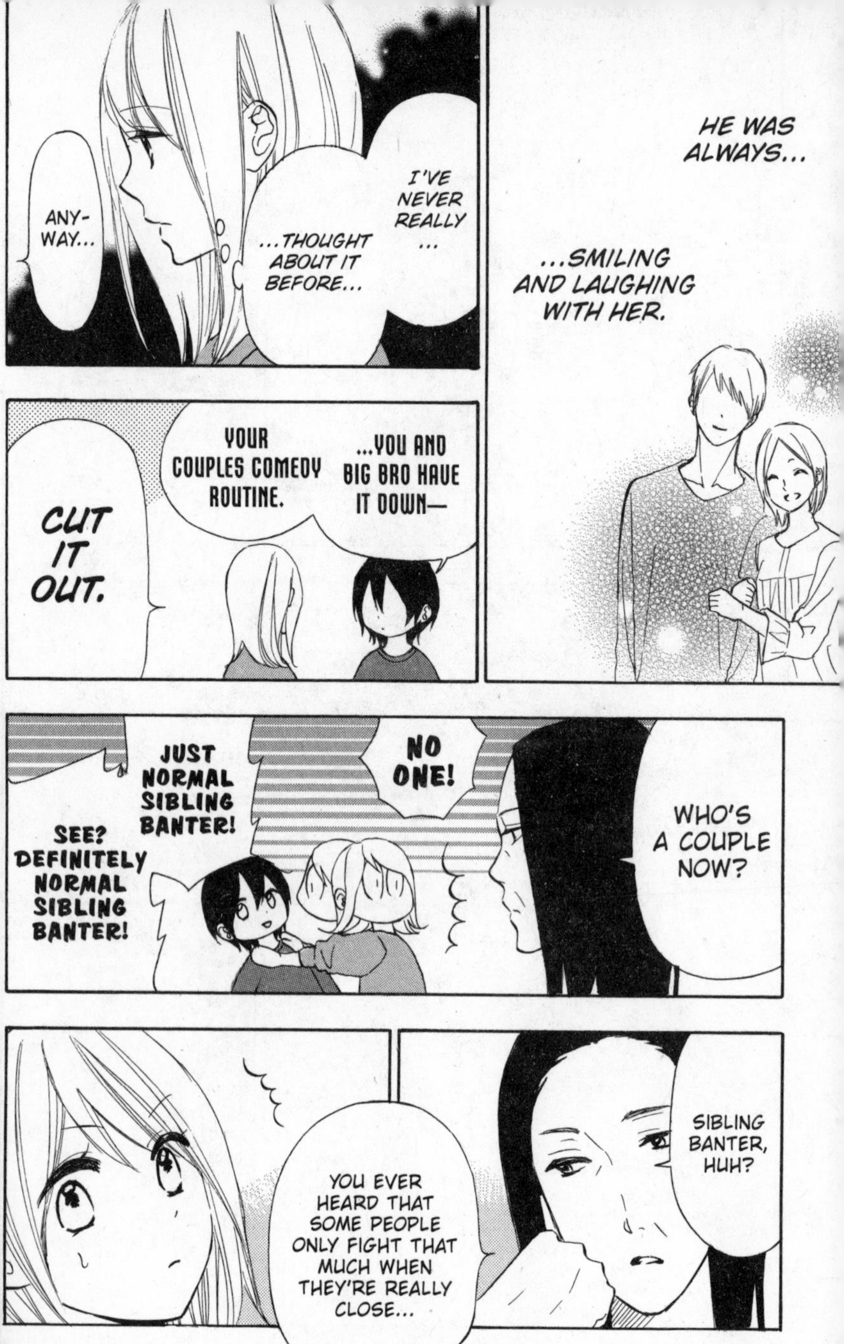
HE WAS ALWAYS...
...SMILING AND LAUGHING WITH HER.
I'VE NEVER REALLY...
...THOUGHT ABOUT IT BEFORE...
ANY-WAY...
...YOU AND BIG BRO HAVE IT DOWN—
YOUR COUPLES COMEDY ROUTINE.
CUT IT OUT.
WHO'S A COUPLE NOW?
NO ONE!
JUST NORMAL SIBLING BANTER!
SEE? DEFINITELY NORMAL SIBLING BANTER!
SIBLING BANTER, HUH?
YOU EVER HEARD THAT SOME PEOPLE ONLY FIGHT THAT MUCH WHEN THEY'RE REALLY CLOSE...

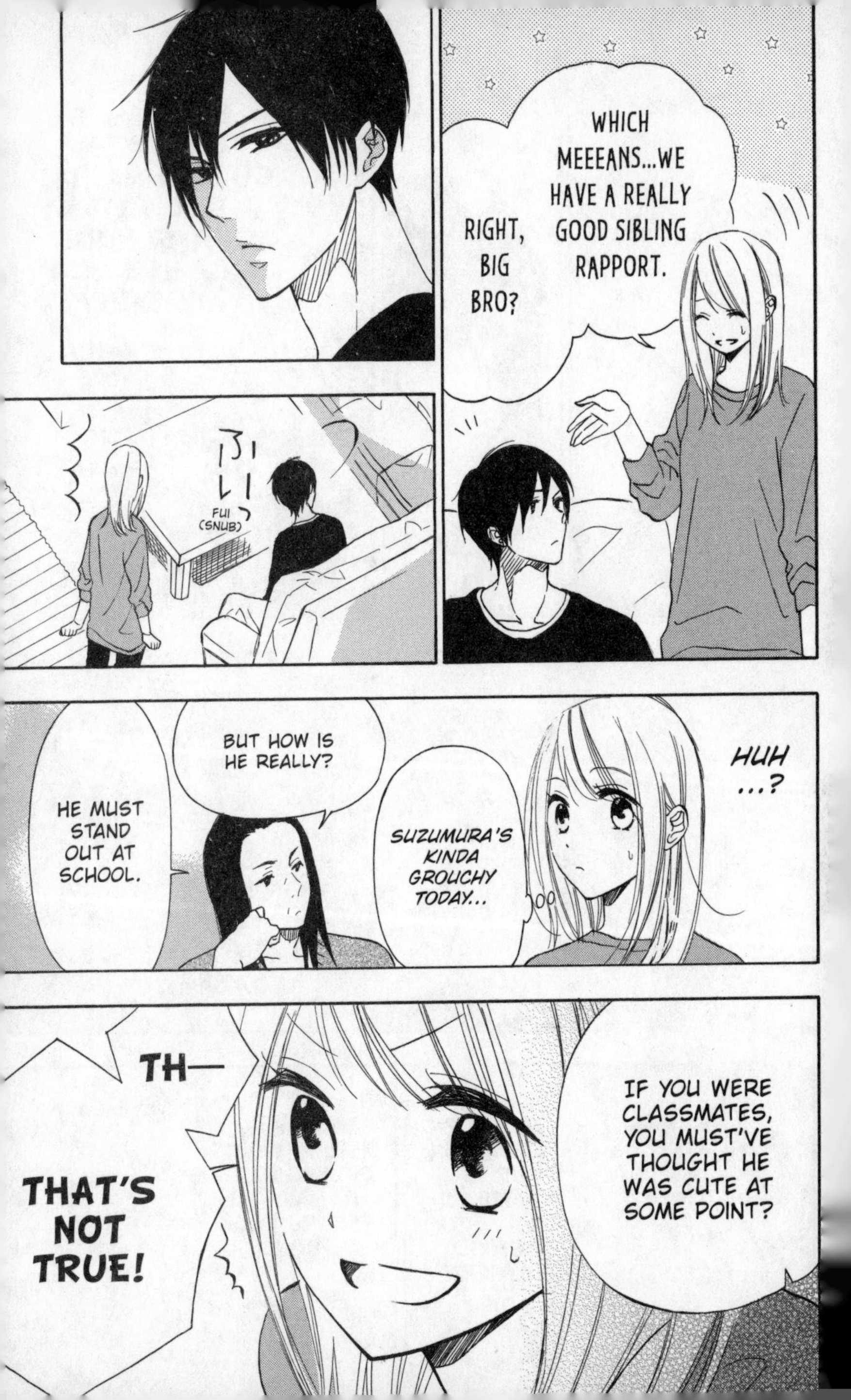
WHICH MEEEANS...WE HAVE A REALLY GOOD SIBLING RAPPORT.
RIGHT, BIG BRO?
ふい
FUI (SNUB)
HUH ...?
SUZUMURA'S KINDA GROUCHY TODAY...
BUT HOW IS HE REALLY?
HE MUST STAND OUT AT SCHOOL.
IF YOU WERE CLASSMATES, YOU MUST'VE THOUGHT HE WAS CUTE AT SOME POINT?
TH—
THAT'S NOT TRUE!

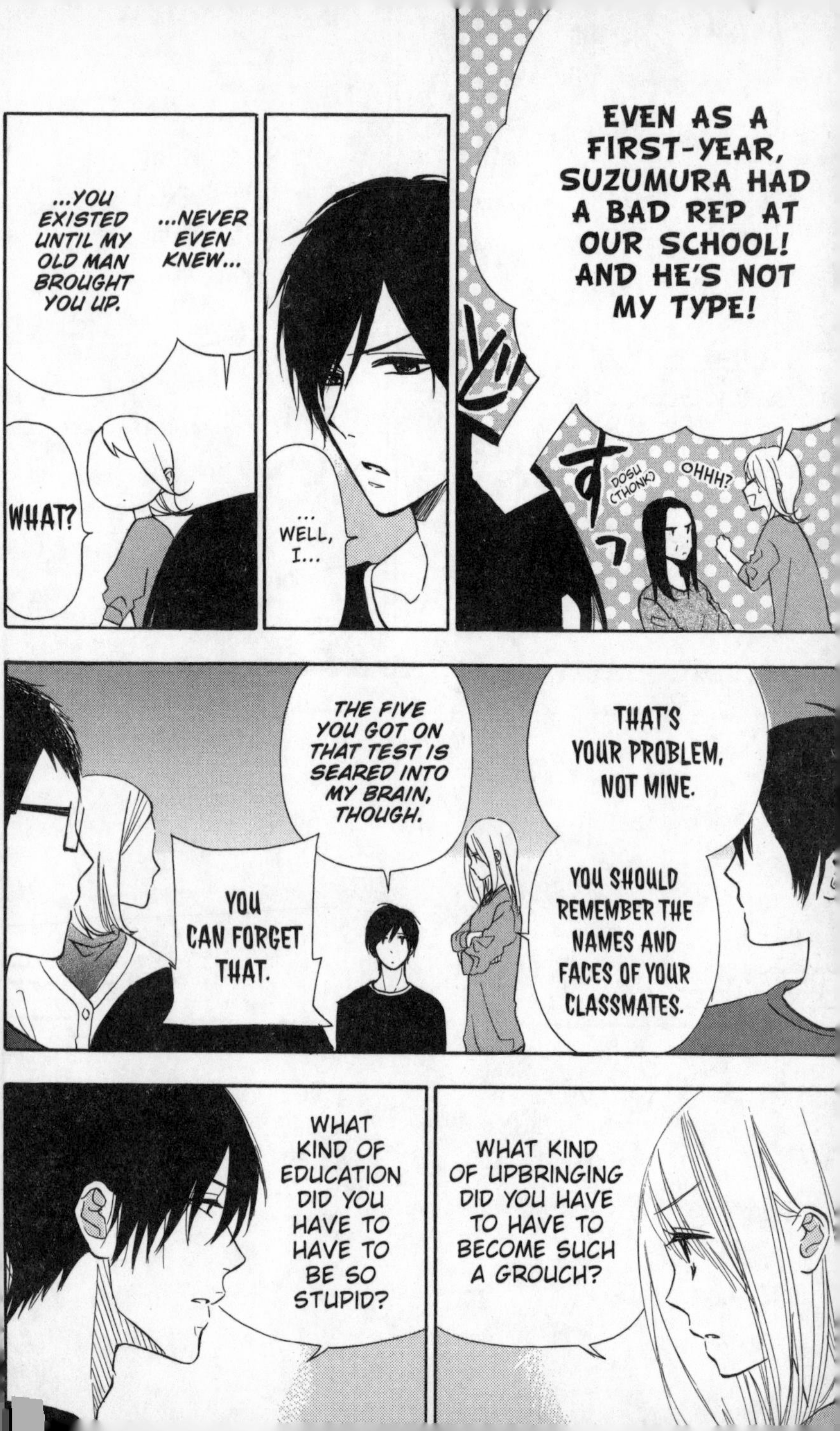
EVEN AS A FIRST-YEAR, SUZUMURA HAD A BAD REP AT OUR SCHOOL! AND HE'S NOT MY TYPE!
すっ
DOSU (THONK)
OHHH?
...WELL, I...
...NEVER EVEN KNEW...
...YOU EXISTED UNTIL MY OLD MAN BROUGHT YOU UP.
WHAT?
THAT'S YOUR PROBLEM, NOT MINE.
YOU SHOULD REMEMBER THE NAMES AND FACES OF YOUR CLASSMATES.
THE FIVE YOU GOT ON THAT TEST IS SEARED INTO MY BRAIN, THOUGH.
YOU CAN FORGET THAT.
WHAT KIND OF UPBRINGING DID YOU HAVE TO HAVE TO BECOME SUCH A GROUCH?
WHAT KIND OF EDUCATION DID YOU HAVE TO HAVE TO BE SO STUPID?

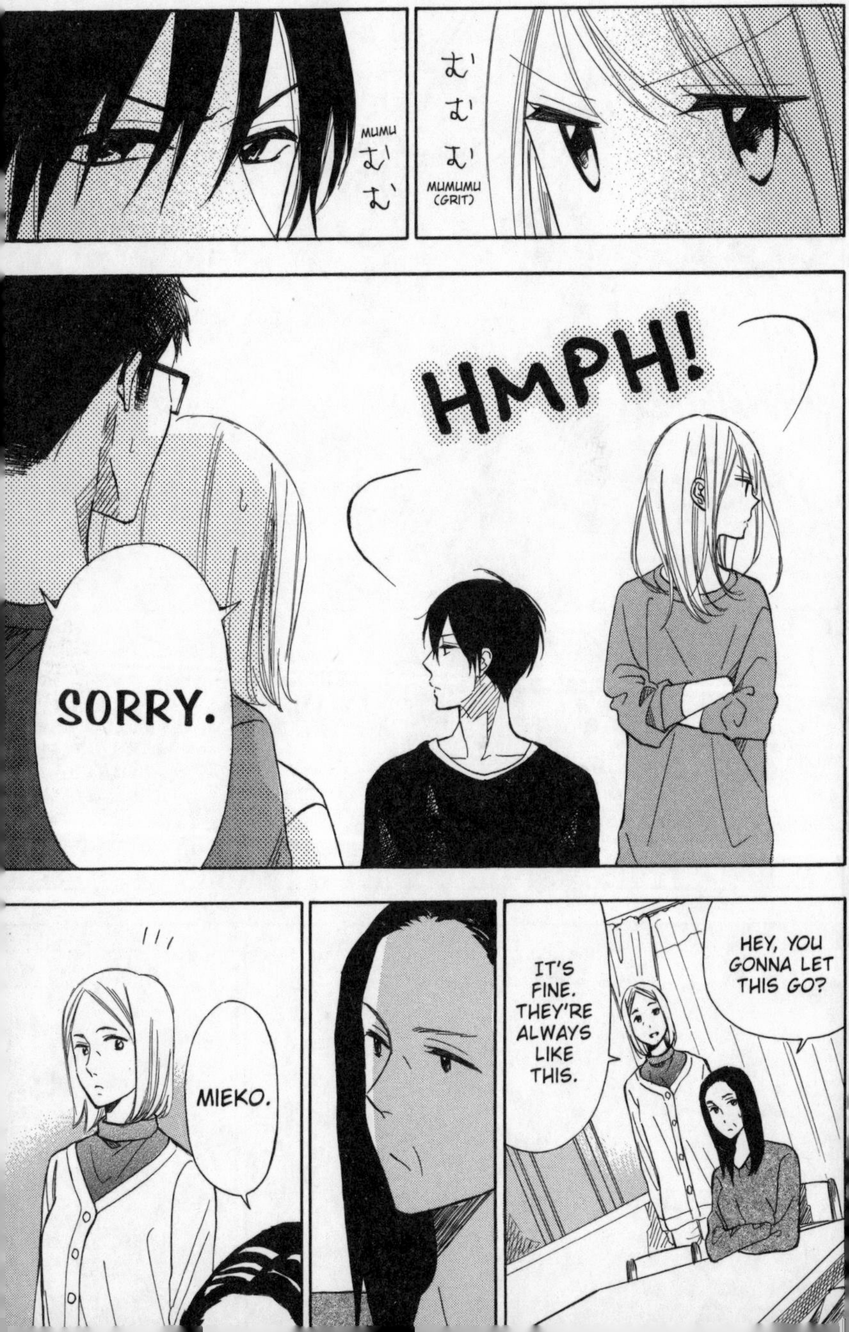
むむむ
MUMUMU (GRIT)
MUMU
むむ
HMPH!
SORRY.
HEY, YOU GONNA LET THIS GO?
IT'S FINE. THEY'RE ALWAYS LIKE THIS.
MIEKO.

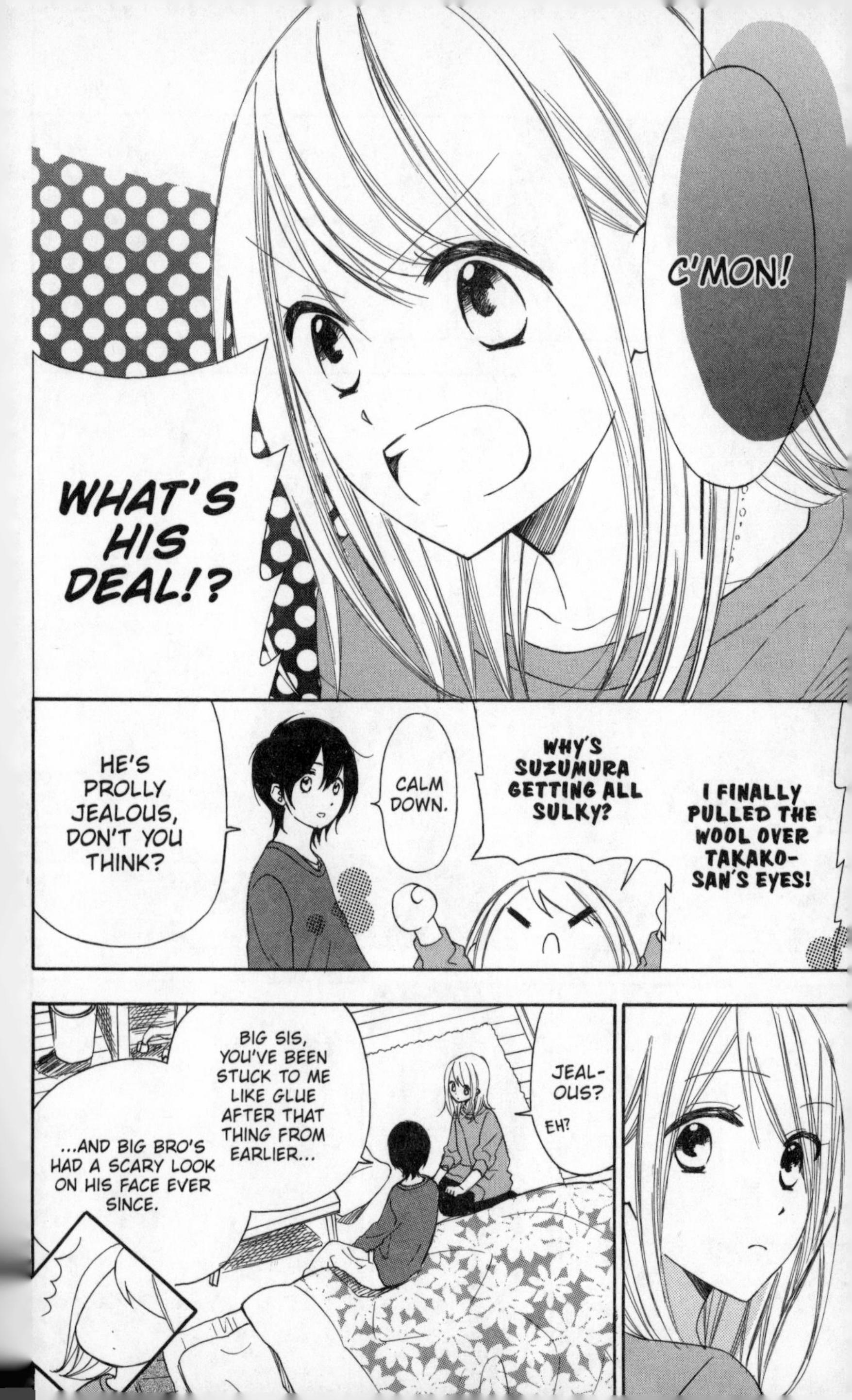
C'MON!
WHAT'S HIS DEAL!?
I FINALLY PULLED THE WOOL OVER TAKAKO-SAN'S EYES!
WHY'S SUZUMURA GETTING ALL SULKY?
CALM DOWN.
HE'S PROLLY JEALOUS, DON'T YOU THINK?
JEAL-OUS?
EH?
BIG SIS, YOU'VE BEEN STUCK TO ME LIKE GLUE AFTER THAT THING FROM EARLIER...
...AND BIG BRO'S HAD A SCARY LOOK ON HIS FACE EVER SINCE.

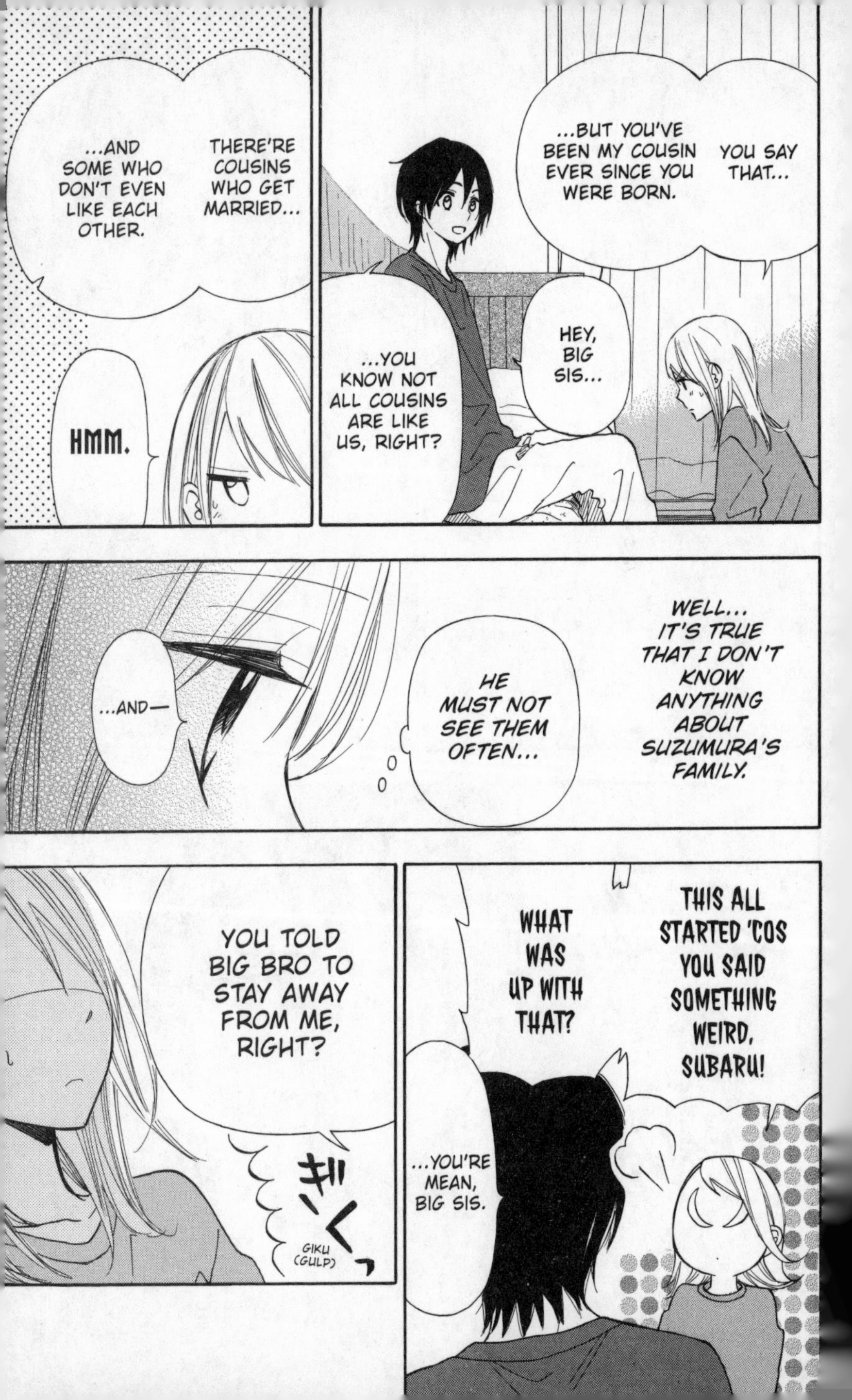
YOU SAY THAT...
...BUT YOU'VE BEEN MY COUSIN EVER SINCE YOU WERE BORN.
HEY, BIG SIS...
...YOU KNOW NOT ALL COUSINS ARE LIKE US, RIGHT?
THERE'RE COUSINS WHO GET MARRIED...
...AND SOME WHO DON'T EVEN LIKE EACH OTHER.
HMM.
WELL... IT'S TRUE THAT I DON'T KNOW ANYTHING ABOUT SUZUMURA'S FAMILY.
HE MUST NOT SEE THEM OFTEN...
...AND—
THIS ALL STARTED 'COS YOU SAID SOMETHING WEIRD, SUBARU!
WHAT WAS UP WITH THAT?
...YOU'RE MEAN, BIG SIS.
YOU TOLD BIG BRO TO STAY AWAY FROM ME, RIGHT?
ぎくっ
GIKU (GULP)

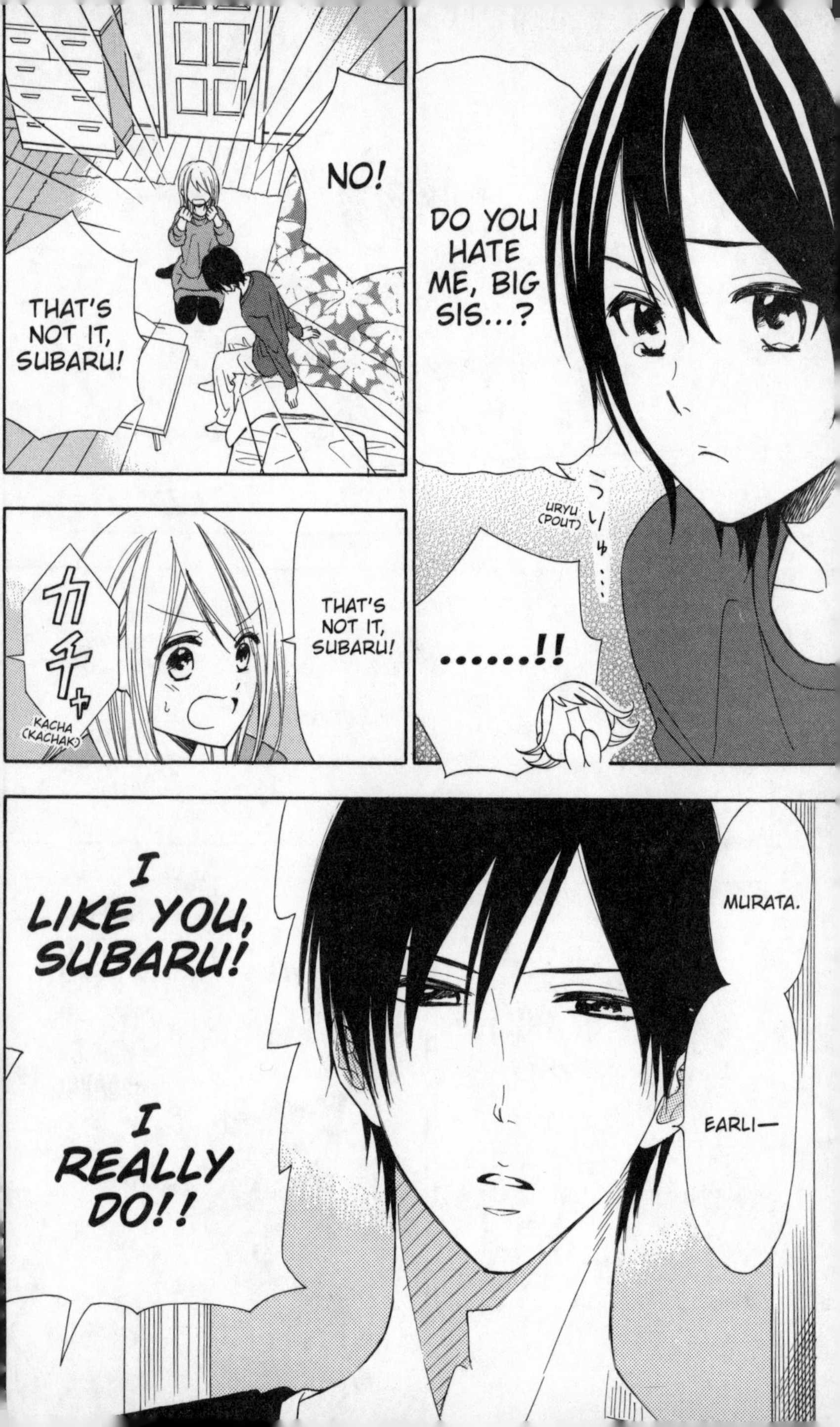
DO YOU HATE ME, BIG SIS...?
うりゅ…
URYU (POUT)
......!!
NO!
THAT'S NOT IT, SUBARU!
THAT'S NOT IT, SUBARU!
カチャ
KACHA (KACHAK)
MURATA.
EARLI—
I LIKE YOU, SUBARU!
I REALLY DO!!

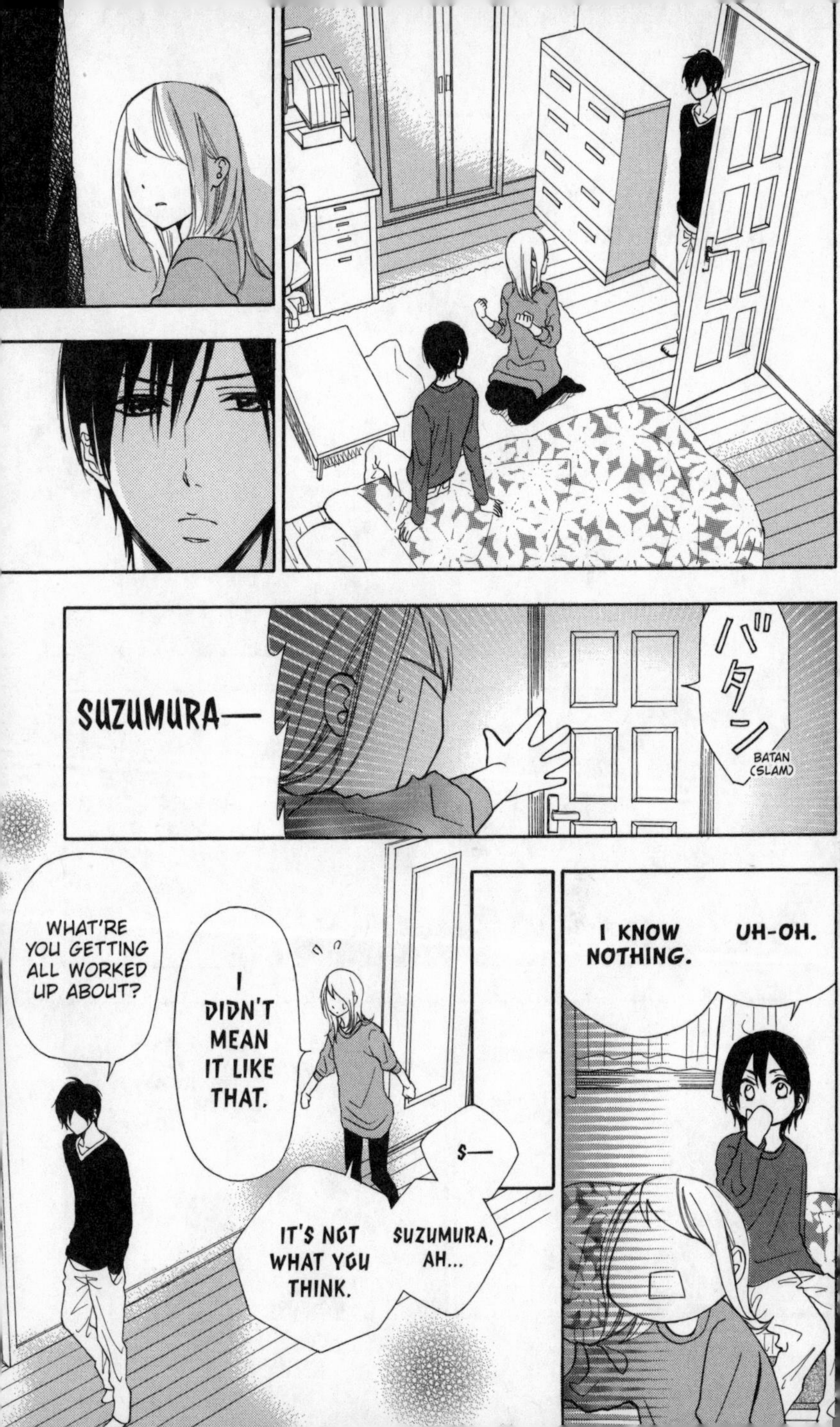
バタン
BATAN (SLAM)
SUZUMURA—
UH-OH.
I KNOW NOTHING.
S—
SUZUMURA, AH...
IT'S NOT WHAT YOU THINK.
I DIDN'T MEAN IT LIKE THAT.
WHAT'RE YOU GETTING ALL WORKED UP ABOUT?

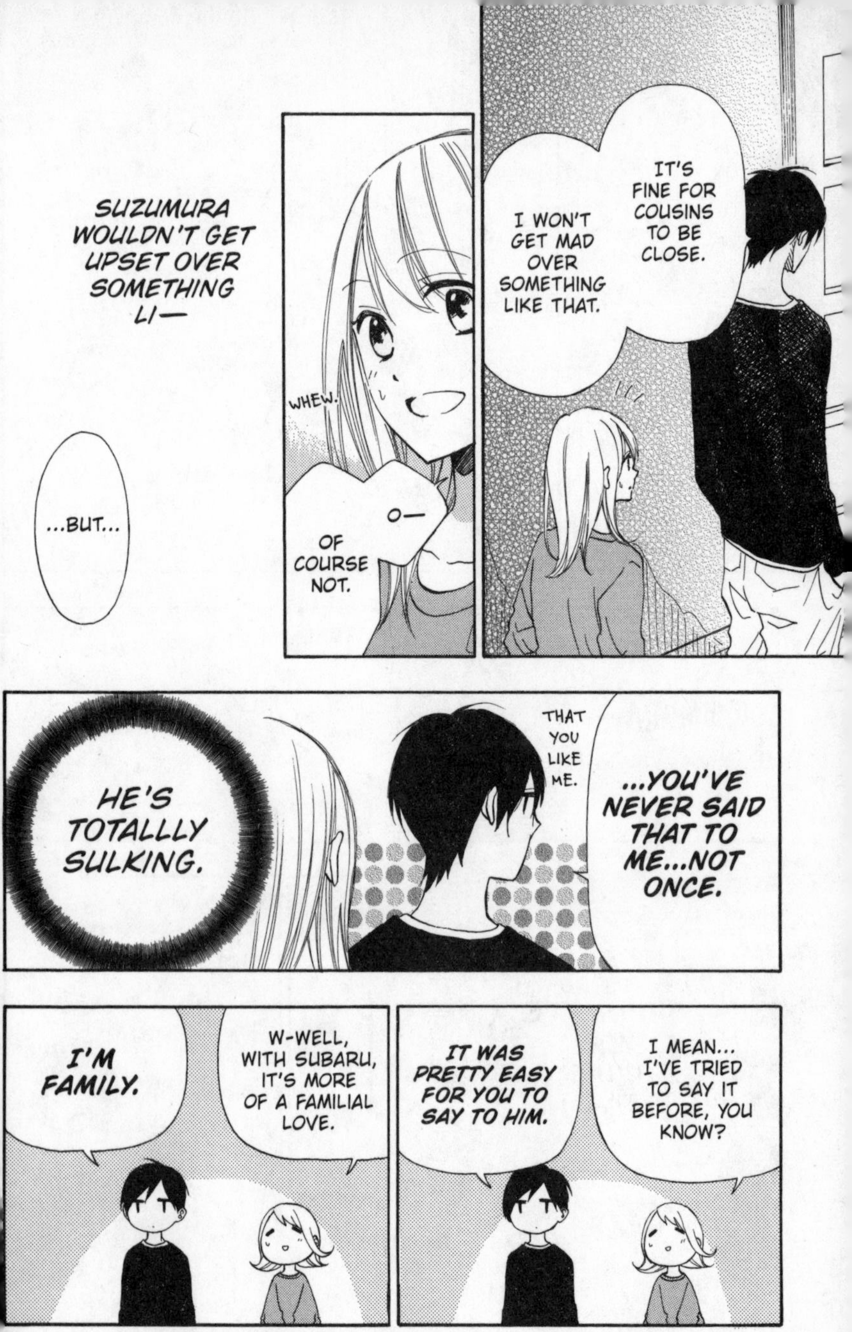
IT'S FINE FOR COUSINS TO BE CLOSE.
I WON'T GET MAD OVER SOMETHING LIKE THAT.
WHEW.
O— OF COURSE NOT.
SUZUMURA WOULDN'T GET UPSET OVER SOMETHING LI—
...BUT...
...YOU'VE NEVER SAID THAT TO ME...NOT ONCE.
THAT YOU LIKE ME.
HE'S TOTALLLY SULKING.
I MEAN... I'VE TRIED TO SAY IT BEFORE, YOU KNOW?
IT WAS PRETTY EASY FOR YOU TO SAY TO HIM.
W-WELL, WITH SUBARU, IT'S MORE OF A FAMILIAL LOVE.
I'M FAMILY.

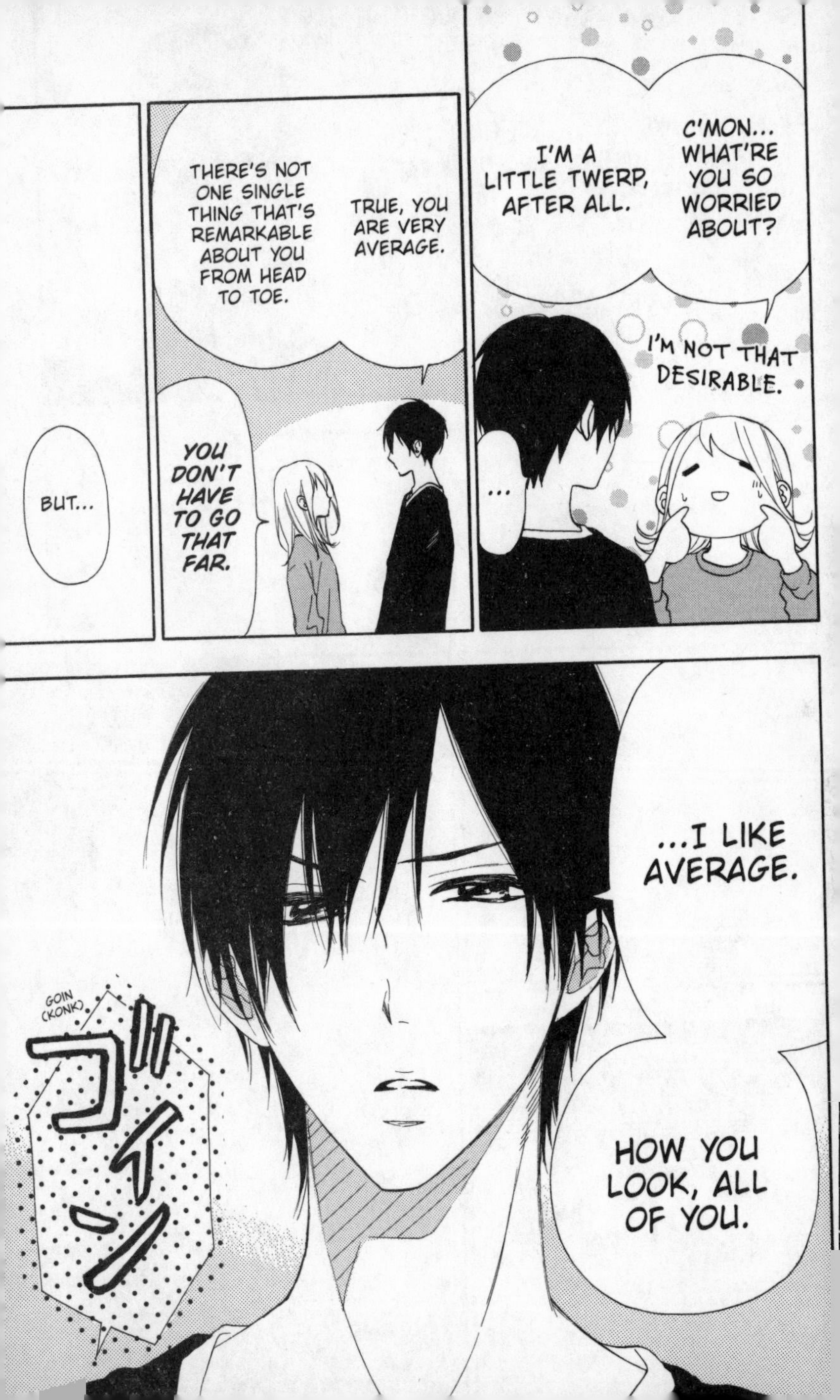
C'MON... WHAT'RE YOU SO WORRIED ABOUT?
I'M A LITTLE TWERP, AFTER ALL.
I'M NOT THAT DESIRABLE.
...
TRUE, YOU ARE VERY AVERAGE.
THERE'S NOT ONE SINGLE THING THAT'S REMARKABLE ABOUT YOU FROM HEAD TO TOE.
YOU DON'T HAVE TO GO THAT FAR.
BUT...
...I LIKE AVERAGE.
HOW YOU LOOK, ALL OF YOU.
GOIN (KONK)

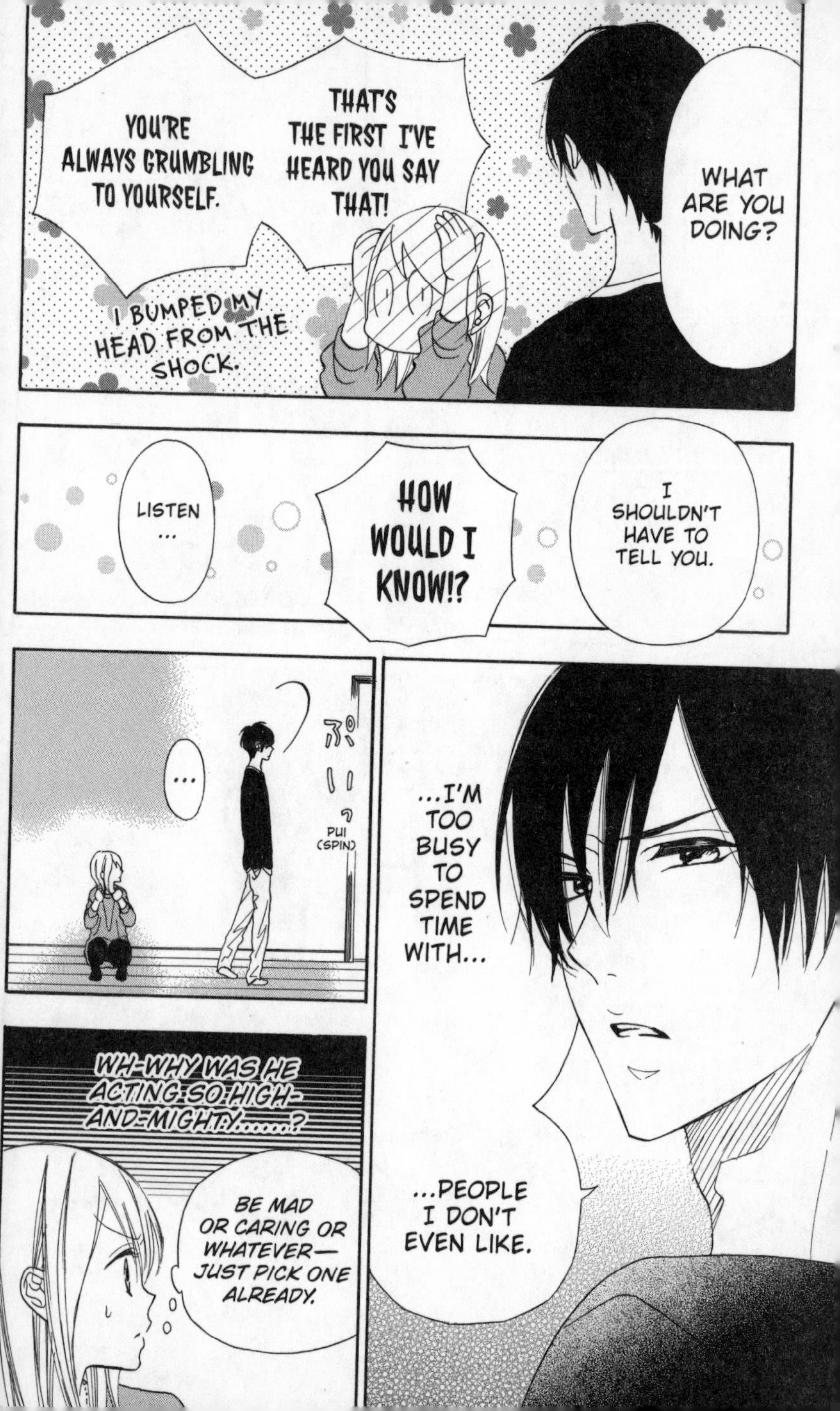
WHAT ARE YOU DOING?
THAT'S THE FIRST I'VE HEARD YOU SAY THAT!
YOU'RE ALWAYS GRUMBLING TO YOURSELF.
I BUMPED MY HEAD FROM THE SHOCK.
I SHOULDN'T HAVE TO TELL YOU.
HOW WOULD I KNOW!?
LISTEN ...
...I'M TOO BUSY TO SPEND TIME WITH...
...PEOPLE I DON'T EVEN LIKE.
ぷい
PUI (SPIN)
...
WH-WHY WAS HE ACTING SO HIGH-AND-MIGHTY.......?
BE MAD OR CARING OR WHATEVER— JUST PICK ONE ALREADY.

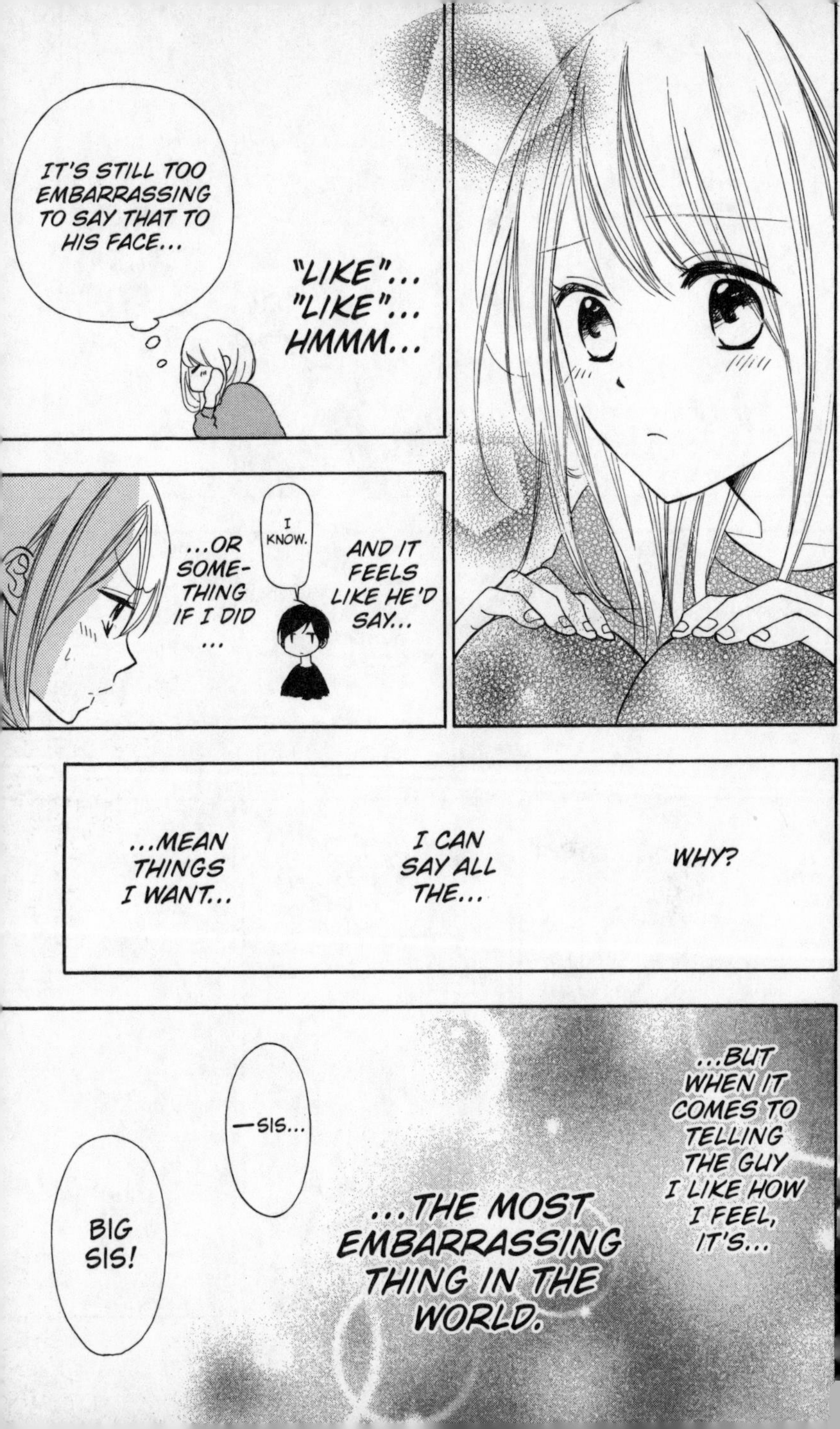
"LIKE"... "LIKE"... HMMM...
IT'S STILL TOO EMBARRASSING TO SAY THAT TO HIS FACE...
AND IT FEELS LIKE HE'D SAY...
I KNOW.
...OR SOME-THING IF I DID ...
WHY?
I CAN SAY ALL THE...
...MEAN THINGS I WANT...
...BUT WHEN IT COMES TO TELLING THE GUY I LIKE HOW I FEEL, IT'S...
...THE MOST EMBARRASSING THING IN THE WORLD.
—SIS...
BIG SIS!

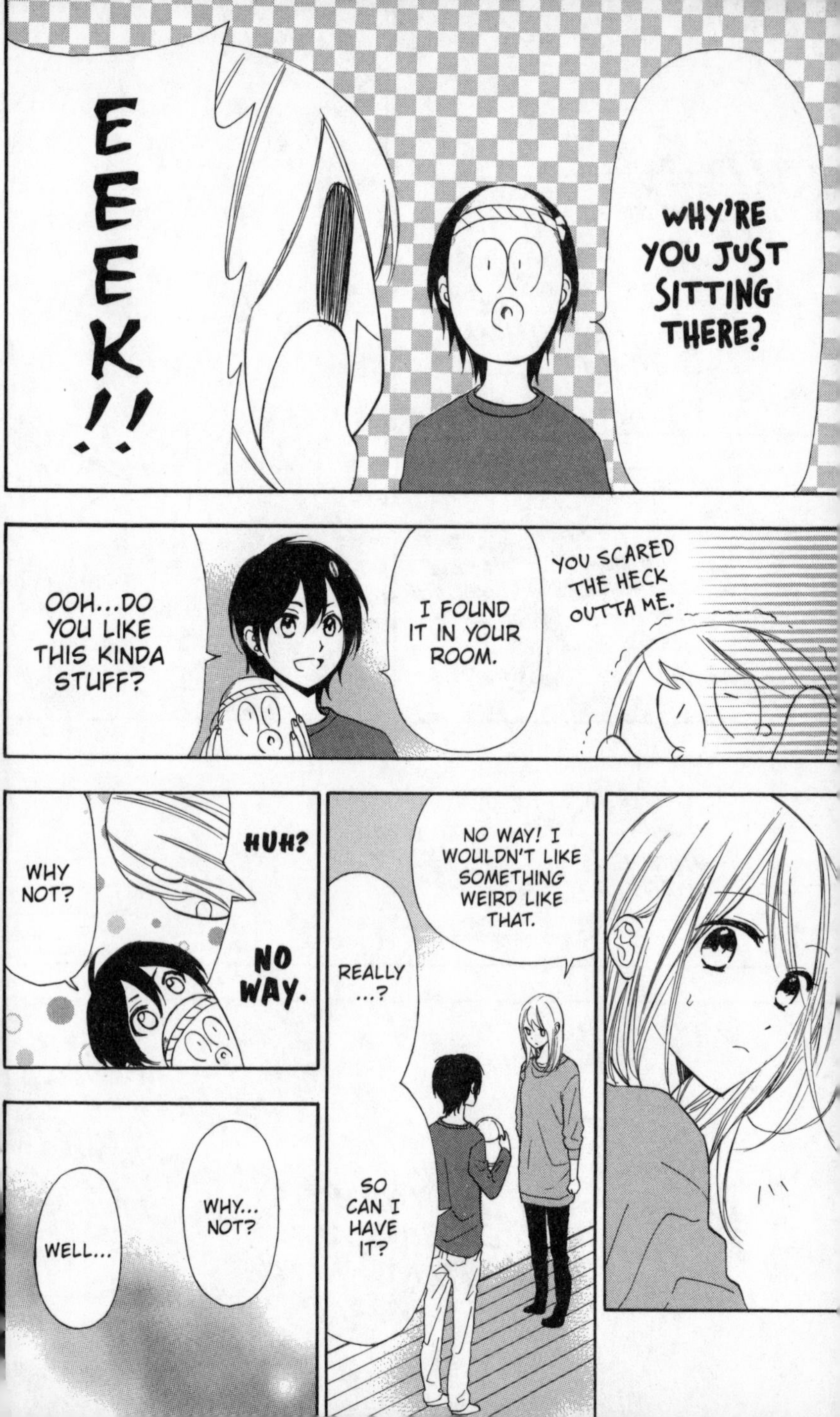

WHY'RE YOU JUST SITTING THERE?
EEEK!!
YOU SCARED THE HECK OUTTA ME.
I FOUND IT IN YOUR ROOM.
OOH...DO YOU LIKE THIS KINDA STUFF?
NO WAY! I WOULDN'T LIKE SOMETHING WEIRD LIKE THAT.
REALLY ...?
SO CAN I HAVE IT?
HUH?
NO WAY.
WHY NOT?
WHY... NOT?
WELL...

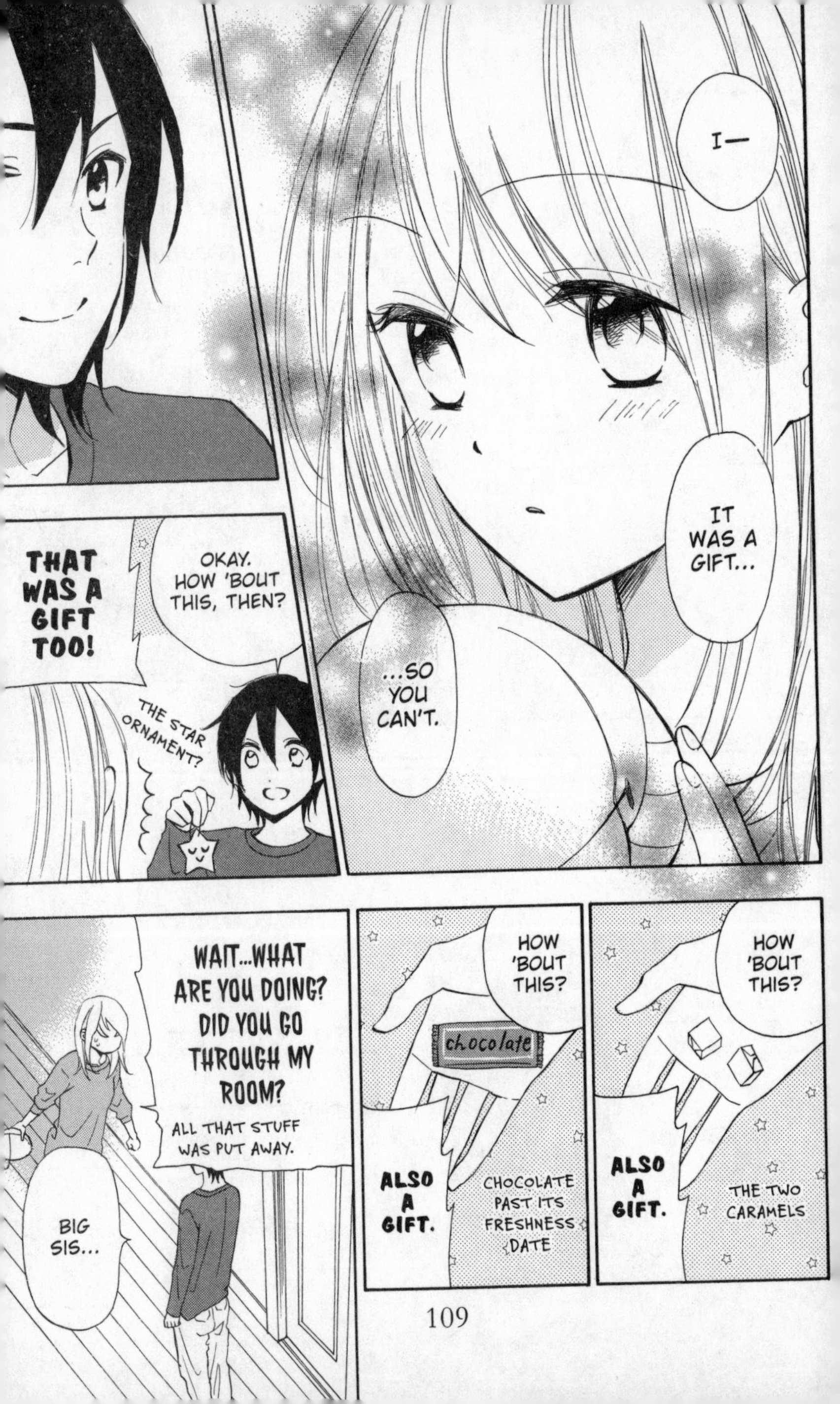
I—
IT WAS A GIFT...
...SO YOU CAN'T.
OKAY. HOW 'BOUT THIS, THEN?
THAT WAS A GIFT TOO!
THE STAR ORNAMENT?
HOW 'BOUT THIS?
ALSO A GIFT.
THE TWO CARAMELS
HOW 'BOUT THIS?
chocolate
ALSO A GIFT.
CHOCOLATE PAST ITS FRESHNESS DATE
WAIT...WHAT ARE YOU DOING? DID YOU GO THROUGH MY ROOM?
ALL THAT STUFF WAS PUT AWAY.
BIG SIS...

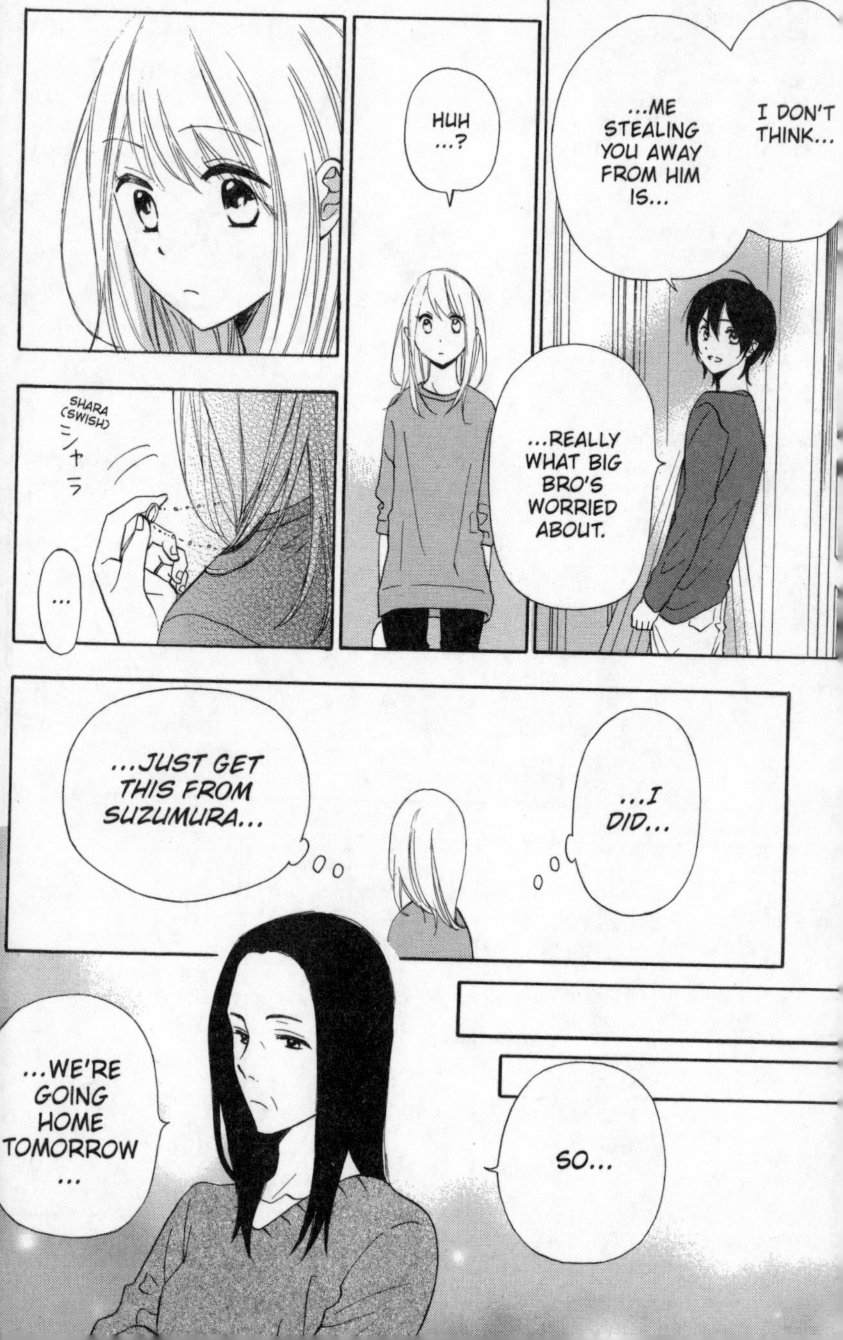
I DON'T THINK...
...ME STEALING YOU AWAY FROM HIM IS...
...REALLY WHAT BIG BRO'S WORRIED ABOUT.
HUH ...?
SHARA (SWISH)
シャラ
...
...I DID...
...JUST GET THIS FROM SUZUMURA...
SO...
...WE'RE GOING HOME TOMORROW ...

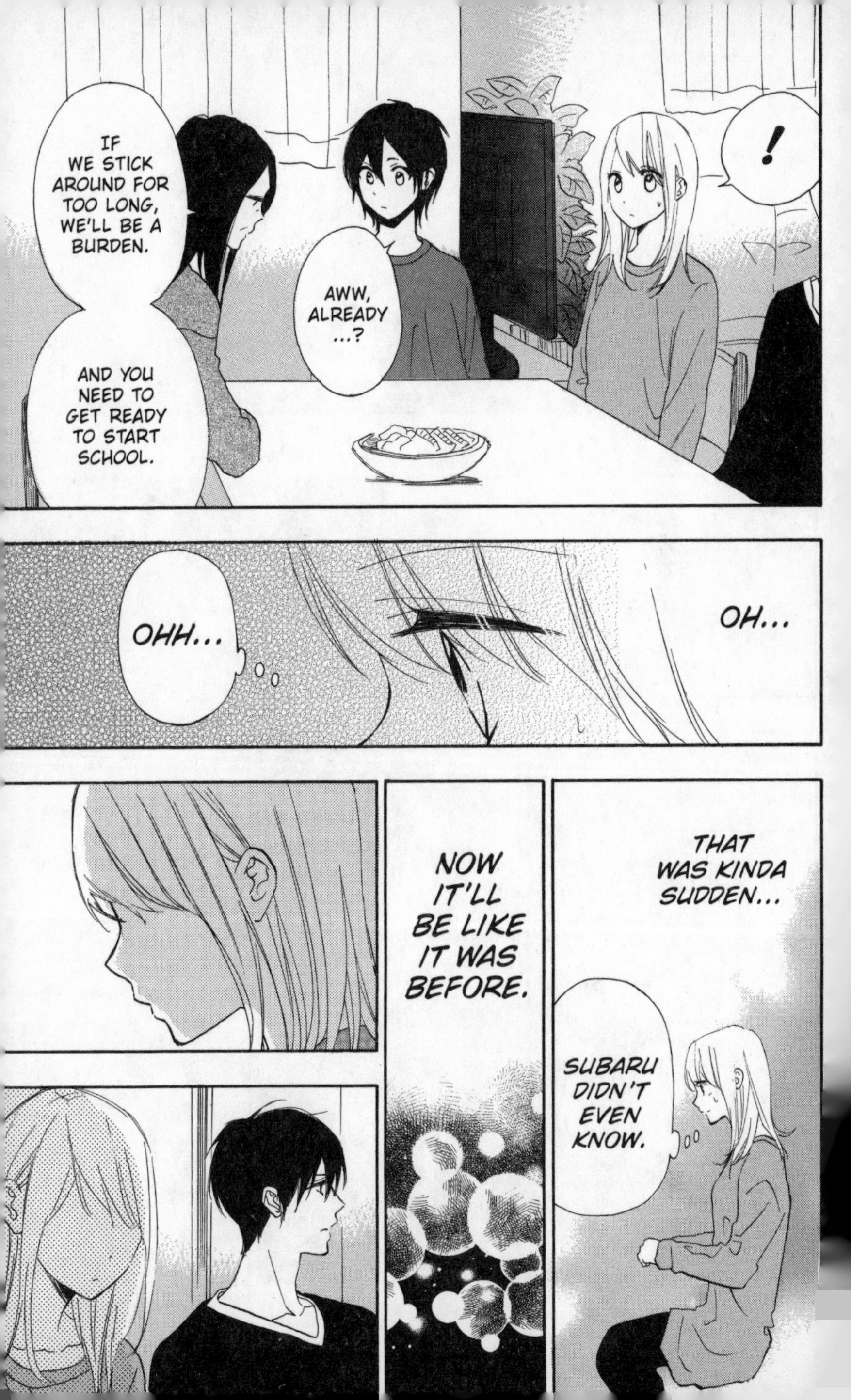
!
IF WE STICK AROUND FOR TOO LONG, WE'LL BE A BURDEN.
AND YOU NEED TO GET READY TO START SCHOOL.
AWW, ALREADY ...?
OH...
OHH...
THAT WAS KINDA SUDDEN...
SUBARU DIDN'T EVEN KNOW.
NOW IT'LL BE LIKE IT WAS BEFORE.

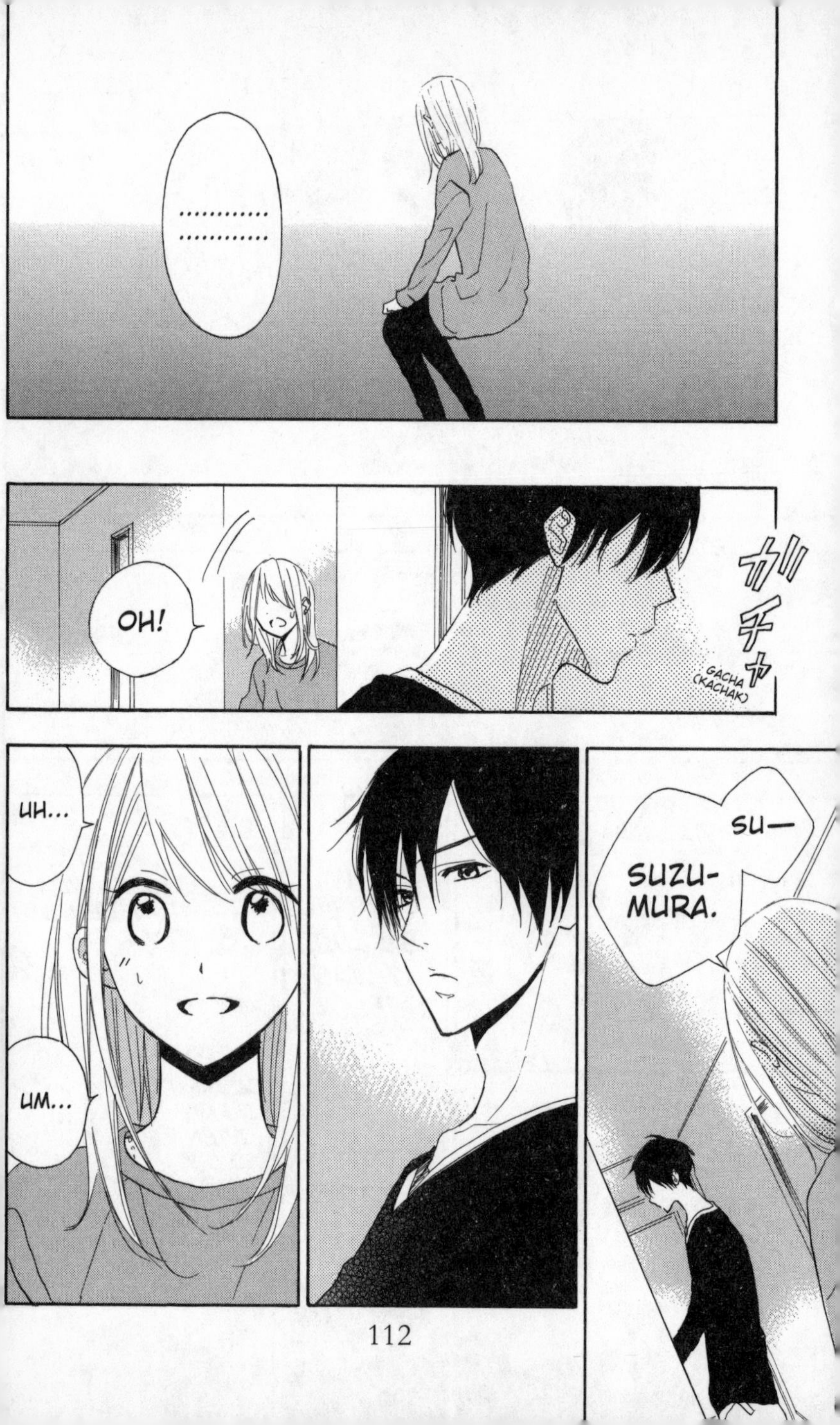
....
....
ガチャ
GACHA (KACHAK)
OH!
SU—
SUZU-MURA.
UH...
UM...

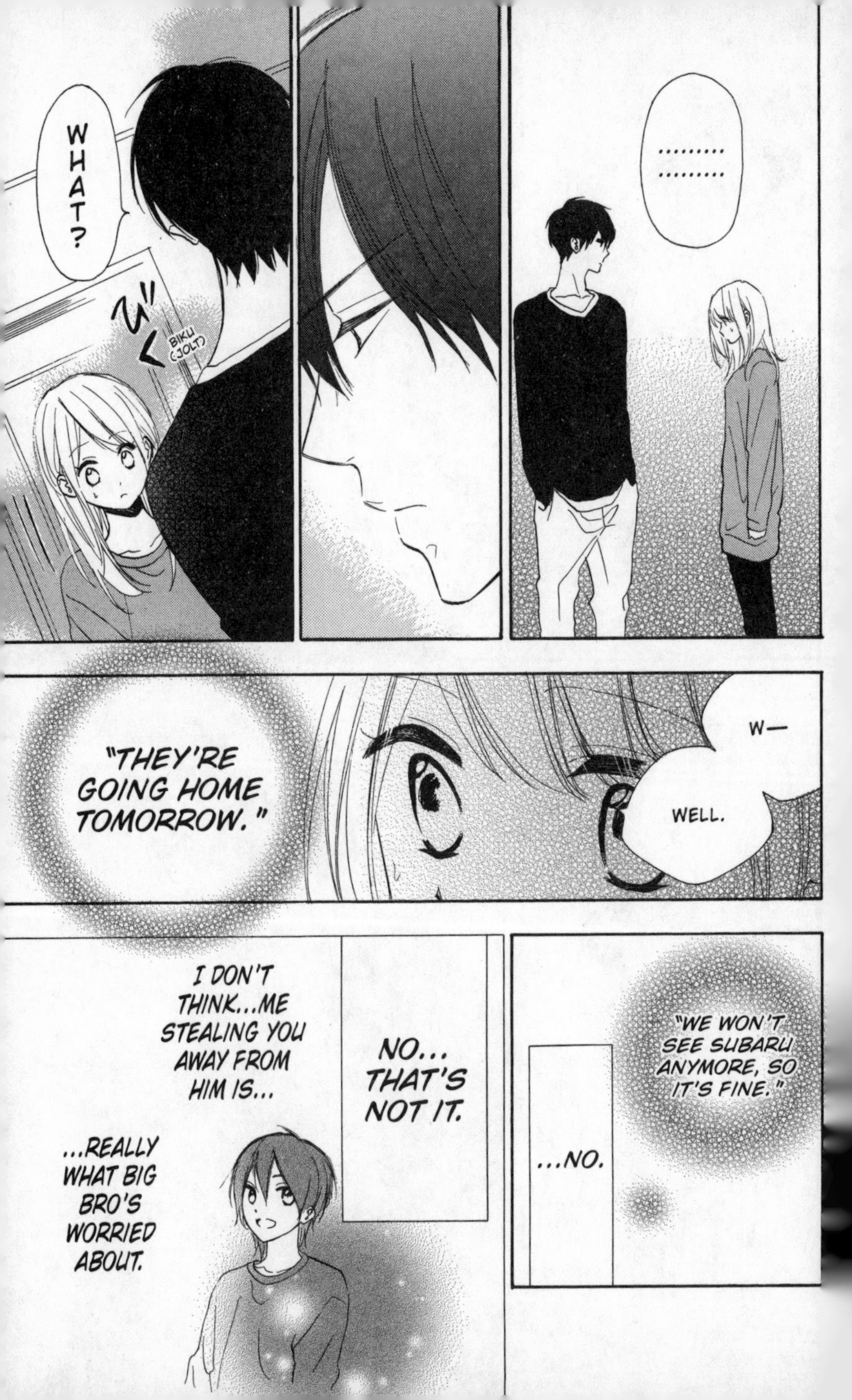
....
....
WHAT?
BIKU (JOLT)
W—
WELL.
"THEY'RE GOING HOME TOMORROW."
"WE WON'T SEE SUBARU ANYMORE, SO IT'S FINE."
...NO.
NO... THAT'S NOT IT.
I DON'T THINK...ME STEALING YOU AWAY FROM HIM IS...
...REALLY WHAT BIG BRO'S WORRIED ABOUT.

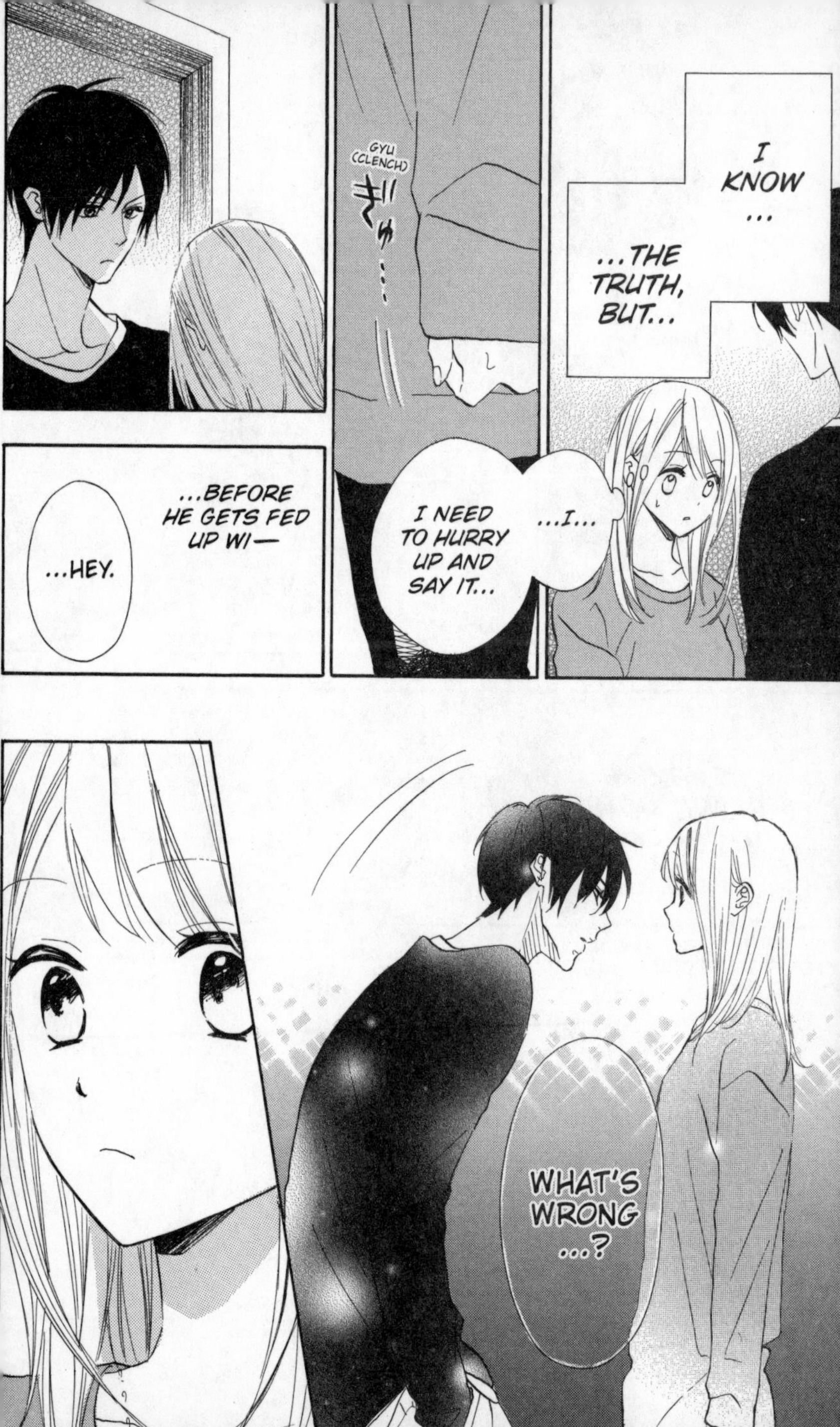
I KNOW...
...THE TRUTH, BUT...
...I...
GYU (CLENCH)
I NEED TO HURRY UP AND SAY IT...
...BEFORE HE GETS FED UP WI—
...HEY.
WHAT'S WRONG...?

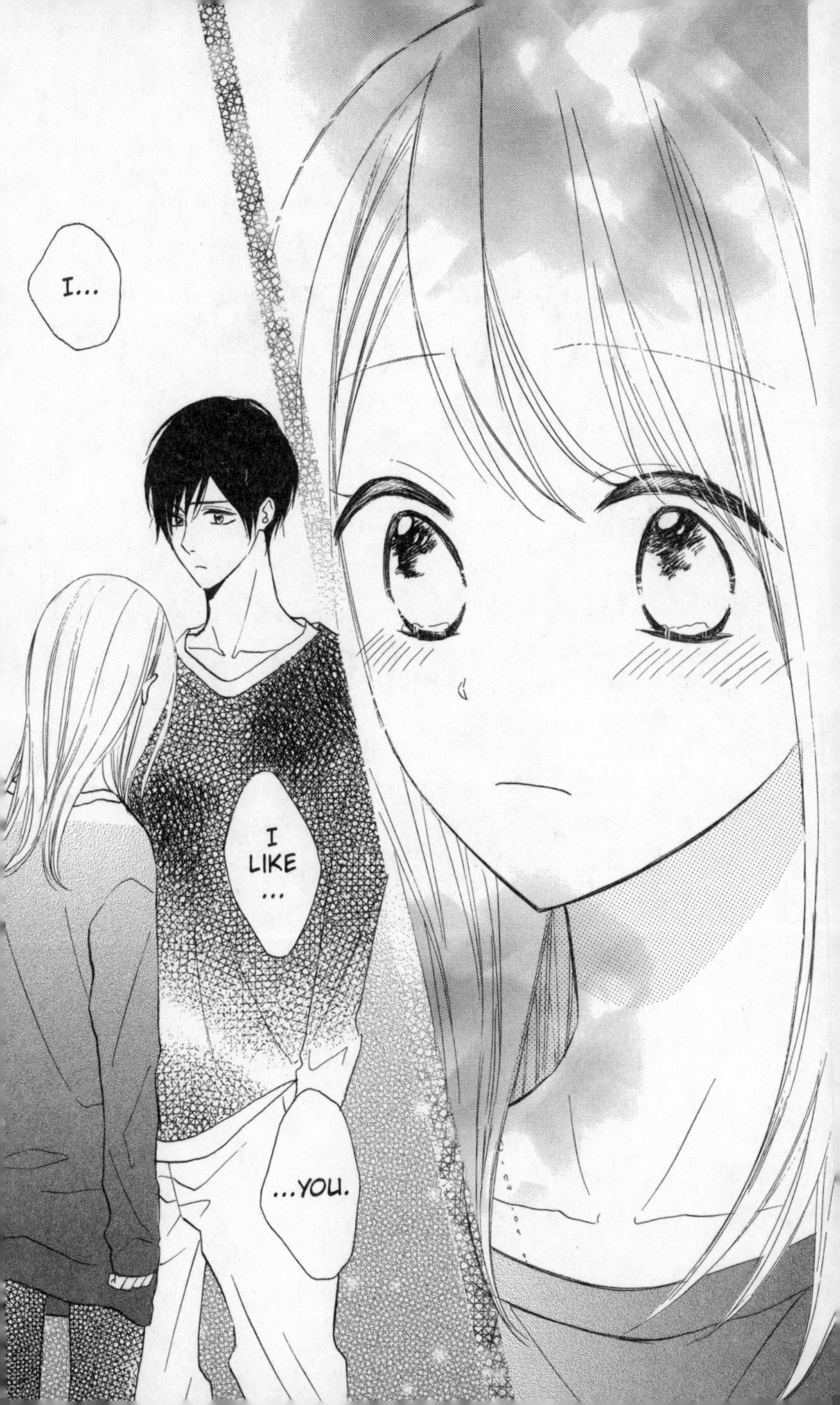
I...
I LIKE ...
...YOU.

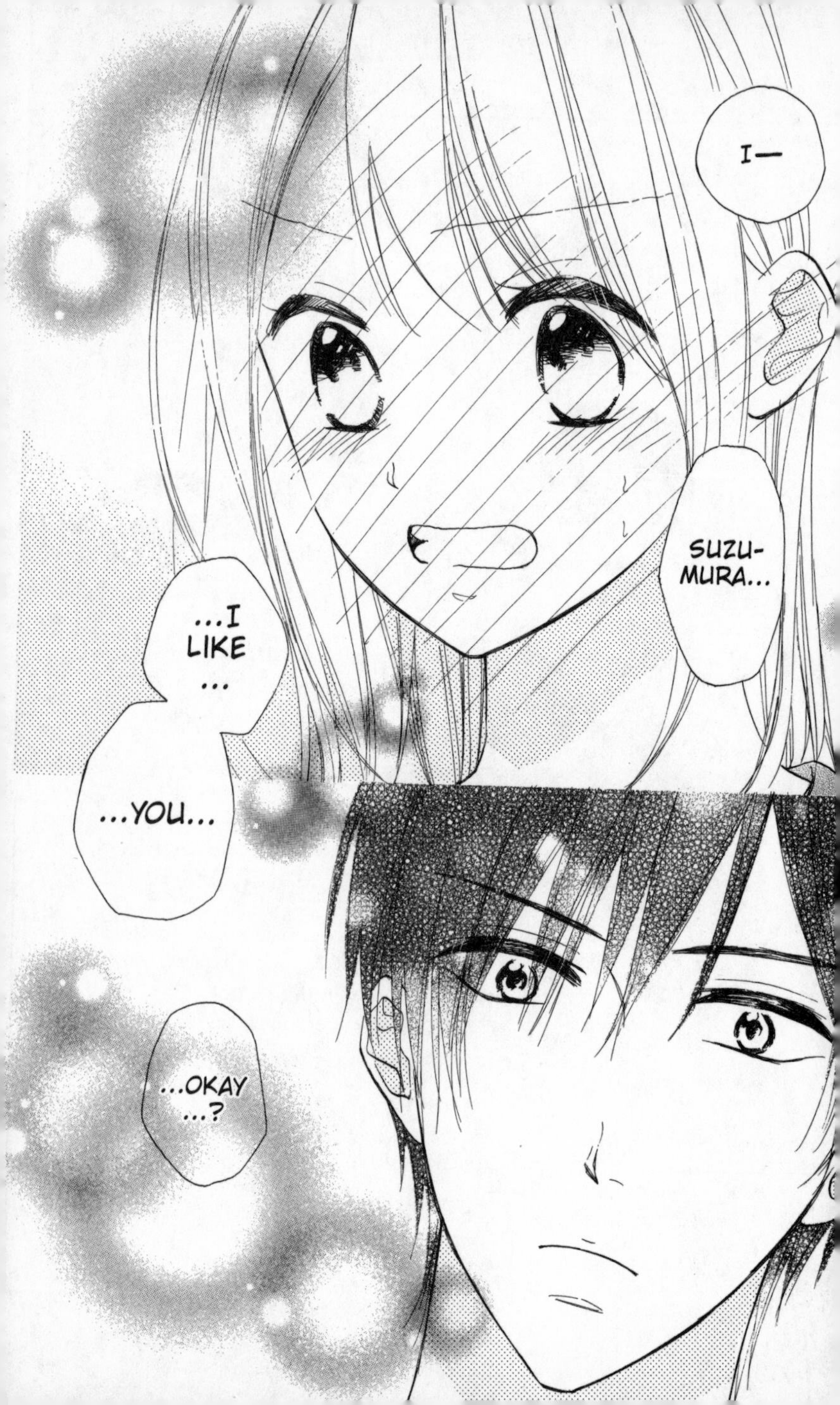
I—
SUZU-MURA...
...I LIKE ...
...YOU...
...OKAY ...?

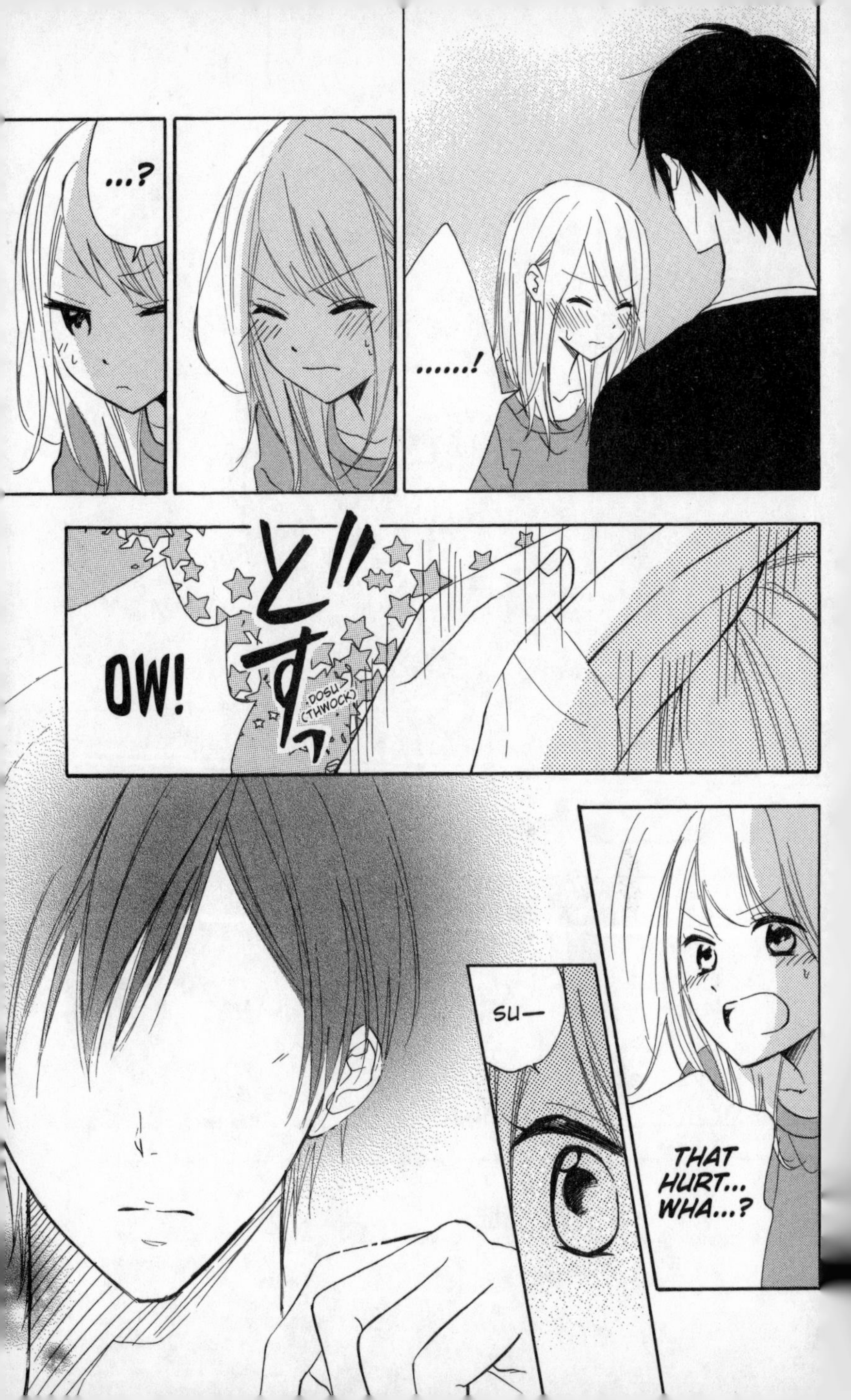
......!
...?
どす
DOSU (THWOCK)
OW!
THAT HURT... WHA...?
SU—

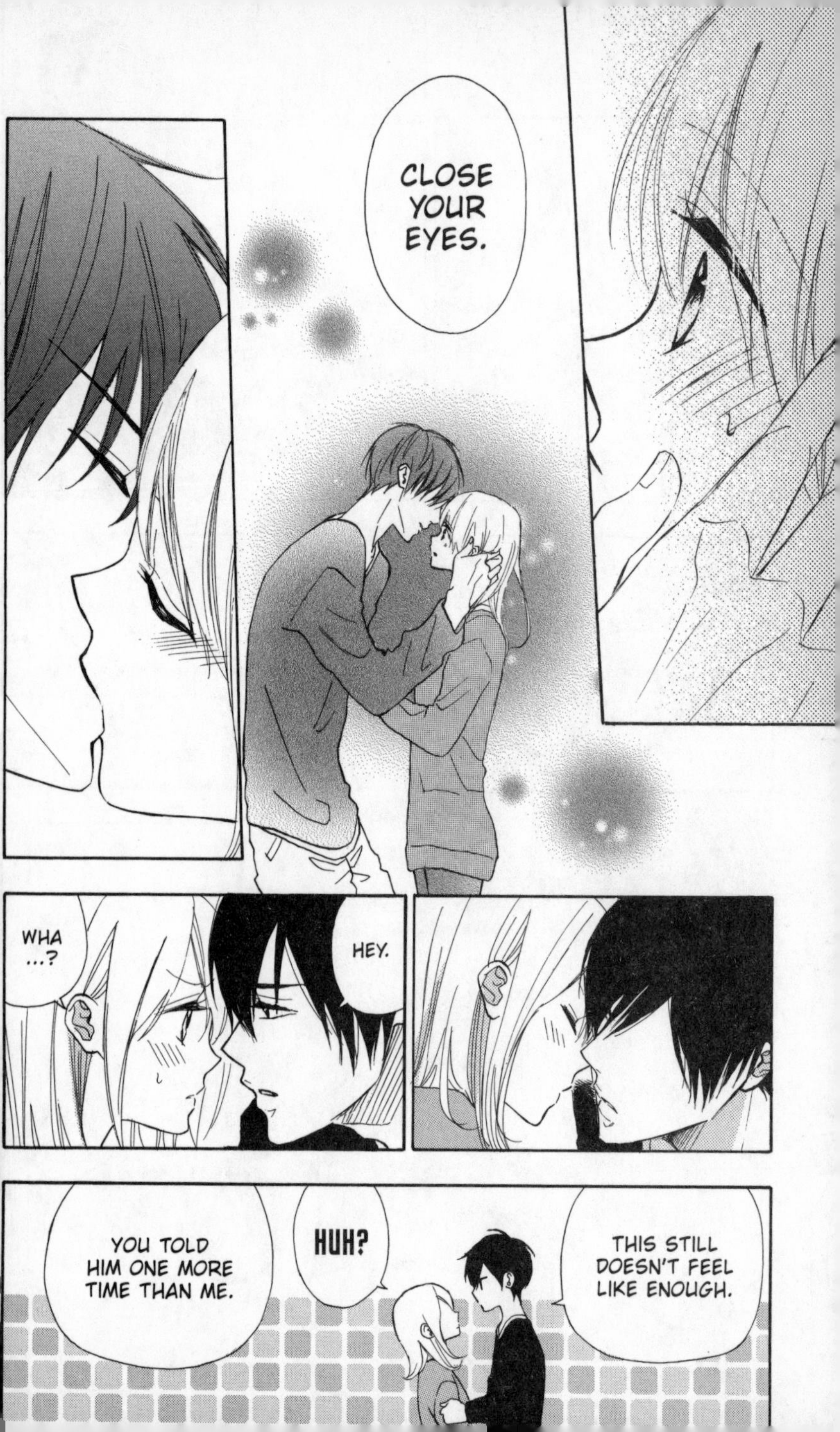
CLOSE YOUR EYES.
HEY.
WHA ...?
THIS STILL DOESN'T FEEL LIKE ENOUGH.
HUH?
YOU TOLD HIM ONE MORE TIME THAN ME.

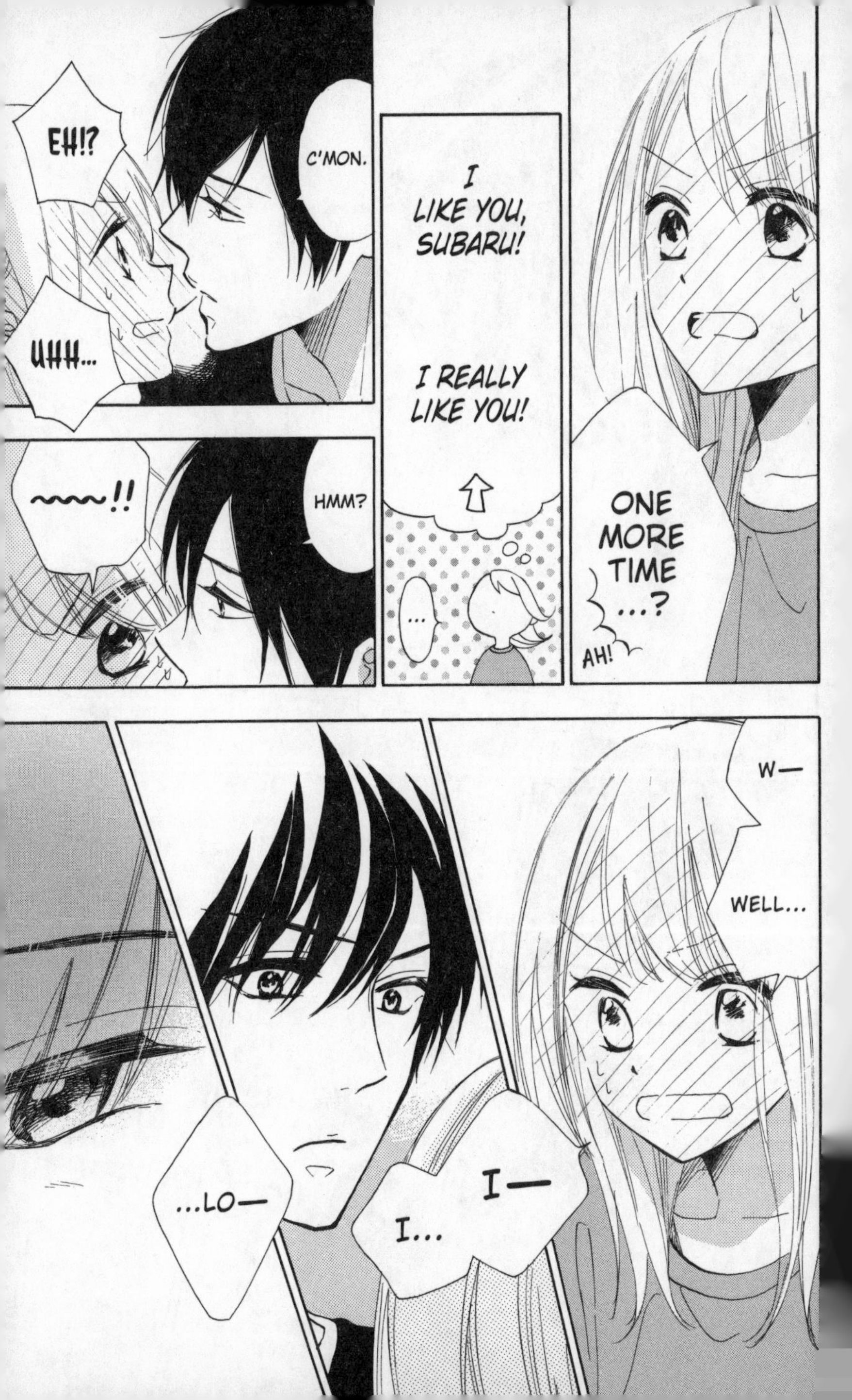
ONE MORE TIME ...?
AH!
I LIKE YOU, SUBARU!
I REALLY LIKE YOU!
...
C'MON.
EH!?
UHH...
HMM?
~~~~!!
W—
WELL...
I—
I...
...LO—
~~~~

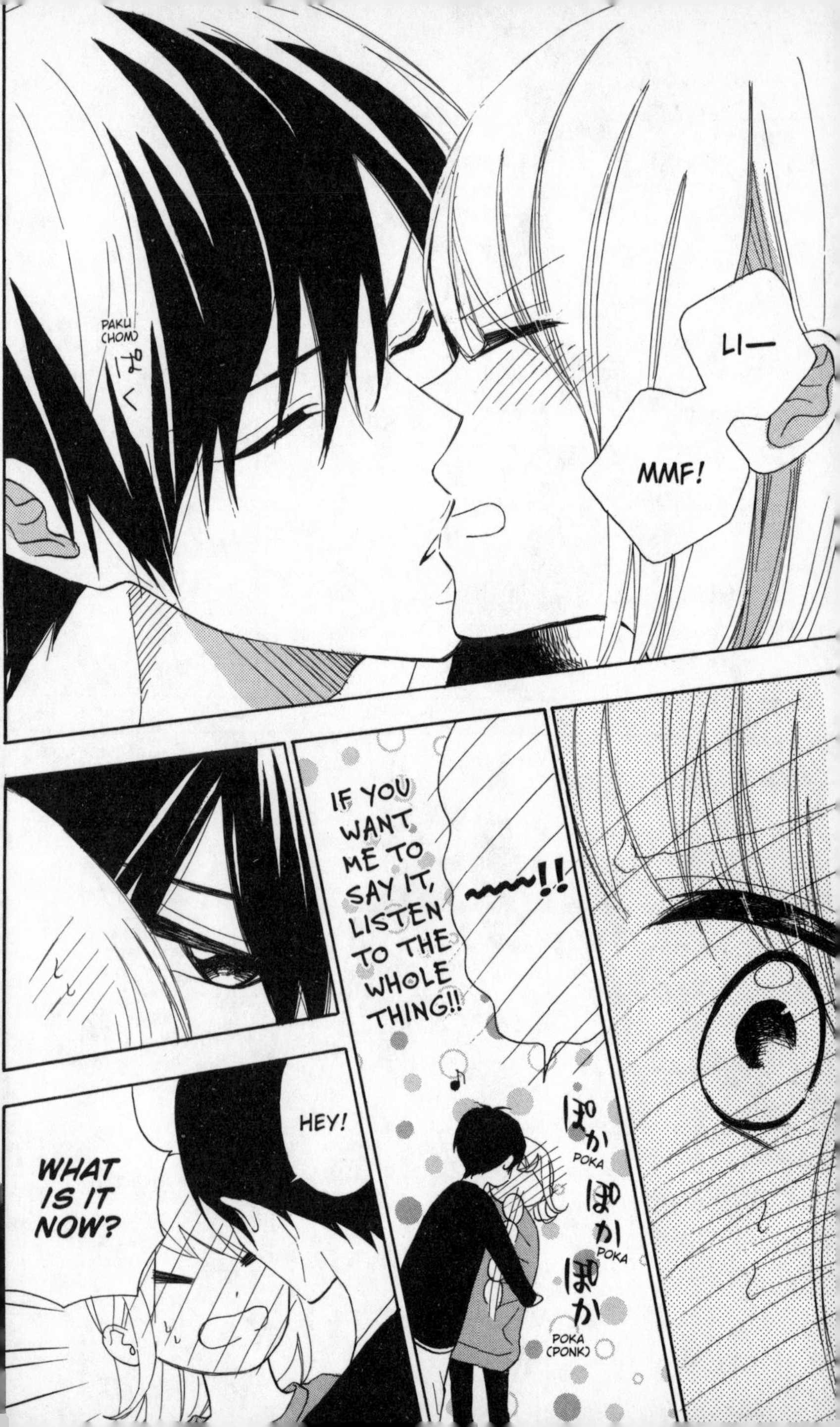
LI—
MMF!
PAKU (HOM)
ぱく
~~~!!
IF YOU WANT ME TO SAY IT, LISTEN TO THE WHOLE THING!!
ぽか
POKA
ぽか
POKA
ぽか
POKA (PONK)
HEY!
WHAT IS IT NOW?
~~~

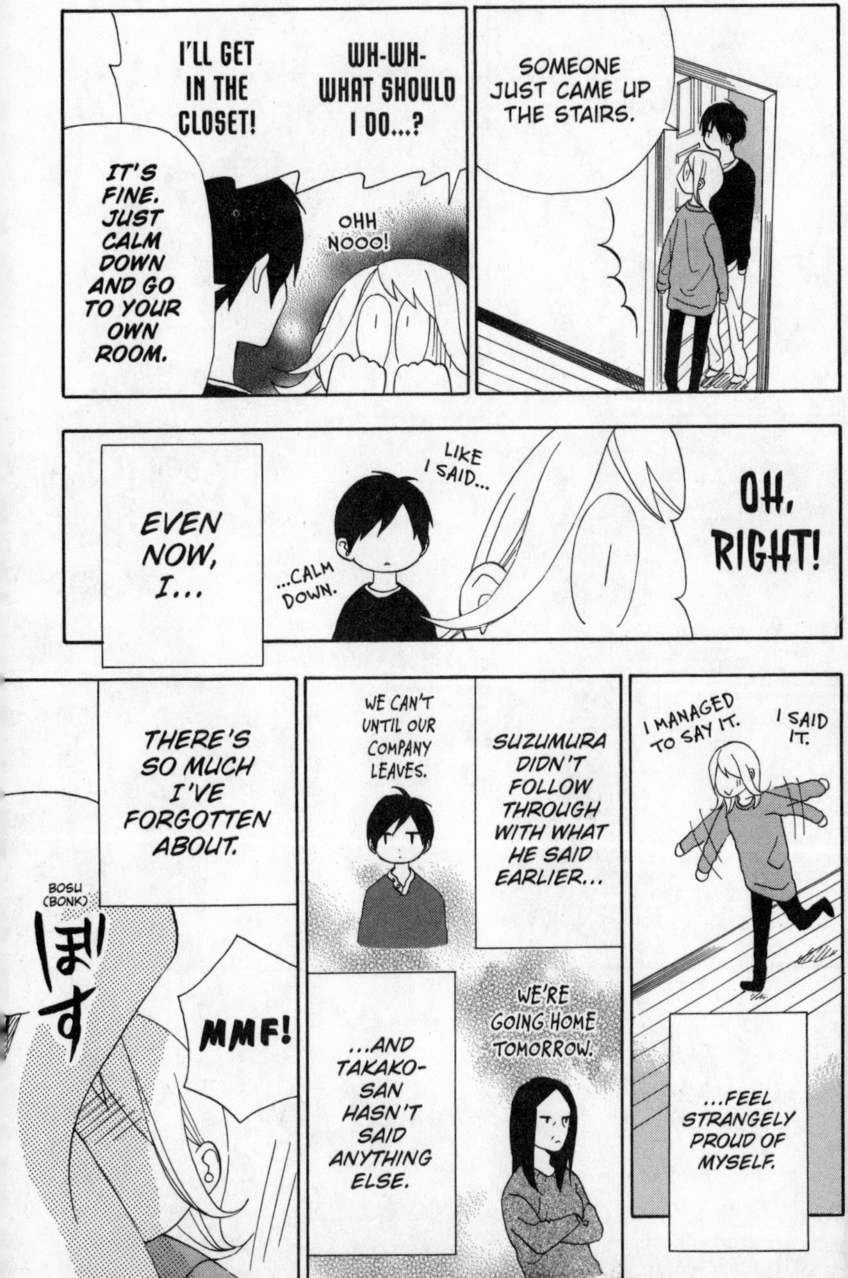
SOMEONE JUST CAME UP THE STAIRS.
WH-WH-WHAT SHOULD I DO...?
I'LL GET IN THE CLOSET!
OHH NOOO!
IT'S FINE. JUST CALM DOWN AND GO TO YOUR OWN ROOM.
OH, RIGHT!
LIKE I SAID...
...CALM DOWN.
EVEN NOW, I...
I SAID IT.
I MANAGED TO SAY IT.
...FEEL STRANGELY PROUD OF MYSELF.
SUZUMURA DIDN'T FOLLOW THROUGH WITH WHAT HE SAID EARLIER...
WE CAN'T UNTIL OUR COMPANY LEAVES.
WE'RE GOING HOME TOMORROW.
...AND TAKAKO-SAN HASN'T SAID ANYTHING ELSE.
THERE'S SO MUCH I'VE FORGOTTEN ABOUT.
MMF!
ぼす
BOSU (BONK)

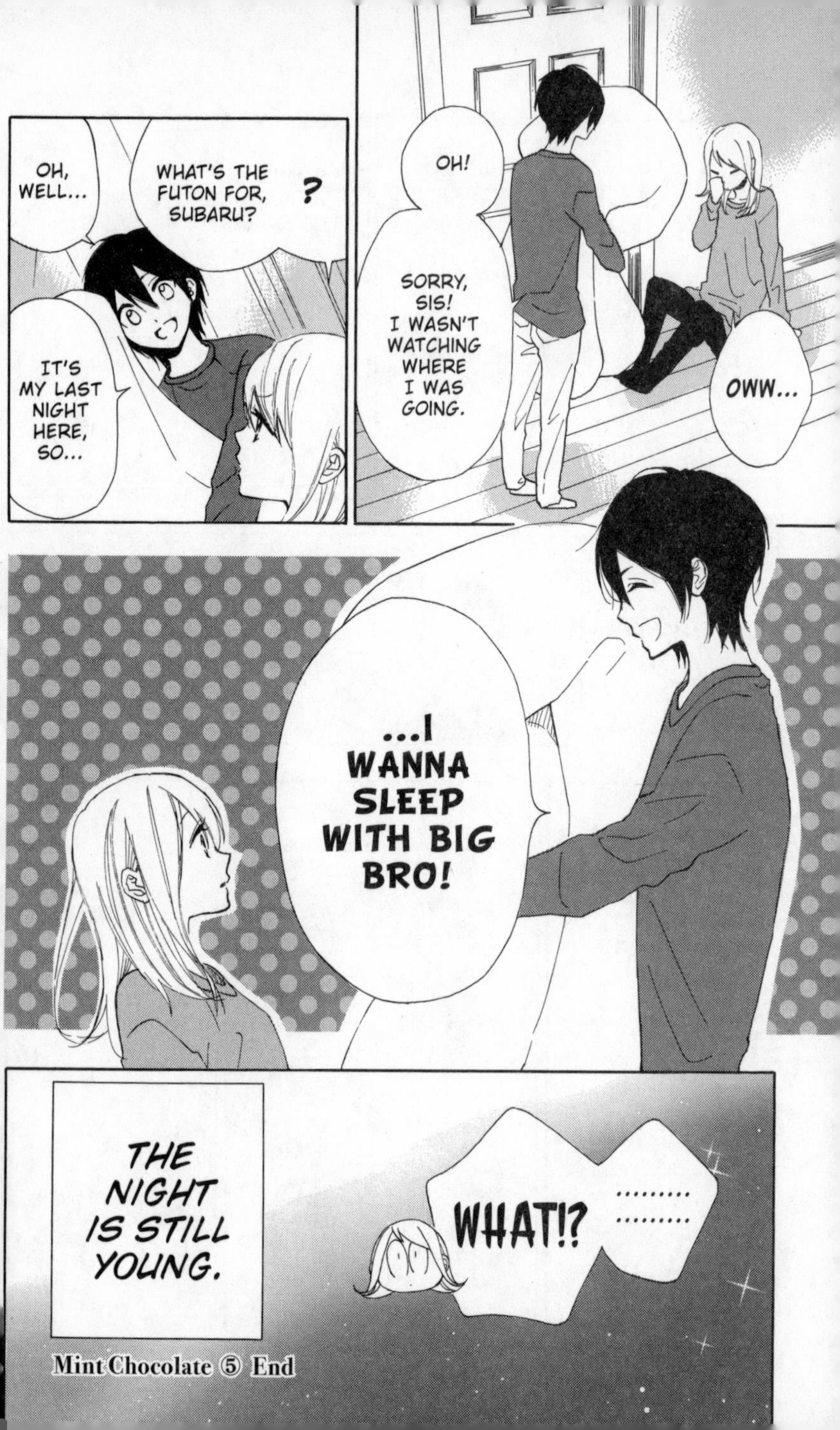
OWW...
OH!
SORRY, SIS! I WASN'T WATCHING WHERE I WAS GOING.
WHAT'S THE FUTON FOR, SUBARU?
?
OH, WELL...
IT'S MY LAST NIGHT HERE, SO...
...I WANNA SLEEP WITH BIG BRO!
....
WHAT!?
THE NIGHT IS STILL YOUNG.
Mint Chocolate ⑤ End

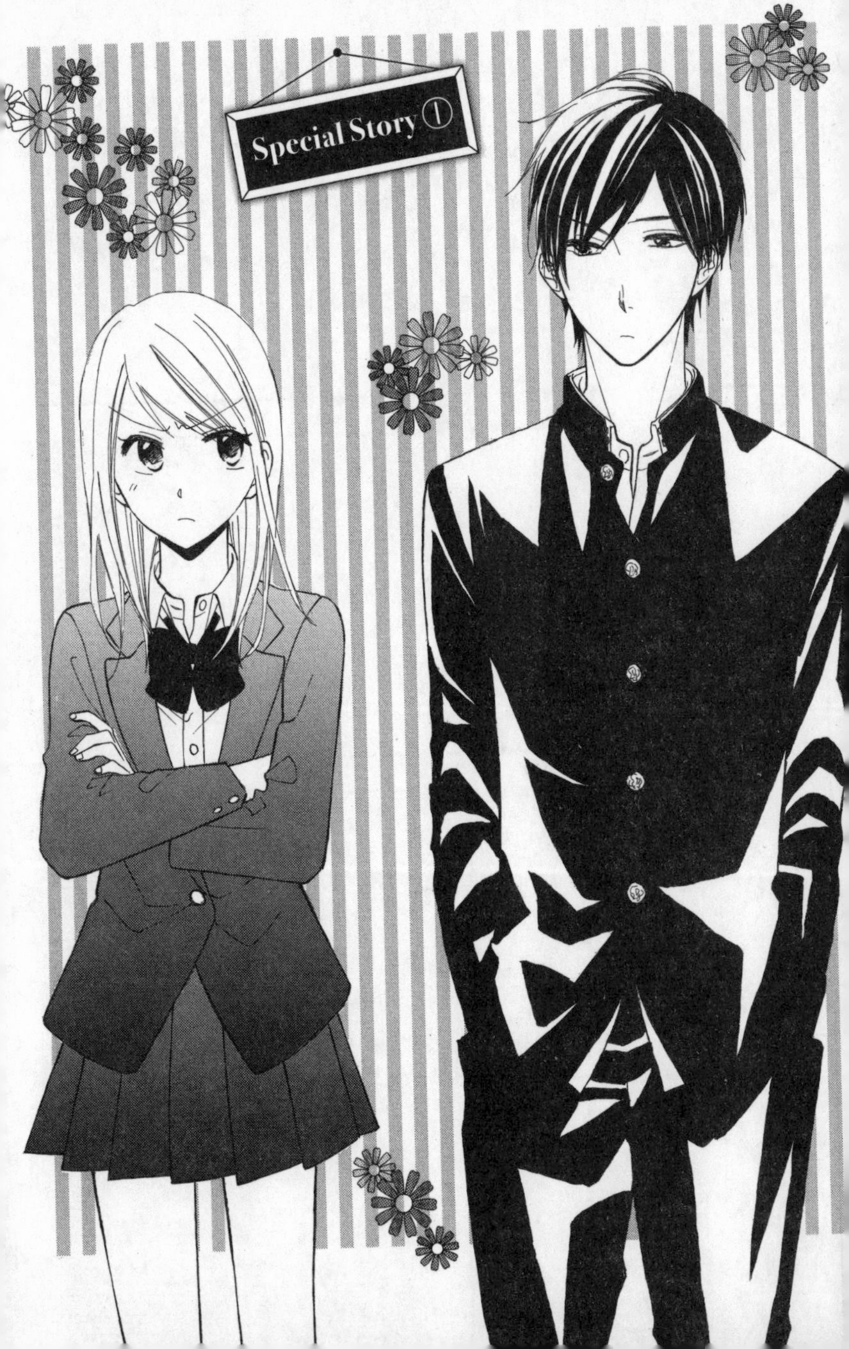
Special Story ①

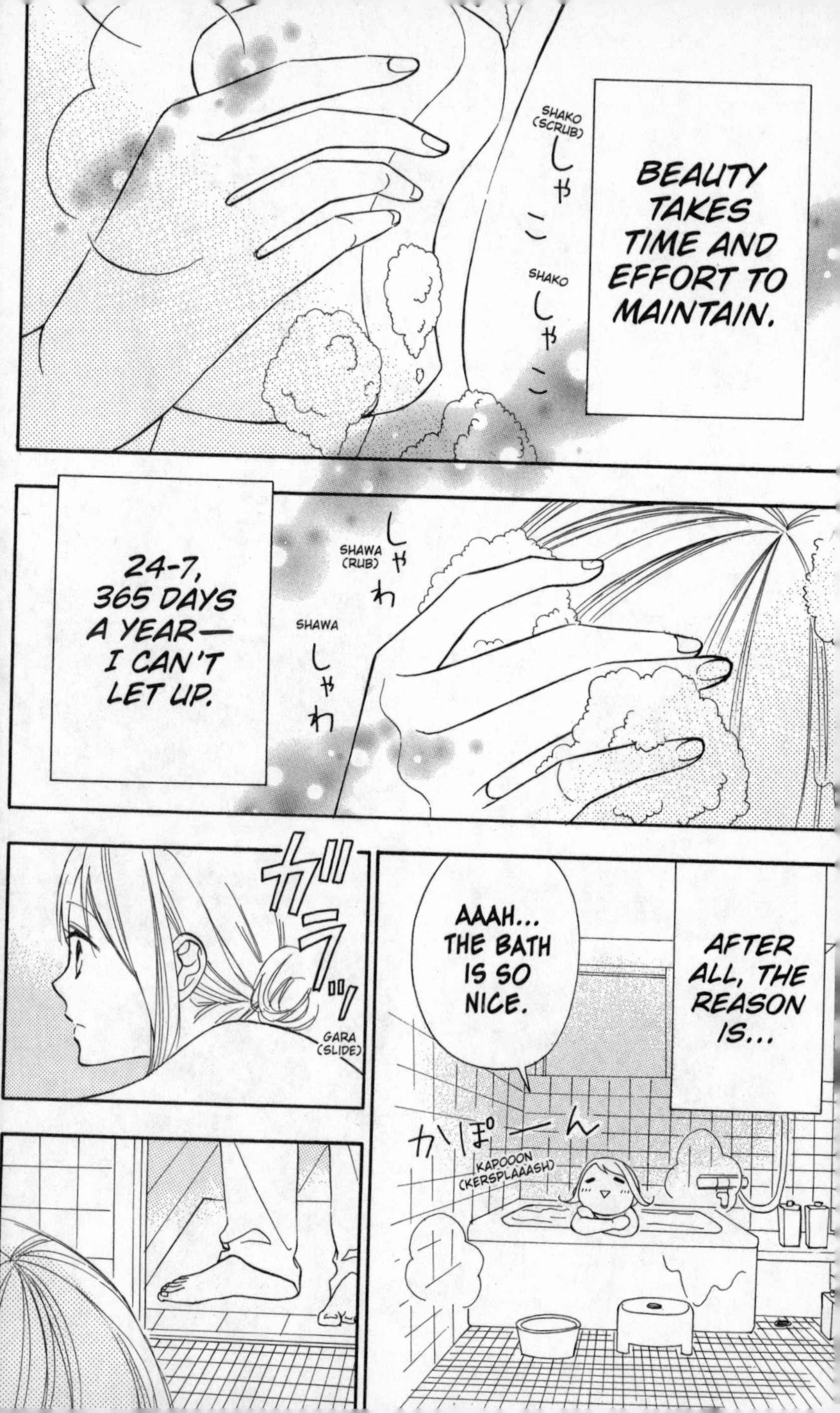
BEAUTY TAKES TIME AND EFFORT TO MAINTAIN.
しゃこ
SHAKO (SCRUB)
しゃこ
SHAKO
しゃわ
SHAWA (RUB)
しゃわ
SHAWA
24-7, 365 DAYS A YEAR— I CAN'T LET UP.
AFTER ALL, THE REASON IS...
AAAH... THE BATH IS SO NICE.
かぽーん
KAPOOON (KERSPLAAASH)
ガラッ
GARA (SLIDE)

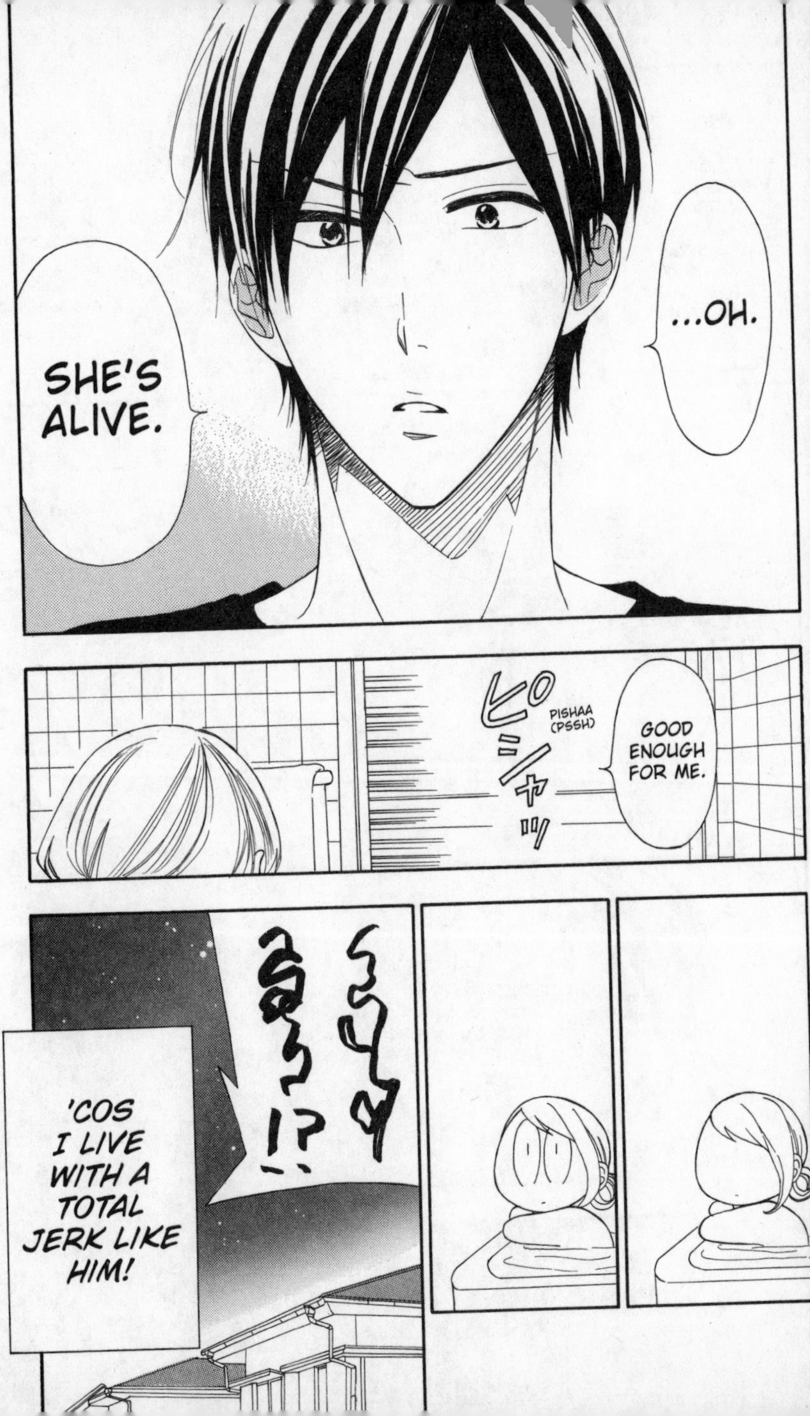
...OH.
SHE'S ALIVE.
ピシャッ
PISHAA (PSSH)
GOOD ENOUGH FOR ME.
'COS I LIVE WITH A TOTAL JERK LIKE HIM!

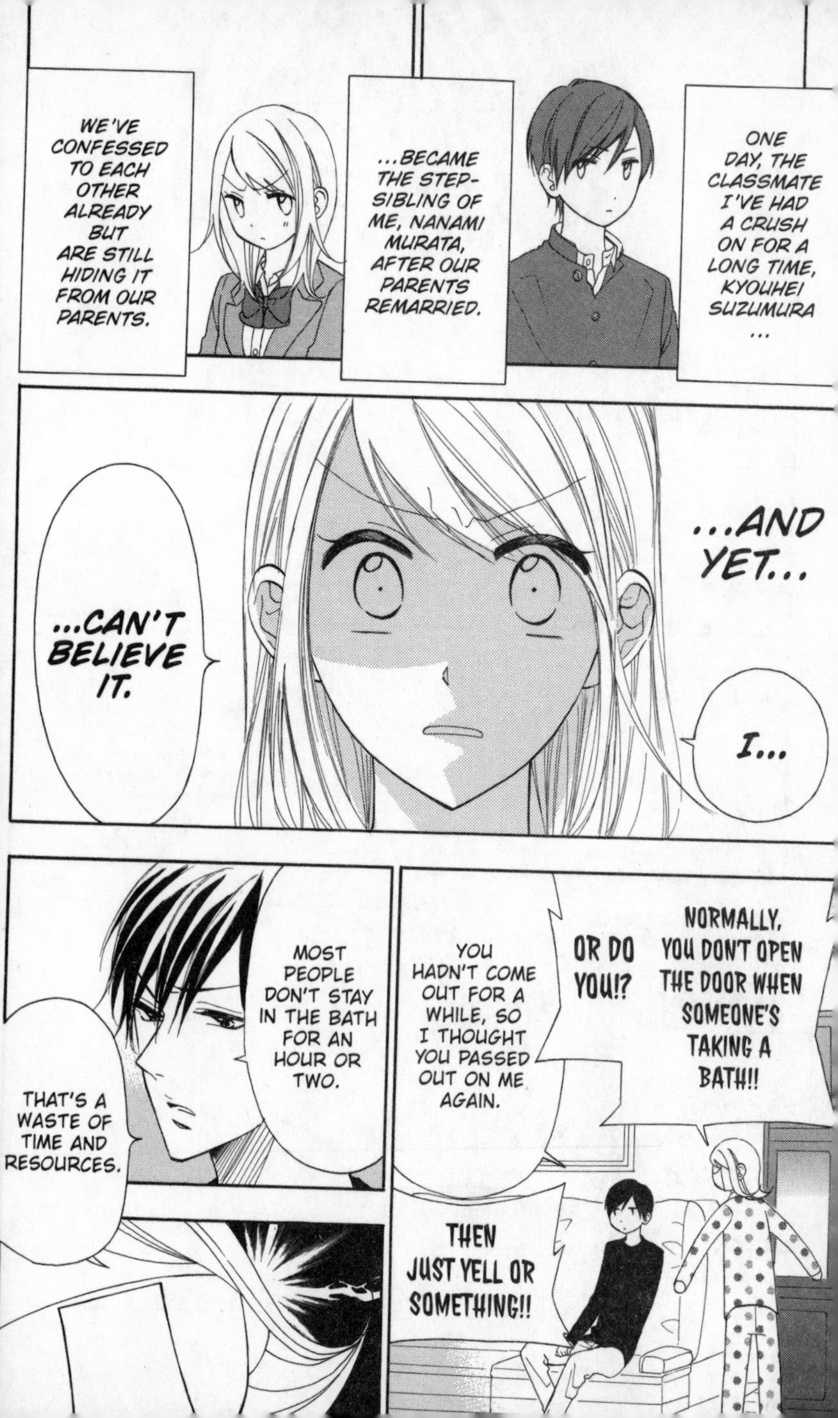
ONE DAY, THE CLASSMATE I'VE HAD A CRUSH ON FOR A LONG TIME, KYOUHEI SUZUMURA ...
...BECAME THE STEP-SIBLING OF ME, NANAMI MURATA, AFTER OUR PARENTS REMARRIED.
WE'VE CONFESSED TO EACH OTHER ALREADY BUT ARE STILL HIDING IT FROM OUR PARENTS.
...AND YET...
I...
...CAN'T BELIEVE IT.
NORMALLY, YOU DON'T OPEN THE DOOR WHEN SOMEONE'S TAKING A BATH!!
OR DO YOU!?
YOU HADN'T COME OUT FOR A WHILE, SO I THOUGHT YOU PASSED OUT ON ME AGAIN.
THEN JUST YELL OR SOMETHING!!
MOST PEOPLE DON'T STAY IN THE BATH FOR AN HOUR OR TWO.
THAT'S A WASTE OF TIME AND RESOURCES.

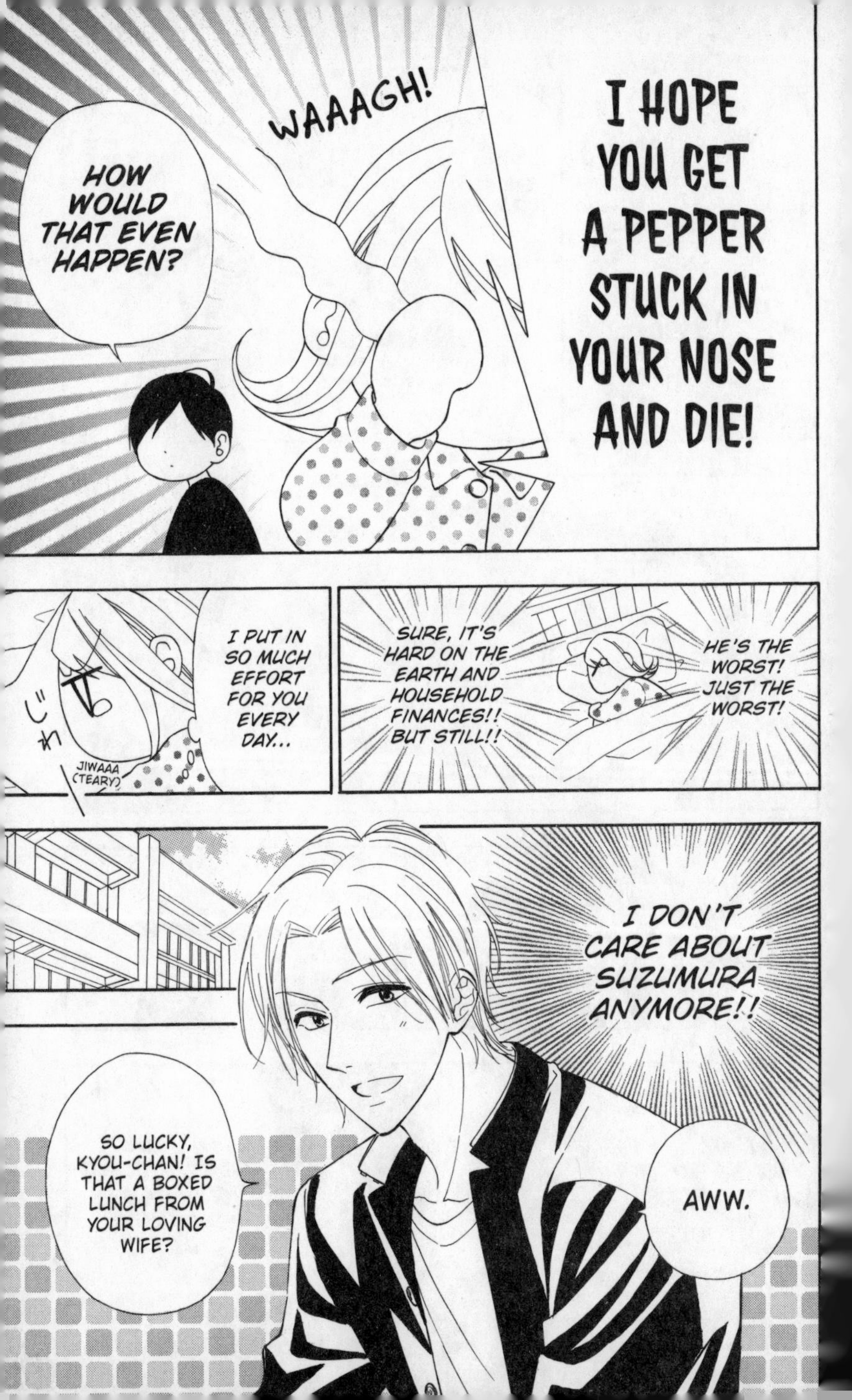
I HOPE YOU GET A PEPPER STUCK IN YOUR NOSE AND DIE!
WAAAGH!
HOW WOULD THAT EVEN HAPPEN?
HE'S THE WORST! JUST THE WORST!
SURE, IT'S HARD ON THE EARTH AND HOUSEHOLD FINANCES!! BUT STILL!!
I PUT IN SO MUCH EFFORT FOR YOU EVERY DAY...
じわ
JIWAAA (TEARY)
I DON'T CARE ABOUT SUZUMURA ANYMORE!!
AWW.
SO LUCKY, KYOU-CHAN! IS THAT A BOXED LUNCH FROM YOUR LOVING WIFE?

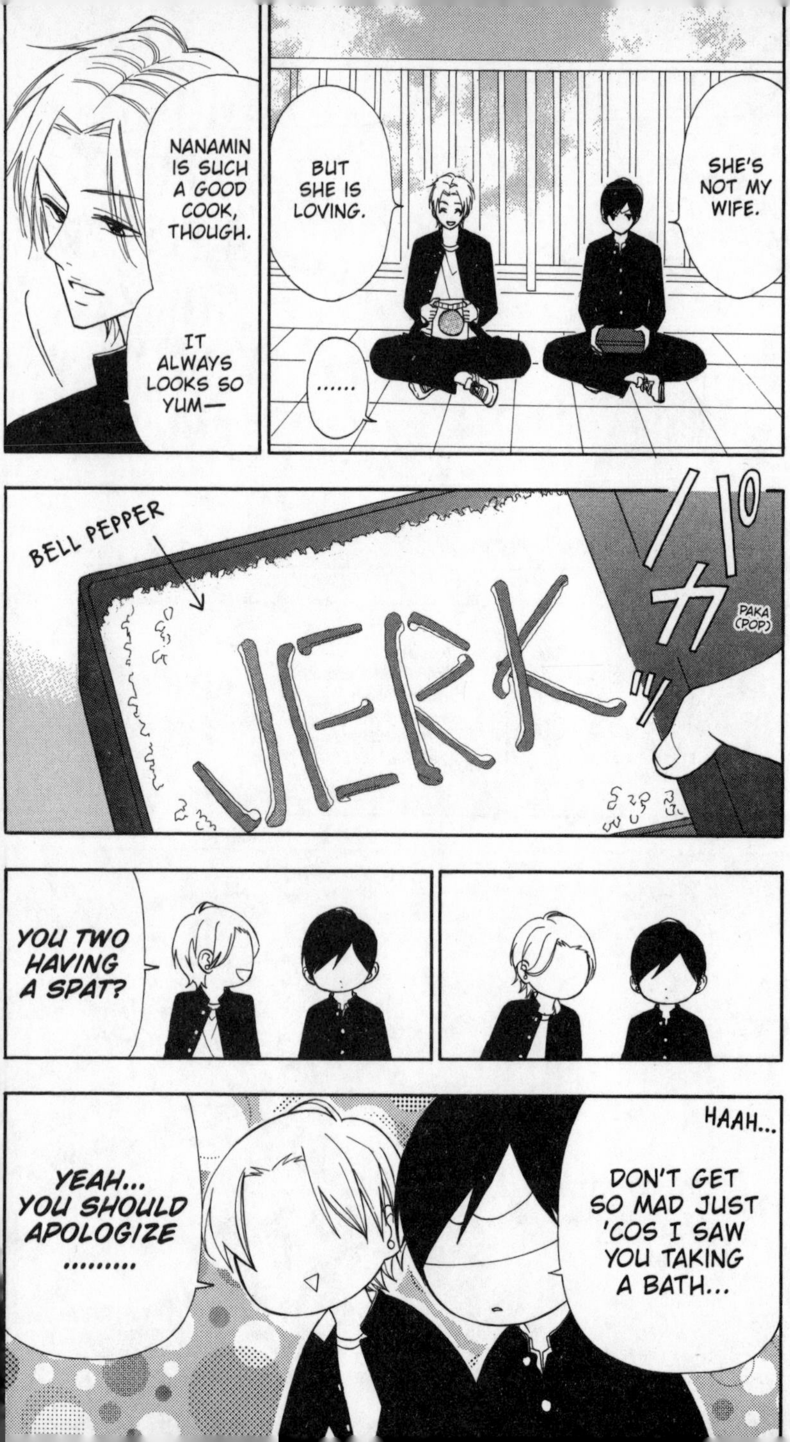
SHE'S NOT MY WIFE.
BUT SHE IS LOVING.
......
NANAMIN IS SUCH A GOOD COOK, THOUGH.
IT ALWAYS LOOKS SO YUM—
パカッ
PAKA (POP)
BELL PEPPER
JERK
YOU TWO HAVING A SPAT?
HAAH...
DON'T GET SO MAD JUST 'COS I SAW YOU TAKING A BATH...
YEAH... YOU SHOULD APOLOGIZE ....

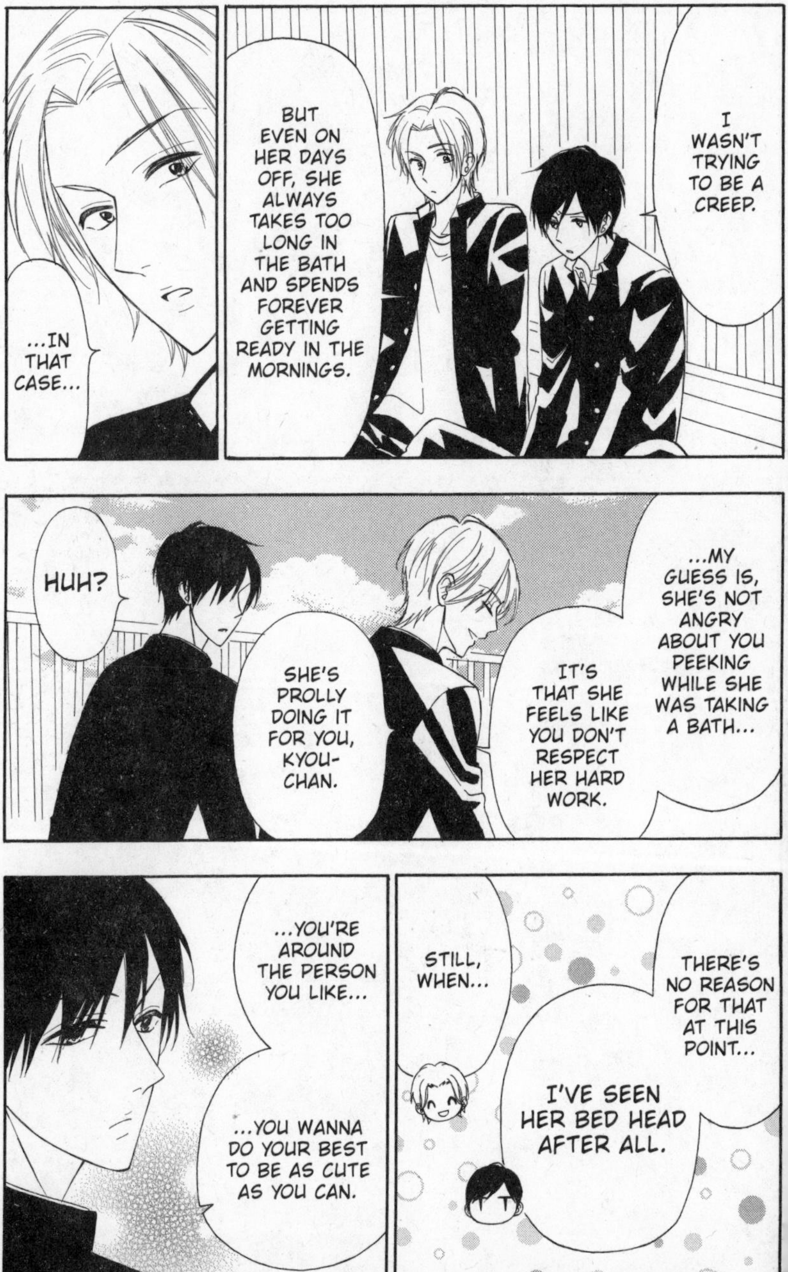
I WASN'T TRYING TO BE A CREEP.
BUT EVEN ON HER DAYS OFF, SHE ALWAYS TAKES TOO LONG IN THE BATH AND SPENDS FOREVER GETTING READY IN THE MORNINGS.
...IN THAT CASE...
...MY GUESS IS, SHE'S NOT ANGRY ABOUT YOU PEEKING WHILE SHE WAS TAKING A BATH...
IT'S THAT SHE FEELS LIKE YOU DON'T RESPECT HER HARD WORK.
SHE'S PROLLY DOING IT FOR YOU, KYOU-CHAN.
HUH?
THERE'S NO REASON FOR THAT AT THIS POINT...
I'VE SEEN HER BED HEAD AFTER ALL.
STILL, WHEN...
...YOU'RE AROUND THE PERSON YOU LIKE...
...YOU WANNA DO YOUR BEST TO BE AS CUTE AS YOU CAN.

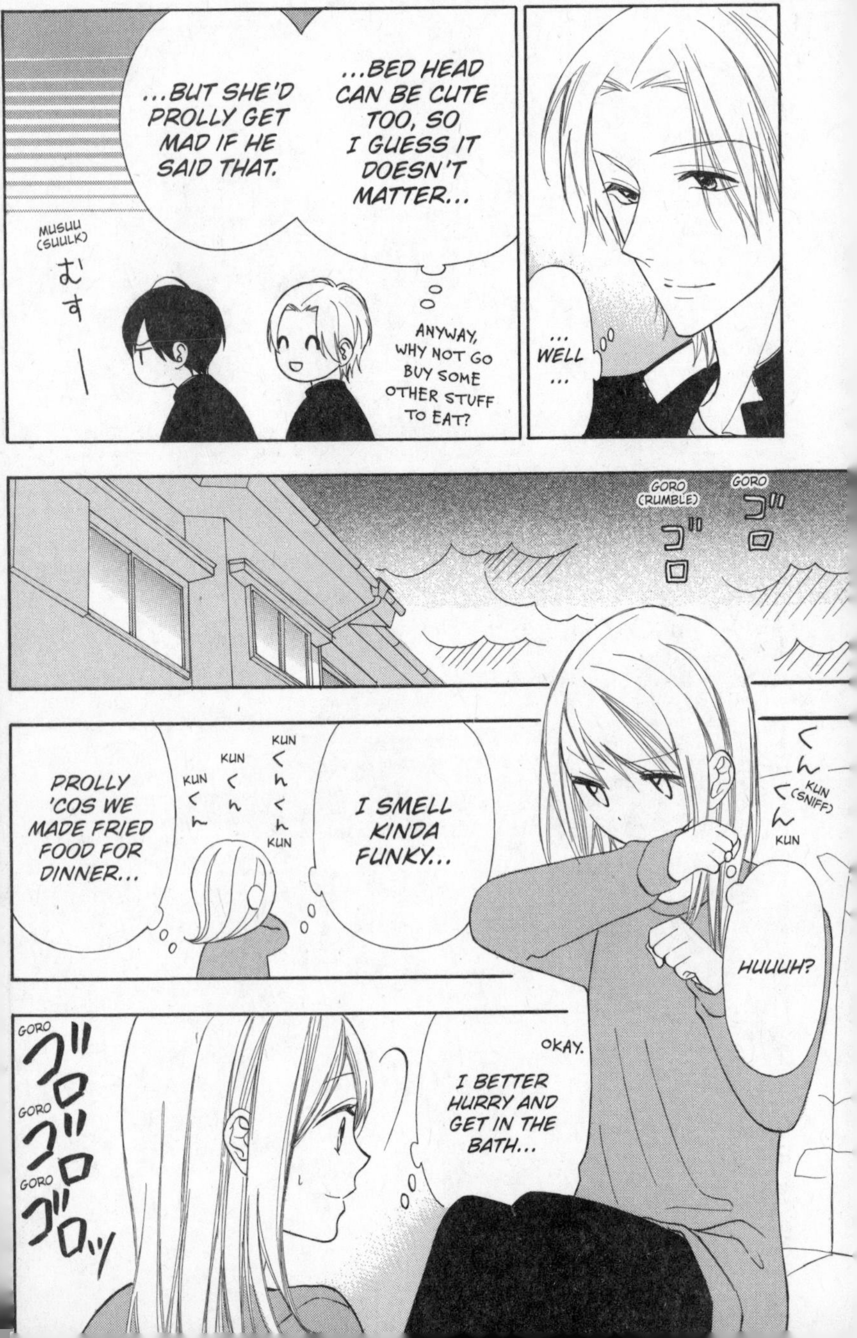
...WELL...
...BED HEAD CAN BE CUTE TOO, SO I GUESS IT DOESN'T MATTER...
...BUT SHE'D PROLLY GET MAD IF HE SAID THAT.
ANYWAY, WHY NOT GO BUY SOME OTHER STUFF TO EAT?
むすー
MUSUU (SUULK)
ゴロ
GORO
ゴロ
GORO (RUMBLE)
くんくん
KUN (SNIFF) KUN
HUUUH?
I SMELL KINDA FUNKY...
くんくん
KUN KUN
くん
KUN
くん
KUN
PROLLY 'COS WE MADE FRIED FOOD FOR DINNER...
OKAY.
I BETTER HURRY AND GET IN THE BATH...
ゴロ
GORO
ゴロ
GORO
ゴロッ
GORO

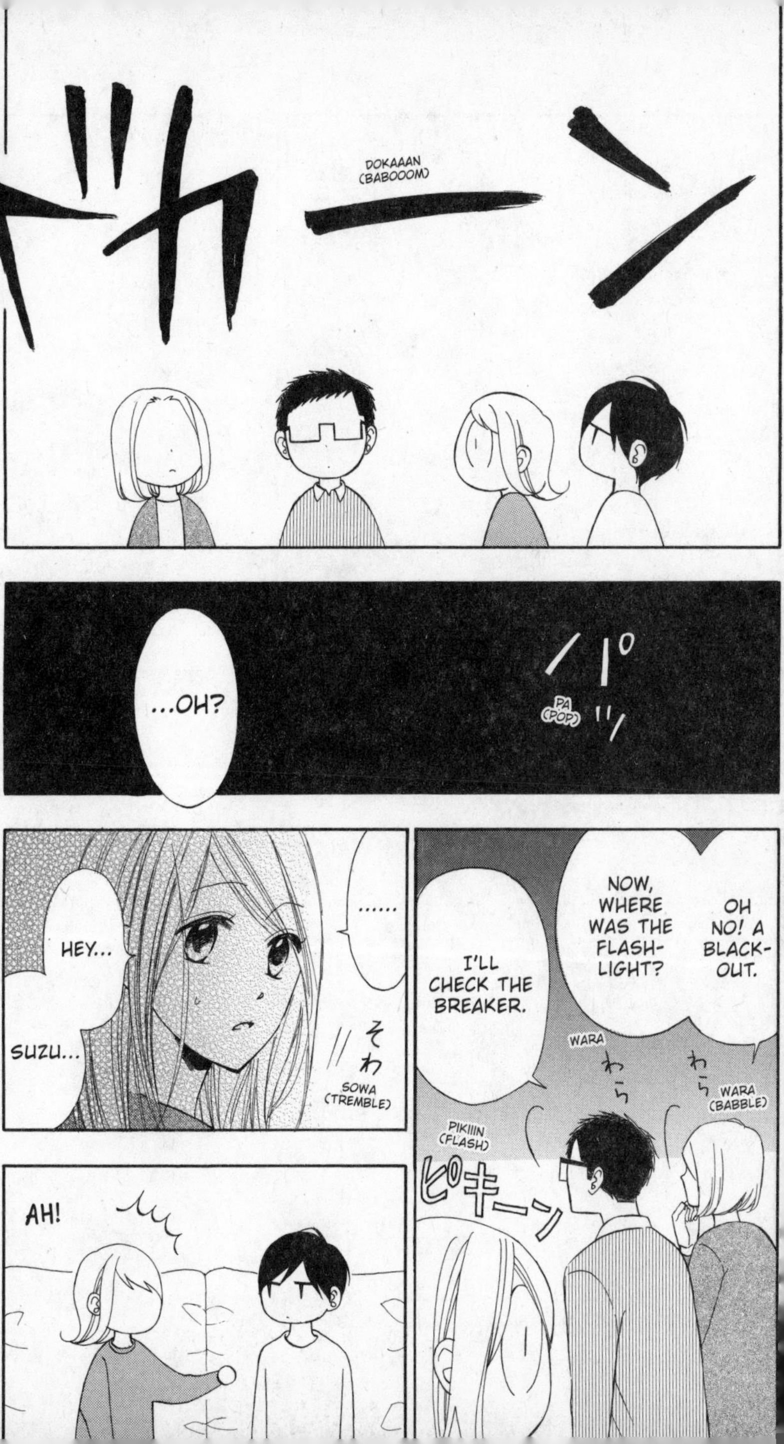

ドカーン
DOKAAAN (BABOOOM)
パッ
PA (POP)
...OH?
OH NO! A BLACK-OUT.
NOW, WHERE WAS THE FLASH-LIGHT?
I'LL CHECK THE BREAKER.
わら
WARA (BABBLE)
わら
WARA
ピキーン
PIKIIIN (FLASH)
......
HEY... SUZU...
そわ
SOWA (TREMBLE)
AH!

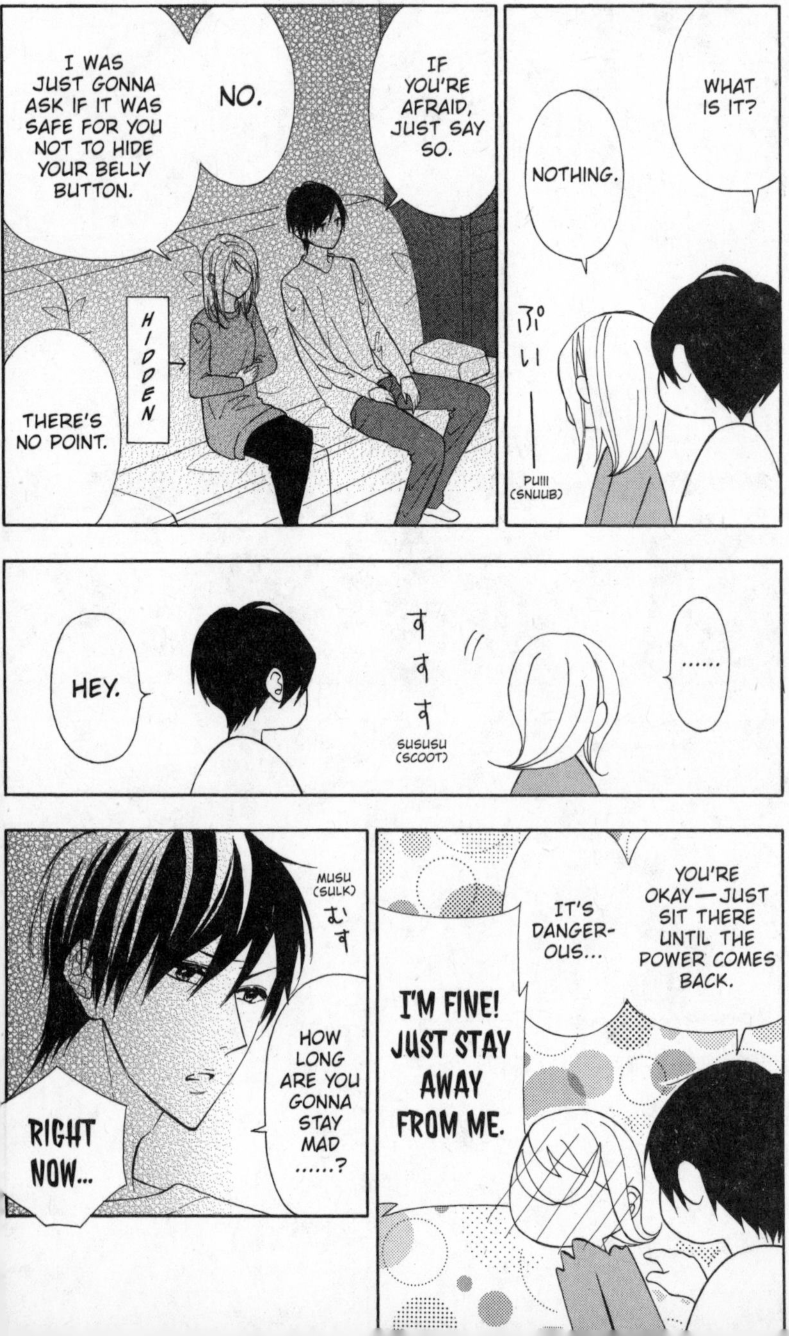
WHAT IS IT?
NOTHING.
ぷい—
PUIII (SNUUB)
IF YOU'RE AFRAID, JUST SAY SO.
NO.
I WAS JUST GONNA ASK IF IT WAS SAFE FOR YOU NOT TO HIDE YOUR BELLY BUTTON.
HIDDEN
THERE'S NO POINT.
......
すすす
SUSUSU (SCOOT)
HEY.
YOU'RE OKAY—JUST SIT THERE UNTIL THE POWER COMES BACK.
IT'S DANGER-OUS...
I'M FINE! JUST STAY AWAY FROM ME.
むす
MUSU (SULK)
HOW LONG ARE YOU GONNA STAY MAD ......?
RIGHT NOW...

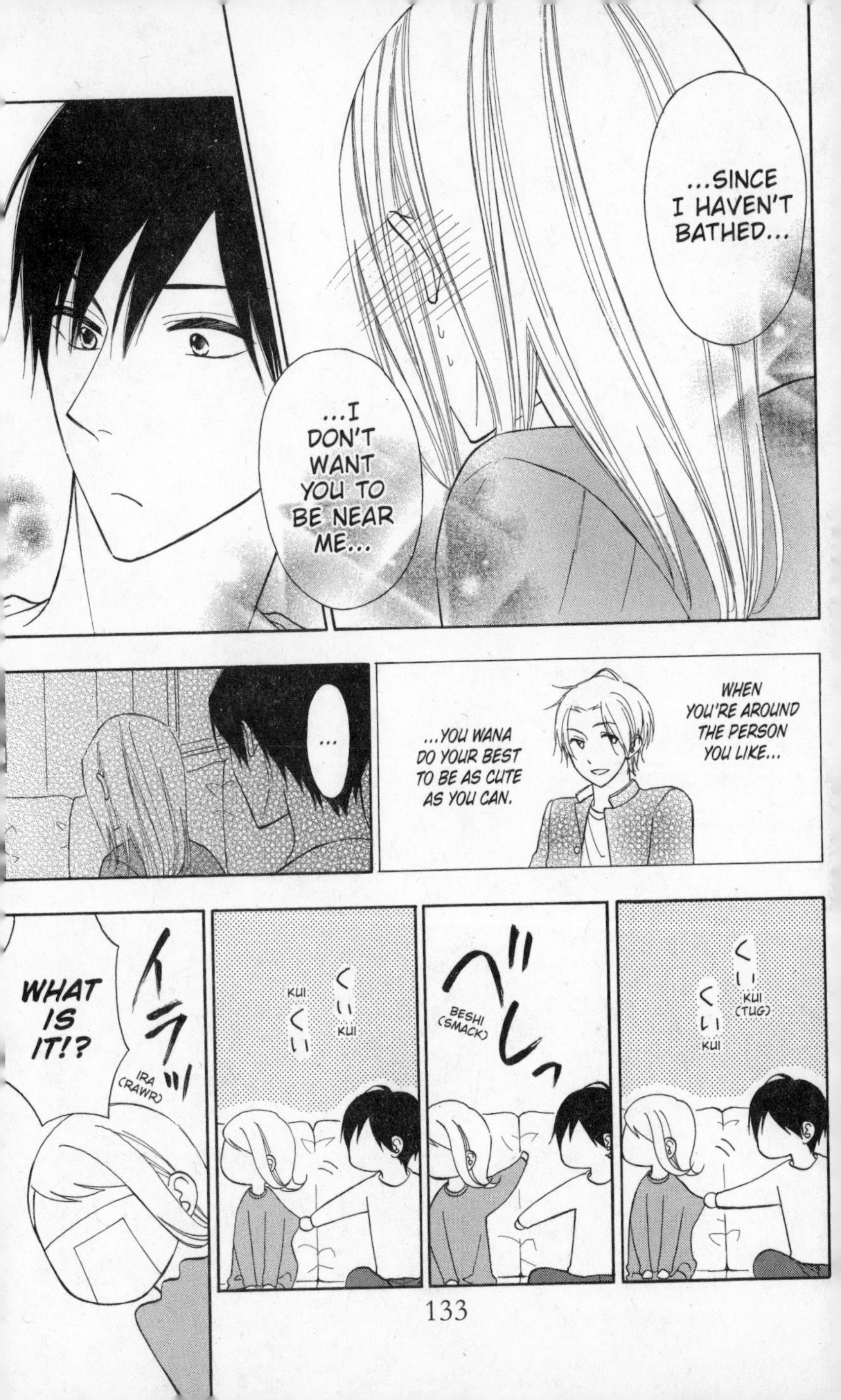
...SINCE I HAVEN'T BATHED...
...I DON'T WANT YOU TO BE NEAR ME...
WHEN YOU'RE AROUND THE PERSON YOU LIKE...
...YOU WANA DO YOUR BEST TO BE AS CUTE AS YOU CAN.
...
くい
KUI (TUG)
くい
KUI
べしっ
BESHI (SMACK)
くい
KUI
くい
KUI
イラッ
IRA (RAWR)
WHAT IS IT!?

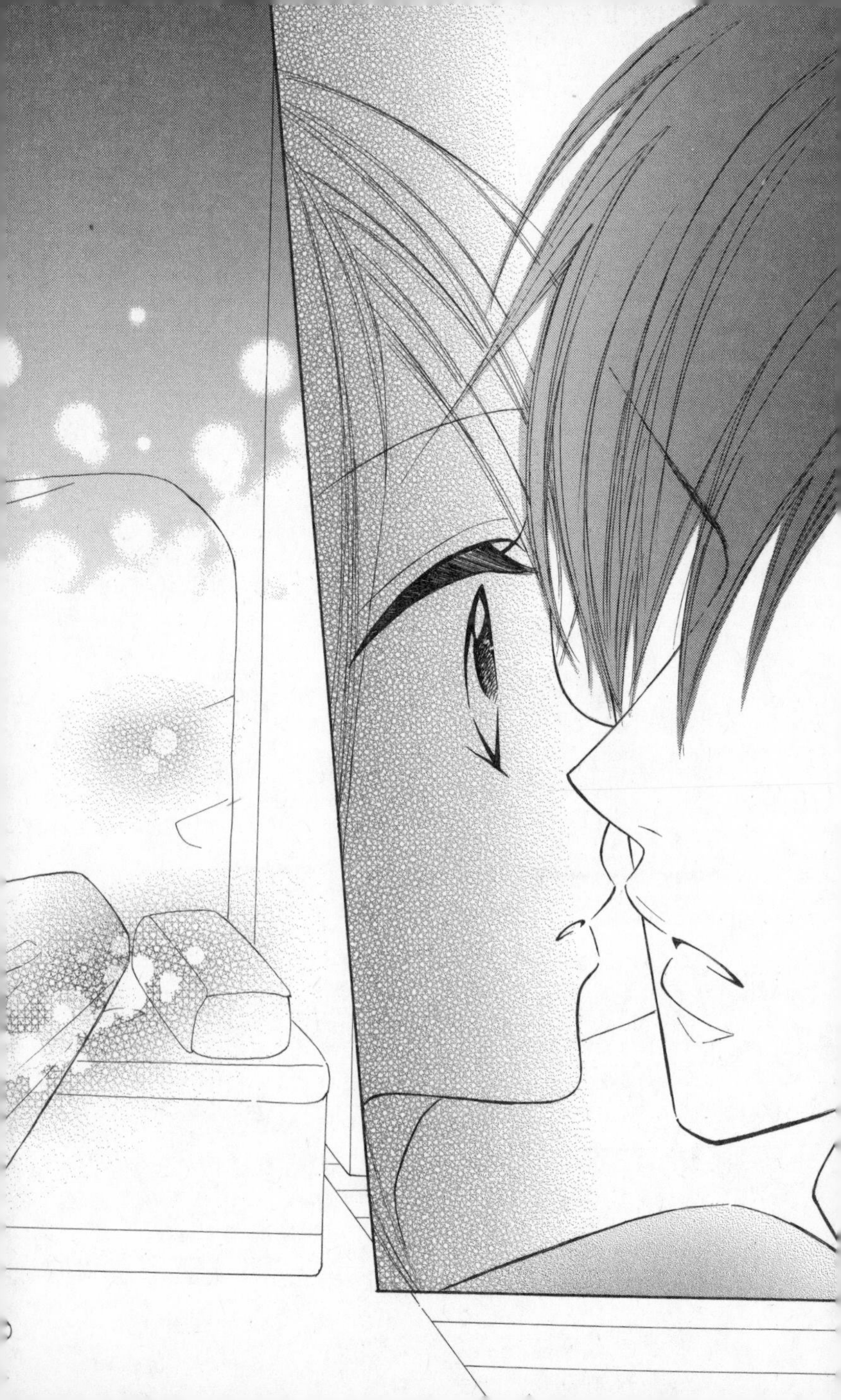

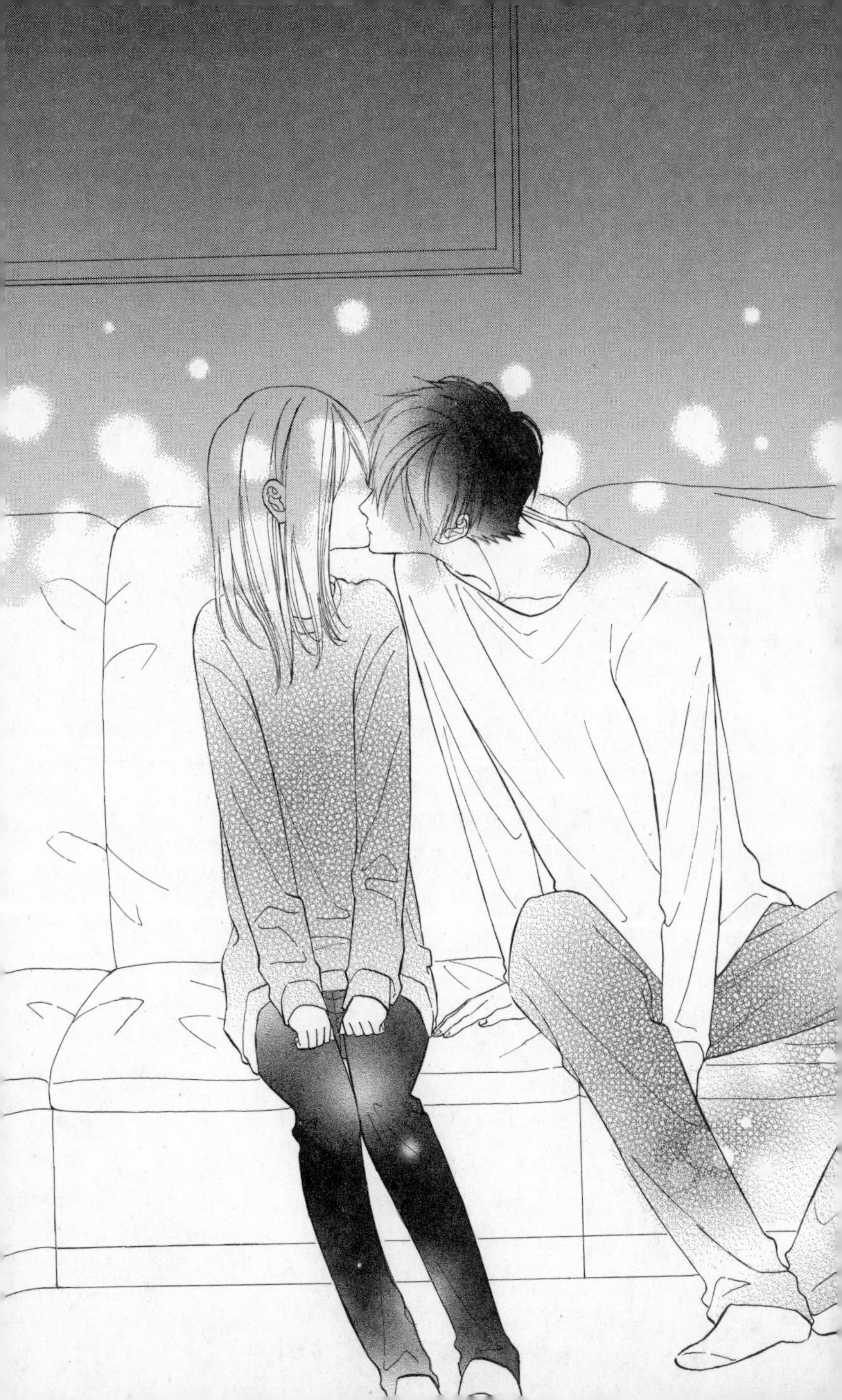

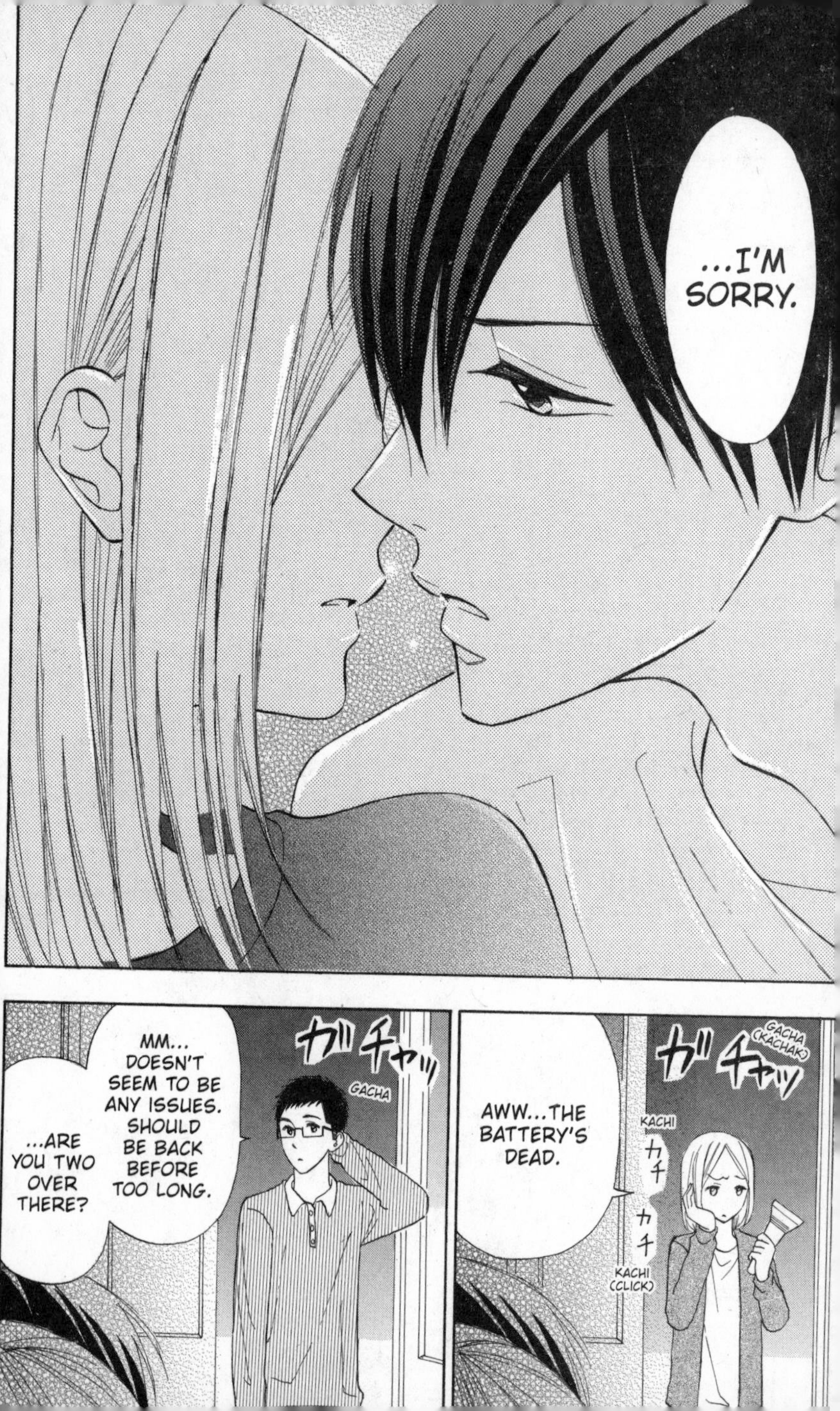
...I'M SORRY.
ガチャッ
GACHA (KACHAK)
AWW...THE BATTERY'S DEAD.
カチ
KACHI
カチ
KACHI (CLICK)
ガチャッ
GACHA
MM... DOESN'T SEEM TO BE ANY ISSUES. SHOULD BE BACK BEFORE TOO LONG.
...ARE YOU TWO OVER THERE?

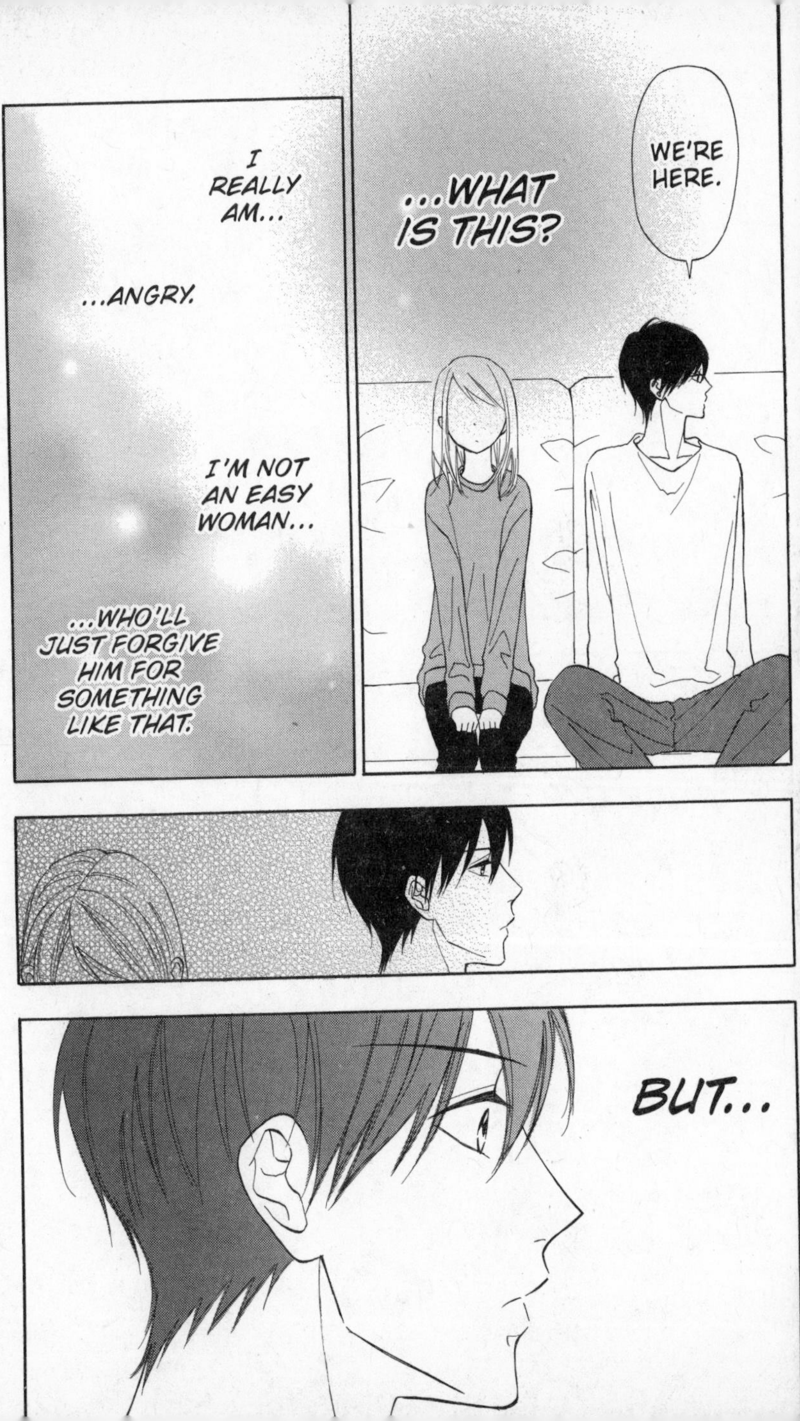
WE'RE HERE.
...WHAT IS THIS?
I REALLY AM...
...ANGRY.
I'M NOT AN EASY WOMAN...
...WHO'LL JUST FORGIVE HIM FOR SOMETHING LIKE THAT.
BUT...

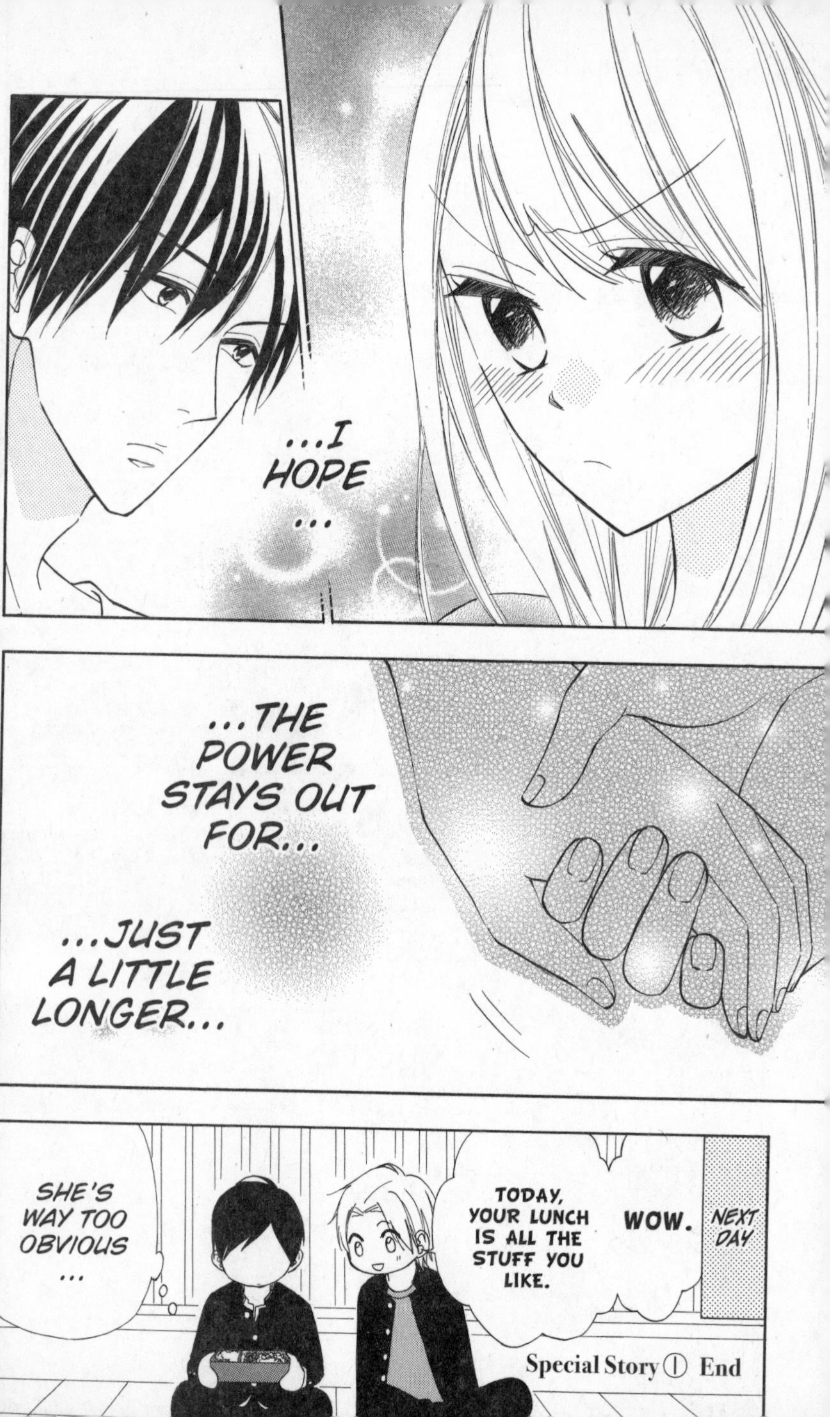
...I HOPE ...
...THE POWER STAYS OUT FOR...
...JUST A LITTLE LONGER...
NEXT DAY
WOW.
TODAY, YOUR LUNCH IS ALL THE STUFF YOU LIKE.
SHE'S WAY TOO OBVIOUS ...
Special Story ① End

Special Story ②

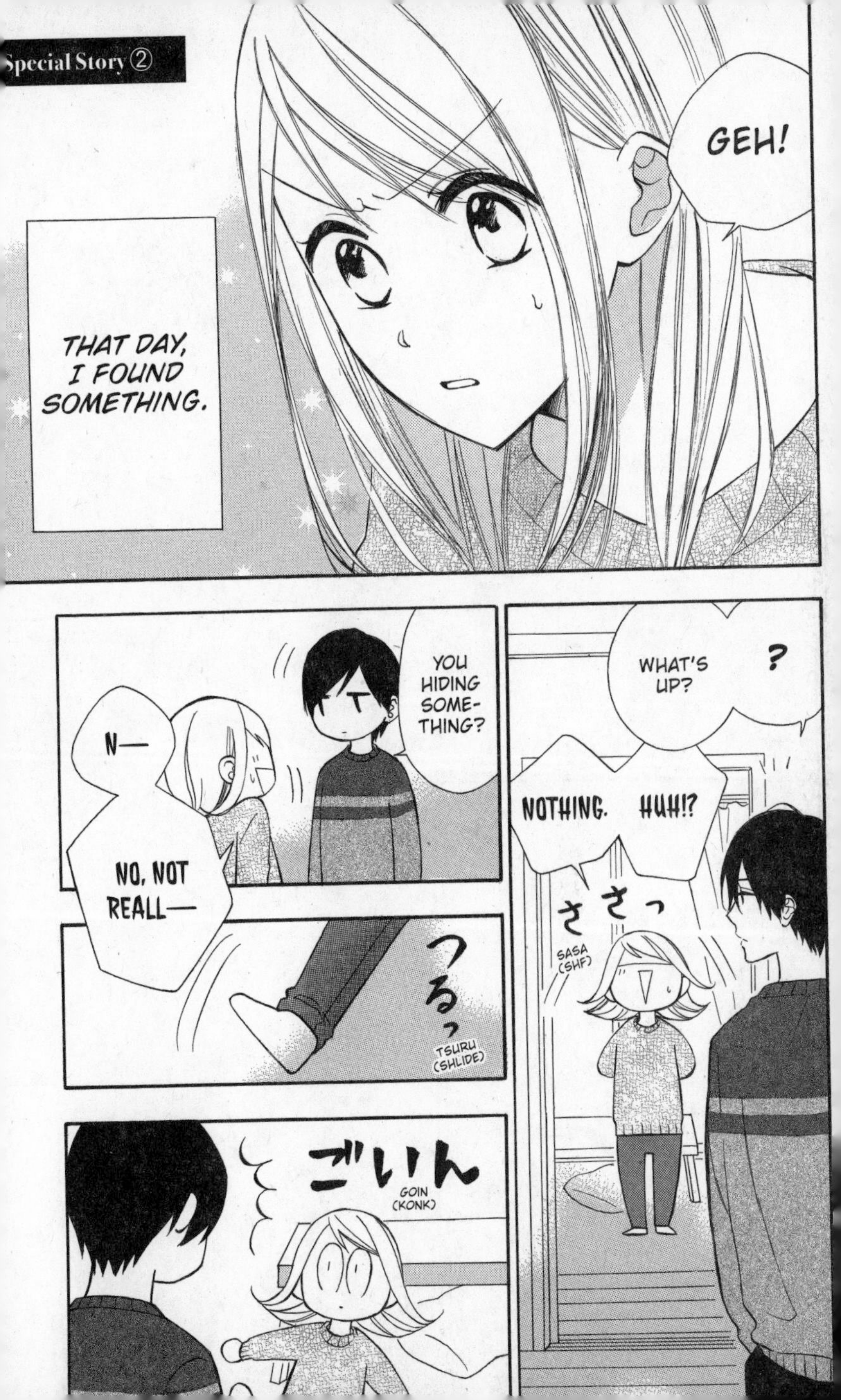

GEH!
THAT DAY, I FOUND SOMETHING.
?
WHAT'S UP?
HUH!?
NOTHING.
ささっ
SASA (SHF)
YOU HIDING SOME-THING?
N—
NO, NOT REALL—
つるっ
TSURU (SHLIDE)
ごいん
GOIN (KONK)

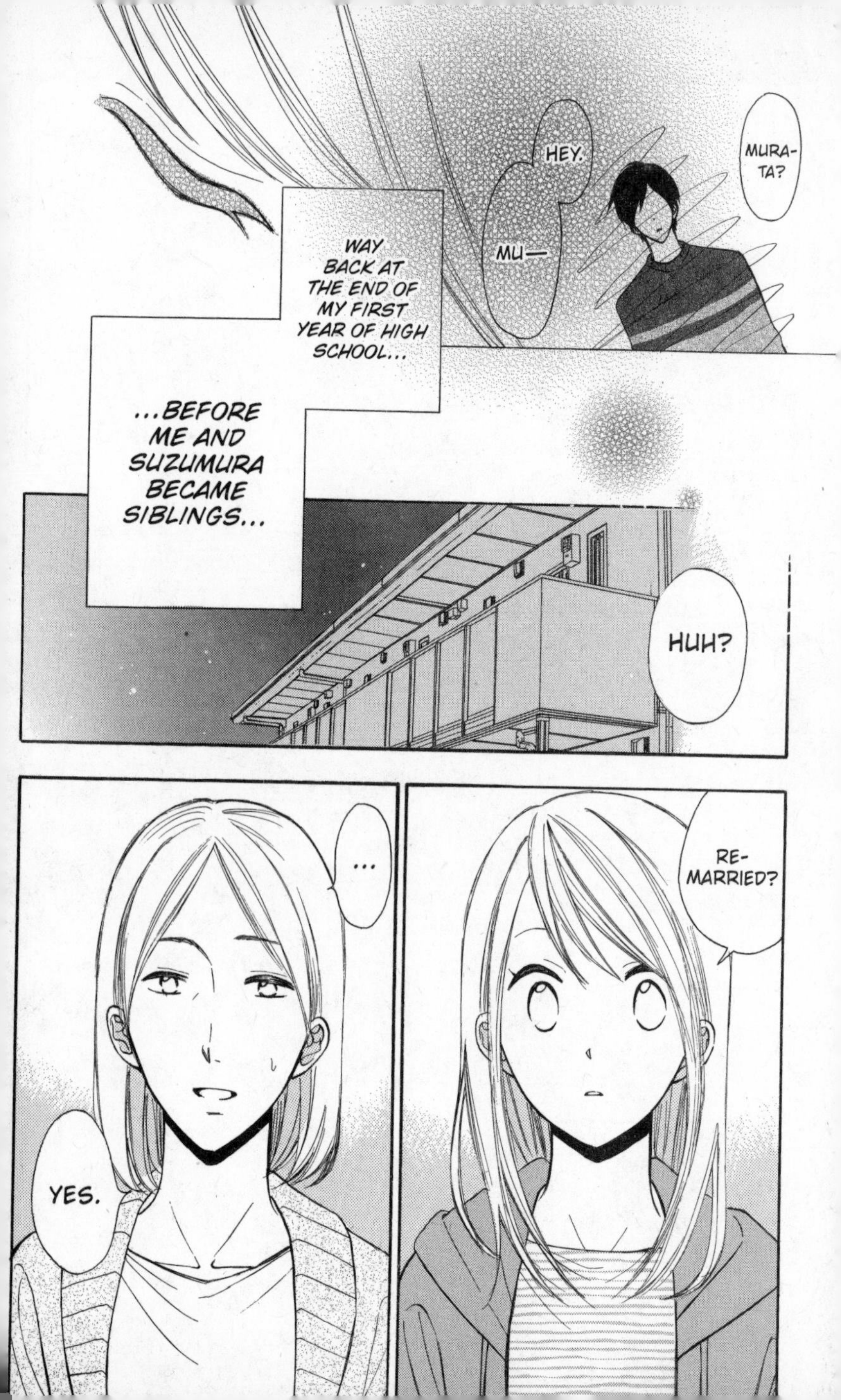
MURA-
TA?
HEY.
MU—
WAY BACK AT THE END OF MY FIRST YEAR OF HIGH SCHOOL...
...BEFORE ME AND SUZUMURA BECAME SIBLINGS...
HUH?
RE-
MARRIED?
...
YES.

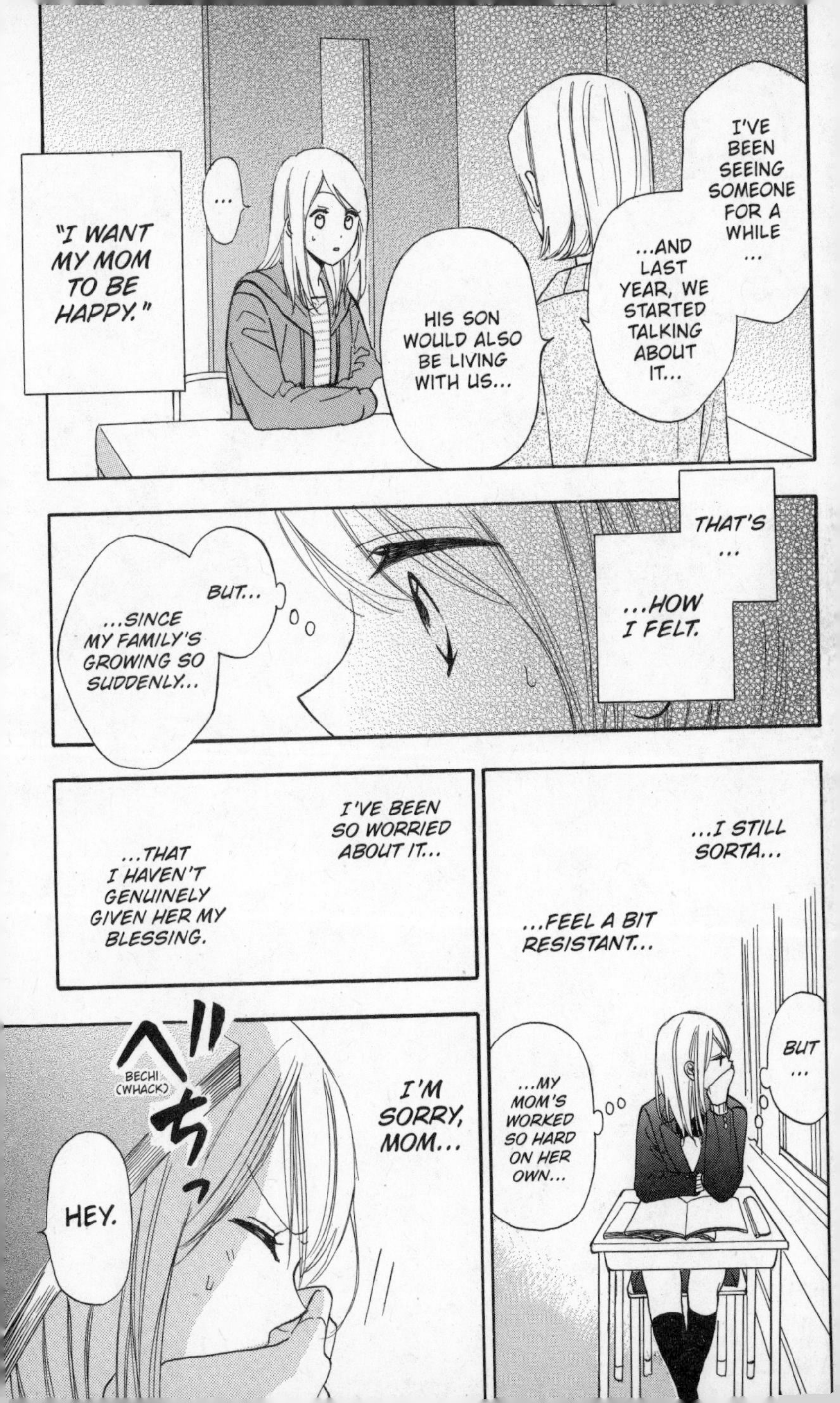
I'VE BEEN SEEING SOMEONE FOR A WHILE...
...AND LAST YEAR, WE STARTED TALKING ABOUT IT...
HIS SON WOULD ALSO BE LIVING WITH US...
...
"I WANT MY MOM TO BE HAPPY."
THAT'S...
...HOW I FELT.
BUT...
...SINCE MY FAMILY'S GROWING SO SUDDENLY...
...I STILL SORTA...
...FEEL A BIT RESISTANT...
I'VE BEEN SO WORRIED ABOUT IT...
...THAT I HAVEN'T GENUINELY GIVEN HER MY BLESSING.
BUT...
...MY MOM'S WORKED SO HARD ON HER OWN...
I'M SORRY, MOM...
べちっ
BECHI (WHACK)
HEY.

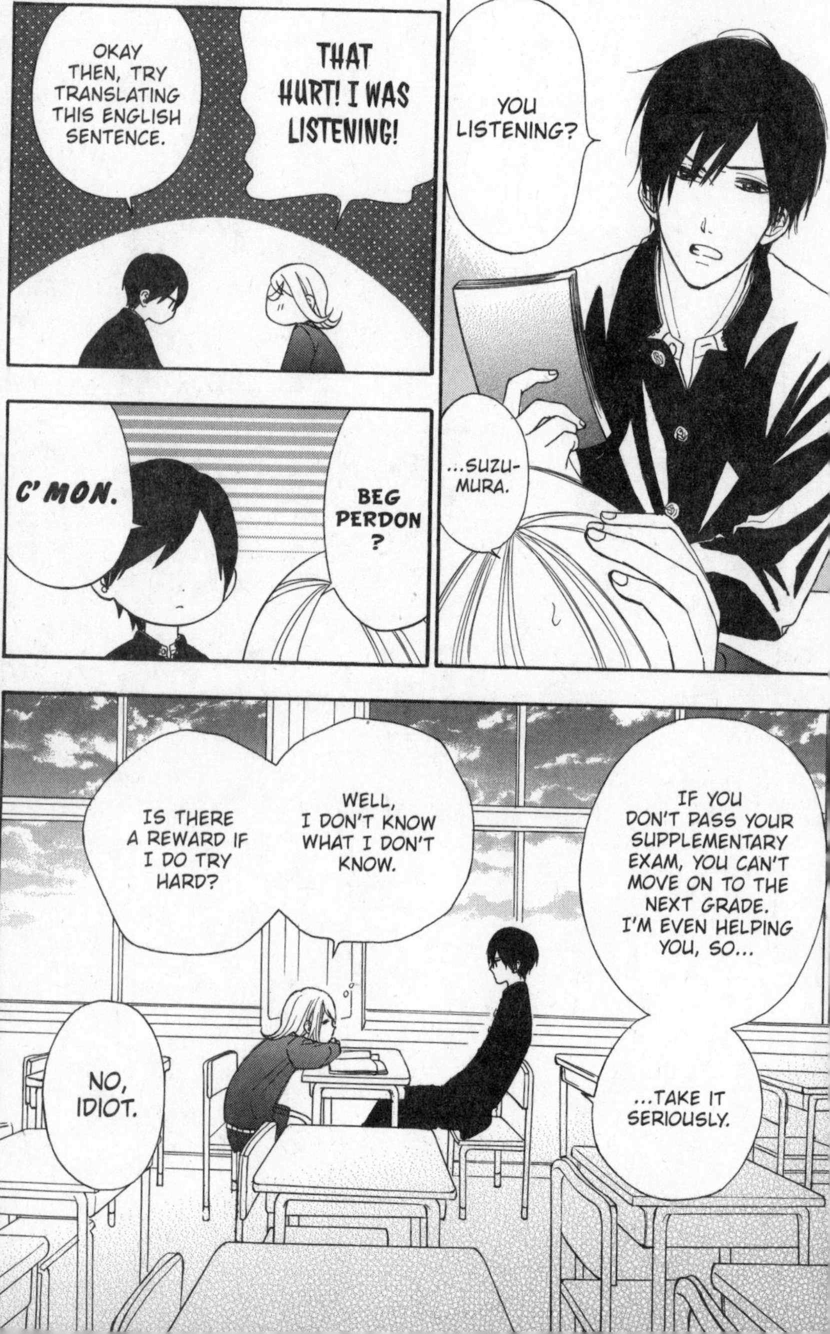
YOU LISTENING?
...SUZU-MURA.
THAT HURT! I WAS LISTENING!
OKAY THEN, TRY TRANSLATING THIS ENGLISH SENTENCE.
BEG PERDON?
C'MON.
IF YOU DON'T PASS YOUR SUPPLEMENTARY EXAM, YOU CAN'T MOVE ON TO THE NEXT GRADE. I'M EVEN HELPING YOU, SO...
...TAKE IT SERIOUSLY.
WELL, I DON'T KNOW WHAT I DON'T KNOW.
IS THERE A REWARD IF I DO TRY HARD?
NO, IDIOT.

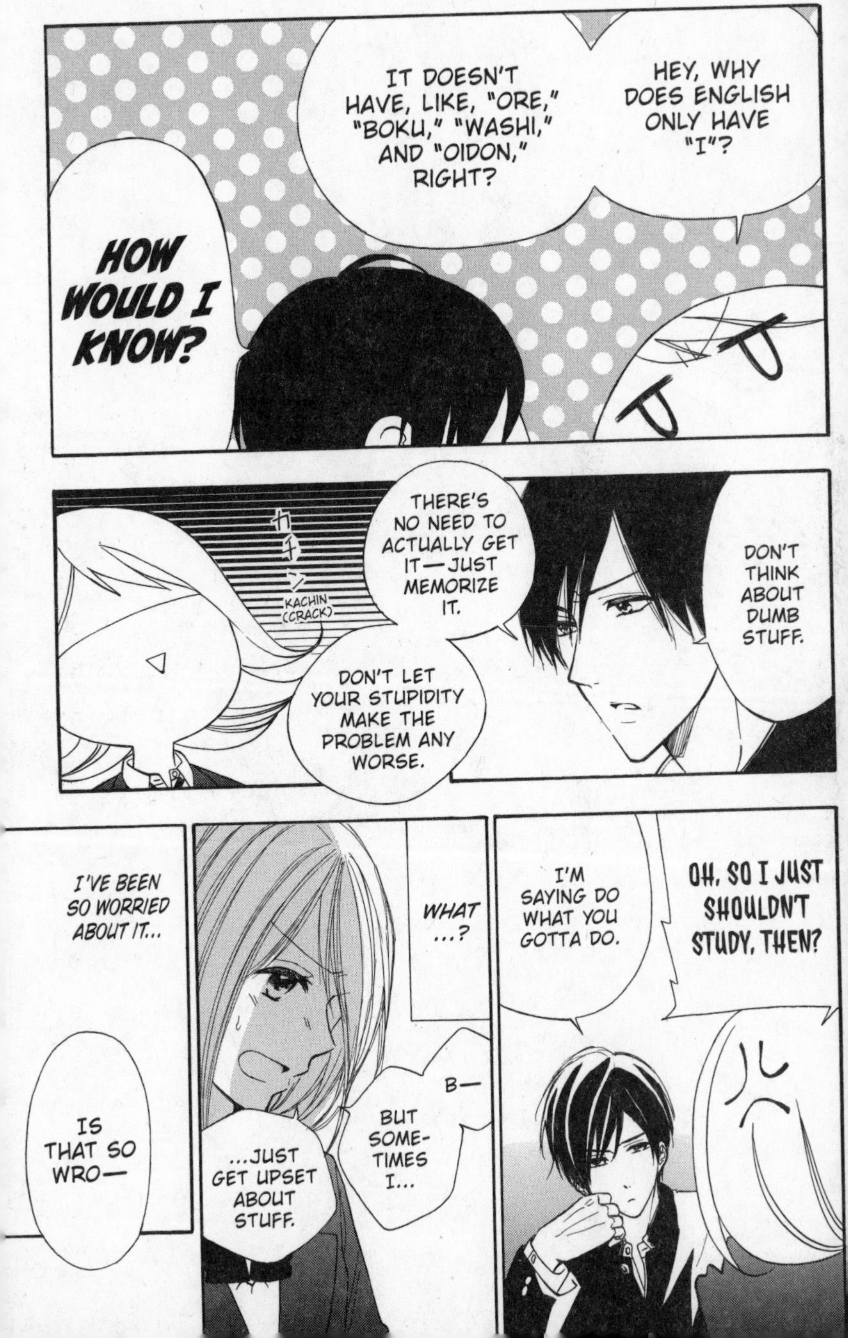
HEY, WHY DOES ENGLISH ONLY HAVE "I"?
IT DOESN'T HAVE, LIKE, "ORE," "BOKU," "WASHI," AND "OIDON," RIGHT?
HOW WOULD I KNOW?
DON'T THINK ABOUT DUMB STUFF.
THERE'S NO NEED TO ACTUALLY GET IT—JUST MEMORIZE IT.
DON'T LET YOUR STUPIDITY MAKE THE PROBLEM ANY WORSE.
KACHIN (CRACK)
OH, SO I JUST SHOULDN'T STUDY, THEN?
I'M SAYING DO WHAT YOU GOTTA DO.
WHAT ...?
B—
BUT SOME-TIMES I...
...JUST GET UPSET ABOUT STUFF.
I'VE BEEN SO WORRIED ABOUT IT...
IS THAT SO WRO—

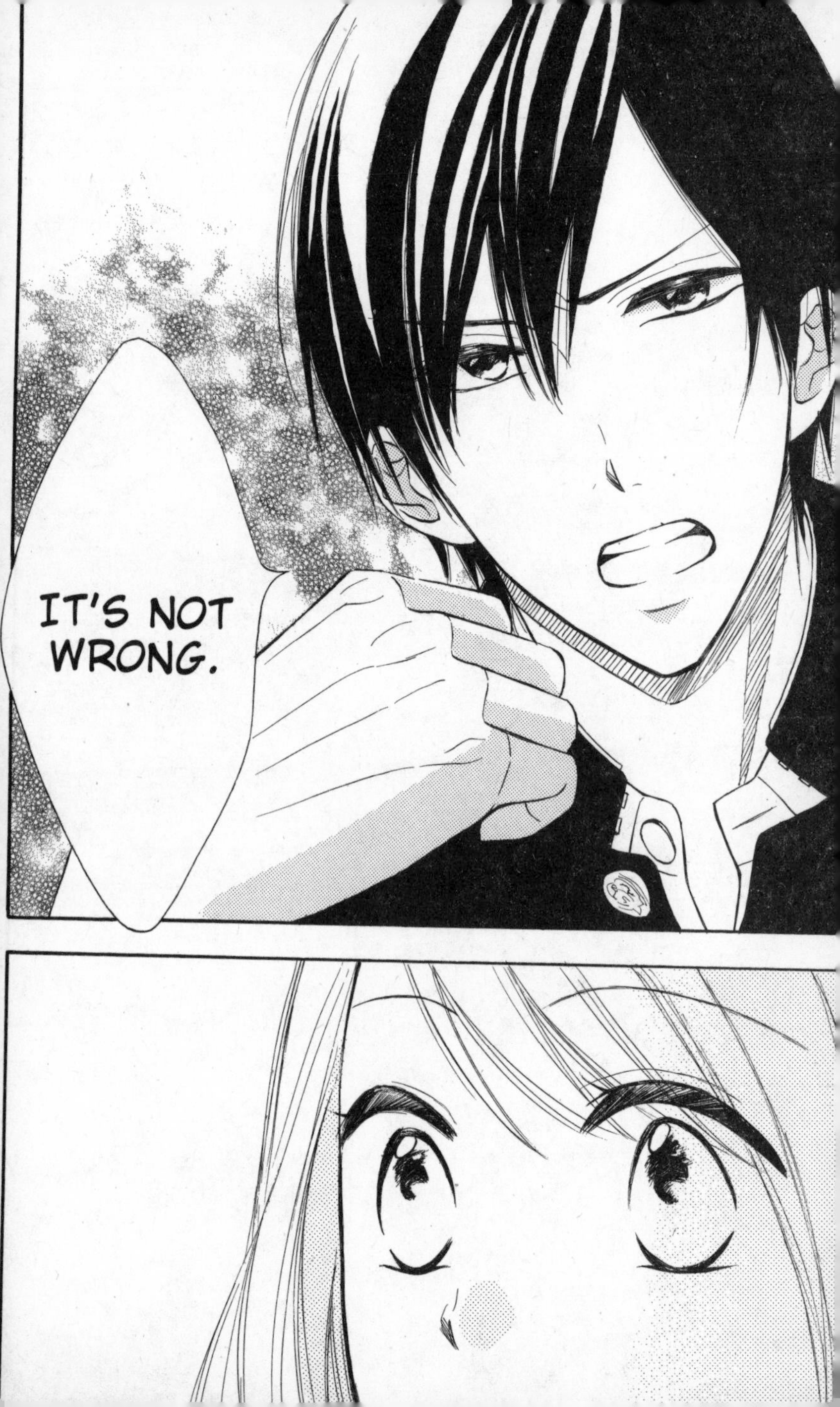
IT'S NOT WRONG.

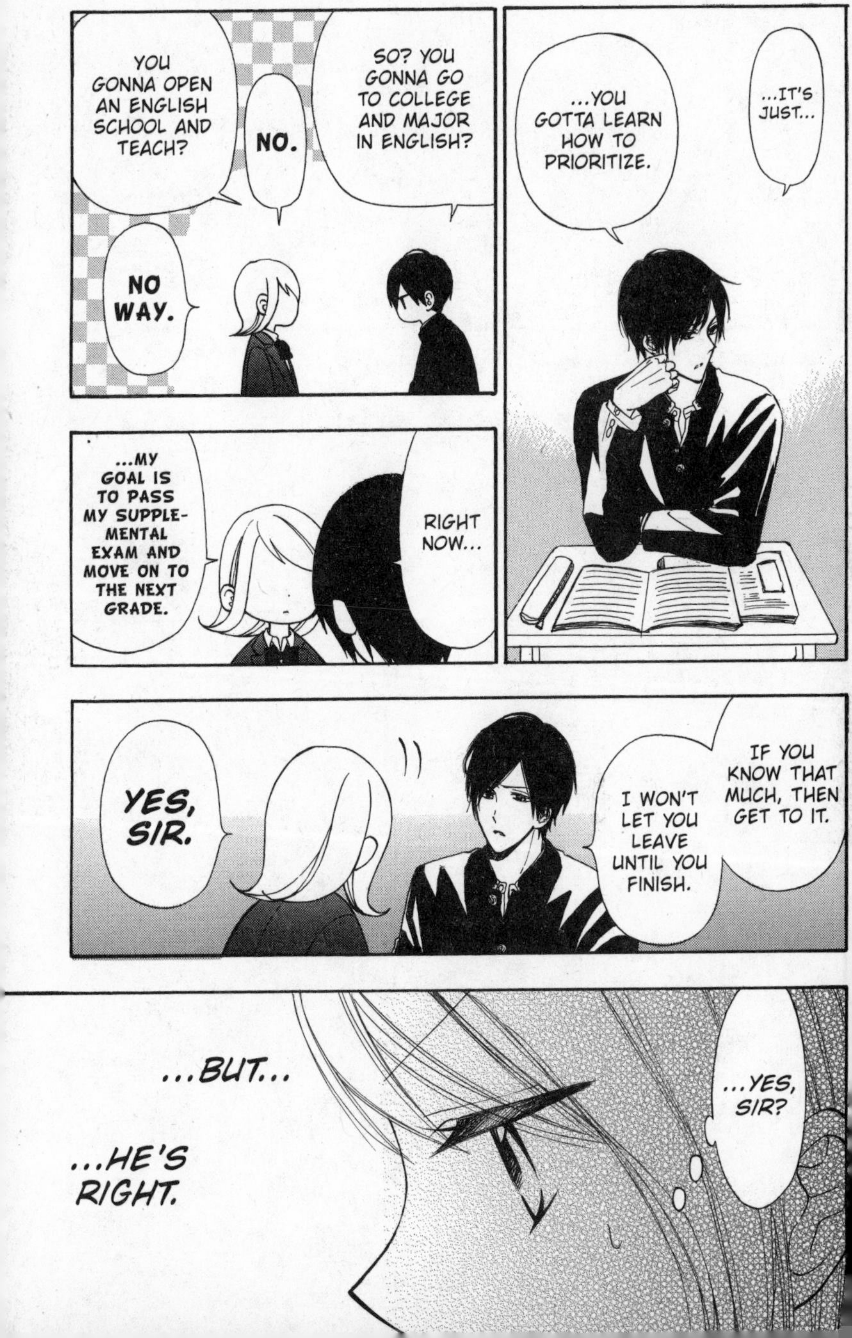
...IT'S JUST...
...YOU GOTTA LEARN HOW TO PRIORITIZE.
SO? YOU GONNA GO TO COLLEGE AND MAJOR IN ENGLISH?
NO.
YOU GONNA OPEN AN ENGLISH SCHOOL AND TEACH?
NO WAY.
RIGHT NOW...
...MY GOAL IS TO PASS MY SUPPLE-MENTAL EXAM AND MOVE ON TO THE NEXT GRADE.
IF YOU KNOW THAT MUCH, THEN GET TO IT.
I WON'T LET YOU LEAVE UNTIL YOU FINISH.
YES, SIR.
...YES, SIR?
...BUT...
...HE'S RIGHT.

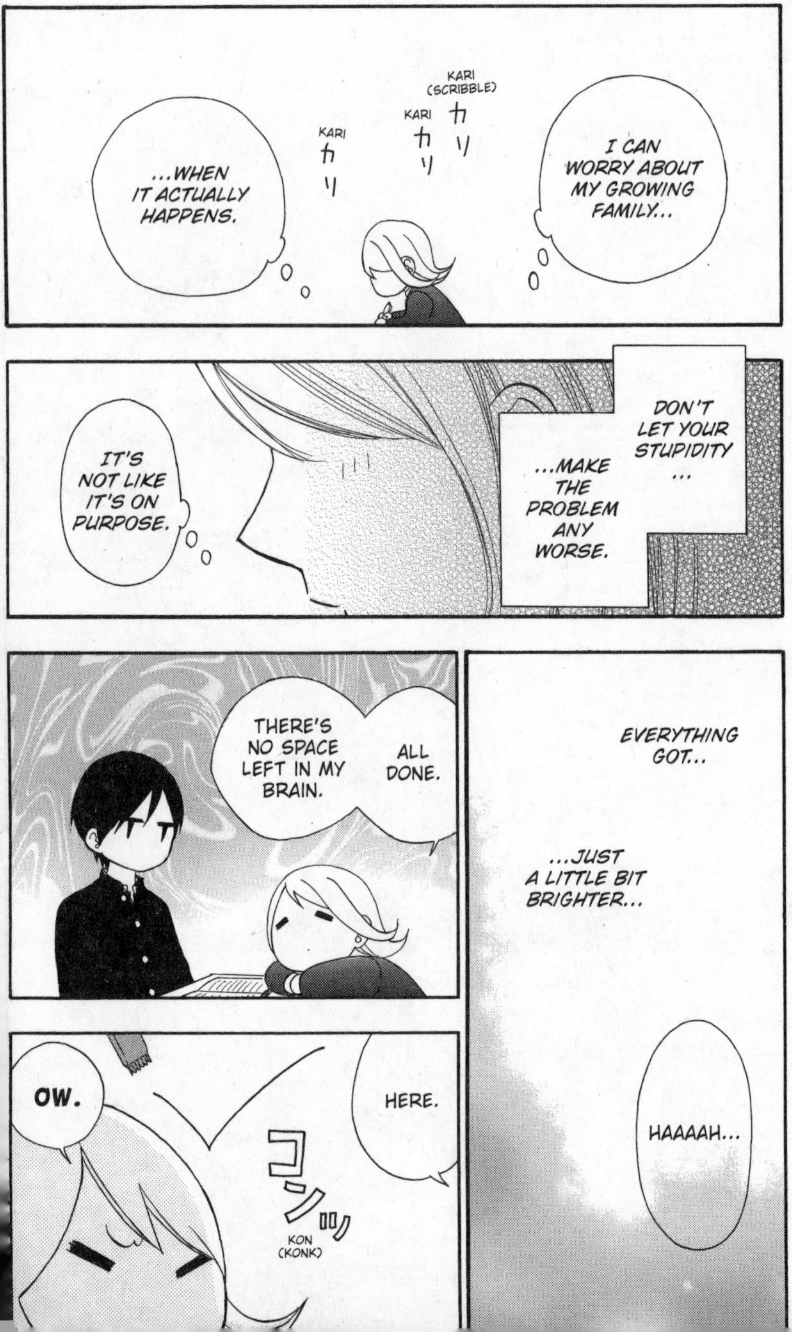
I CAN WORRY ABOUT MY GROWING FAMILY...
KARI (SCRIBBLE)
カリ
KARI
カリ
KARI
カリ
...WHEN IT ACTUALLY HAPPENS.
DON'T LET YOUR STUPIDITY...
...MAKE THE PROBLEM ANY WORSE.
IT'S NOT LIKE IT'S ON PURPOSE.
EVERYTHING GOT...
...JUST A LITTLE BIT BRIGHTER...
HAAAAH...
ALL DONE.
THERE'S NO SPACE LEFT IN MY BRAIN.
HERE.
コン
KON (KONK)
OW.

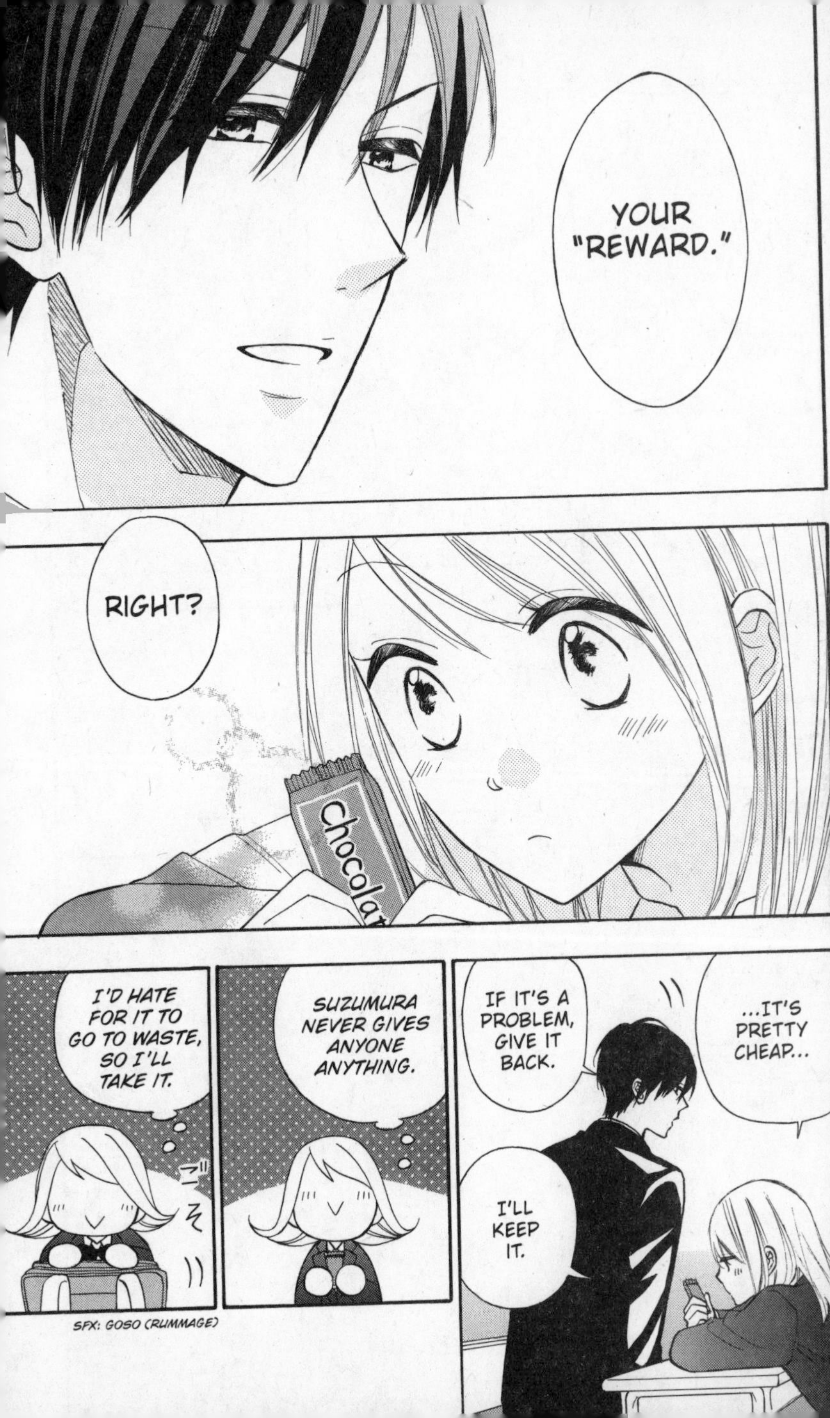
YOUR "REWARD."
RIGHT?
...IT'S PRETTY CHEAP...
IF IT'S A PROBLEM, GIVE IT BACK.
I'LL KEEP IT.
SUZUMURA NEVER GIVES ANYONE ANYTHING.
I'D HATE FOR IT TO GO TO WASTE, SO I'LL TAKE IT.
SFX: GOSO (RUMMAGE)

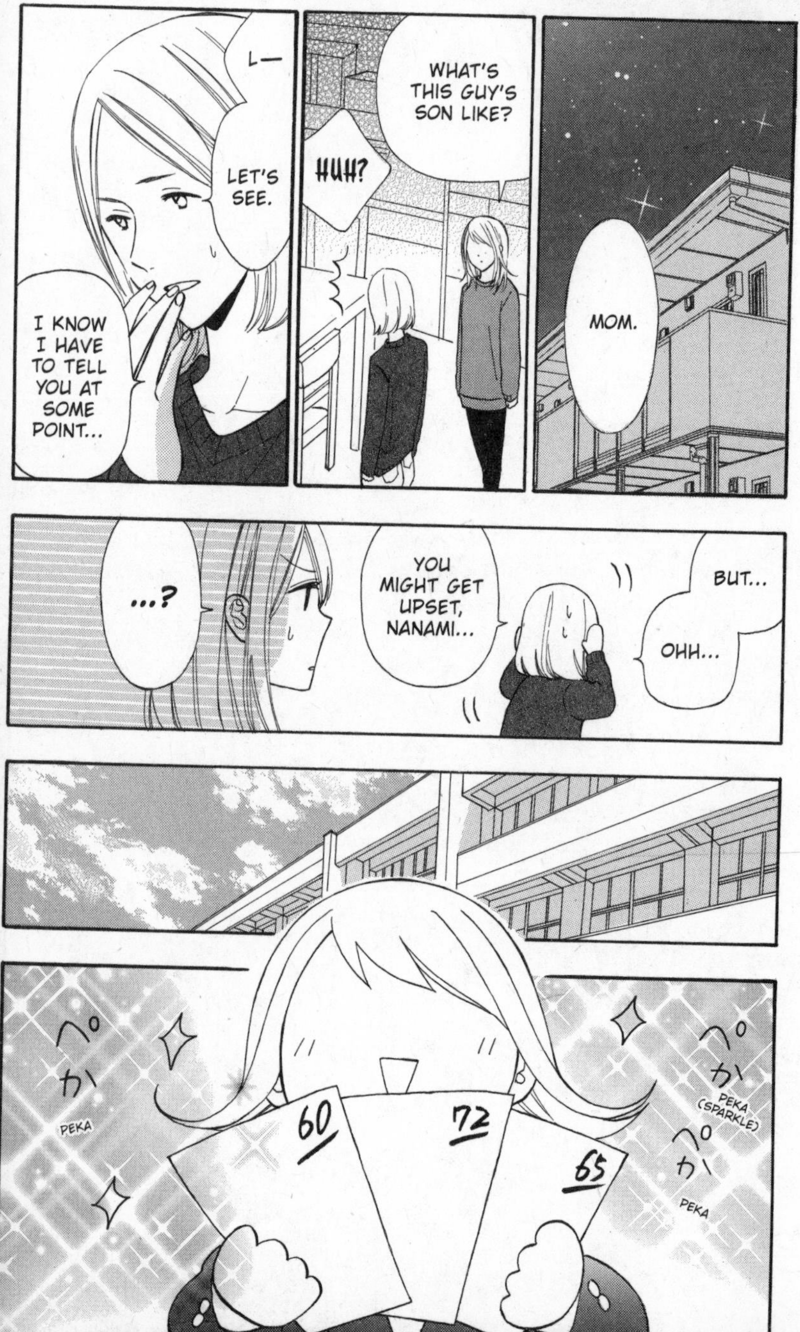
MOM.
WHAT'S THIS GUY'S SON LIKE?
HUH?
I—
LET'S SEE.
I KNOW I HAVE TO TELL YOU AT SOME POINT...
BUT...
OHH...
YOU MIGHT GET UPSET, NANAMI...
...?
ぺか
PEKA (SPARKLE)
ぺか
PEKA
ぺか
PEKA
60
72
65

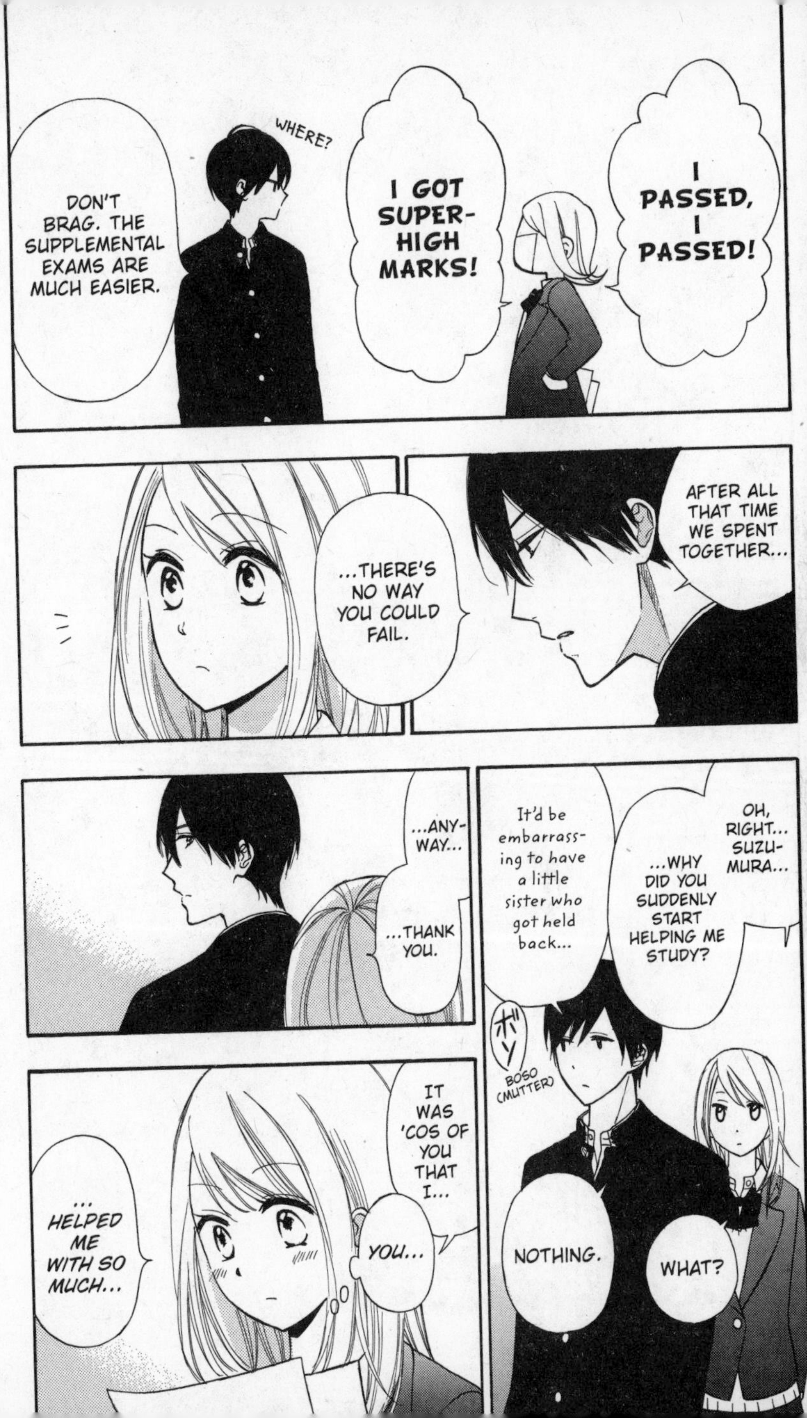

I PASSED, I PASSED!
I GOT SUPER-HIGH MARKS!
WHERE?
DON'T BRAG. THE SUPPLEMENTAL EXAMS ARE MUCH EASIER.
AFTER ALL THAT TIME WE SPENT TOGETHER...
...THERE'S NO WAY YOU COULD FAIL.
OH, RIGHT... SUZUMURA...
...WHY DID YOU SUDDENLY START HELPING ME STUDY?
It'd be embarrassing to have a little sister who got held back...
ボソ
BOSO (MUTTER)
WHAT?
NOTHING.
...ANYWAY...
...THANK YOU.
IT WAS 'COS OF YOU THAT I...
YOU...
...HELPED ME WITH SO MUCH...

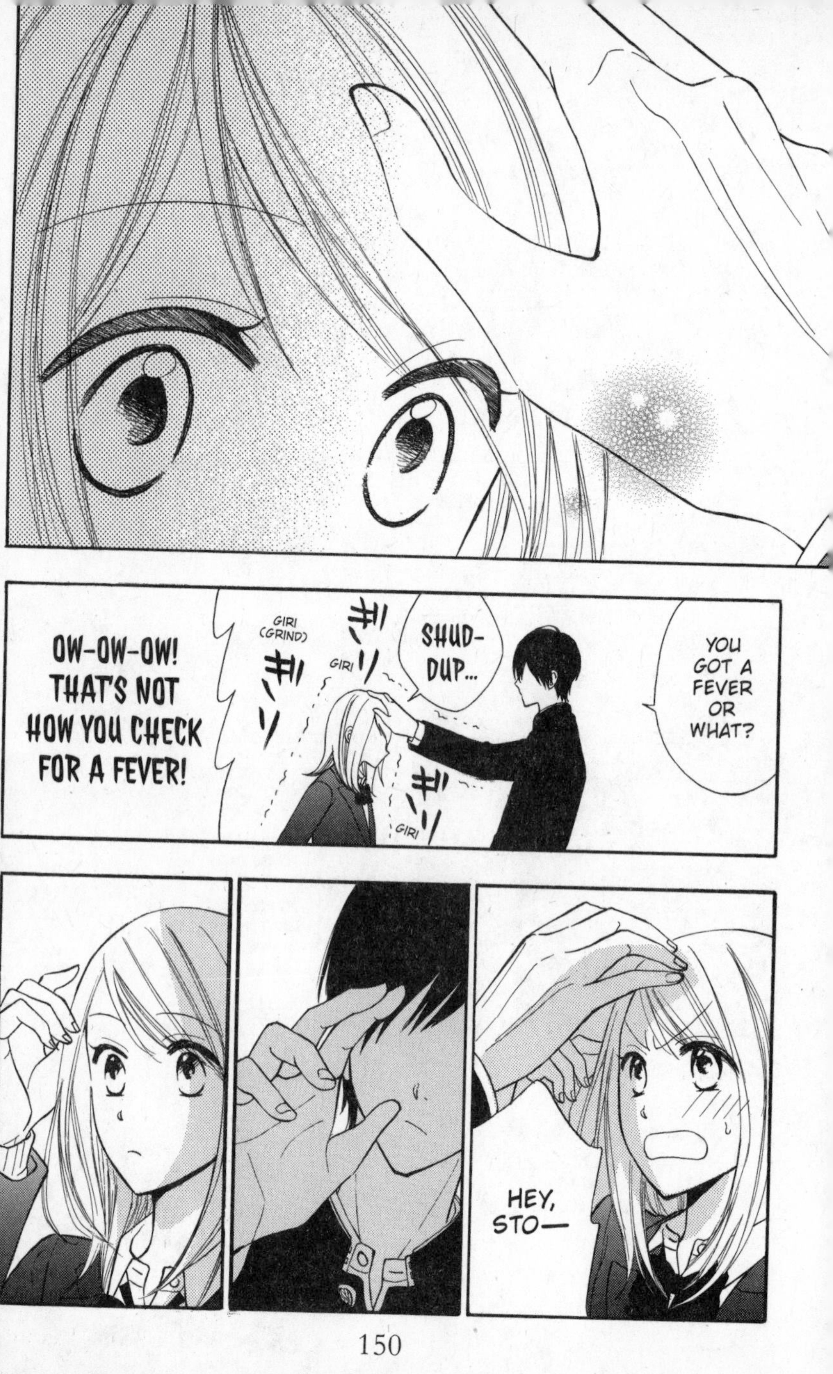
YOU GOT A FEVER OR WHAT?
SHUD-DUP...
ギリ
GIRI (GRIND)
ギリ
GIRI
ギリ
GIRI
OW-OW-OW! THAT'S NOT HOW YOU CHECK FOR A FEVER!
HEY, STO—

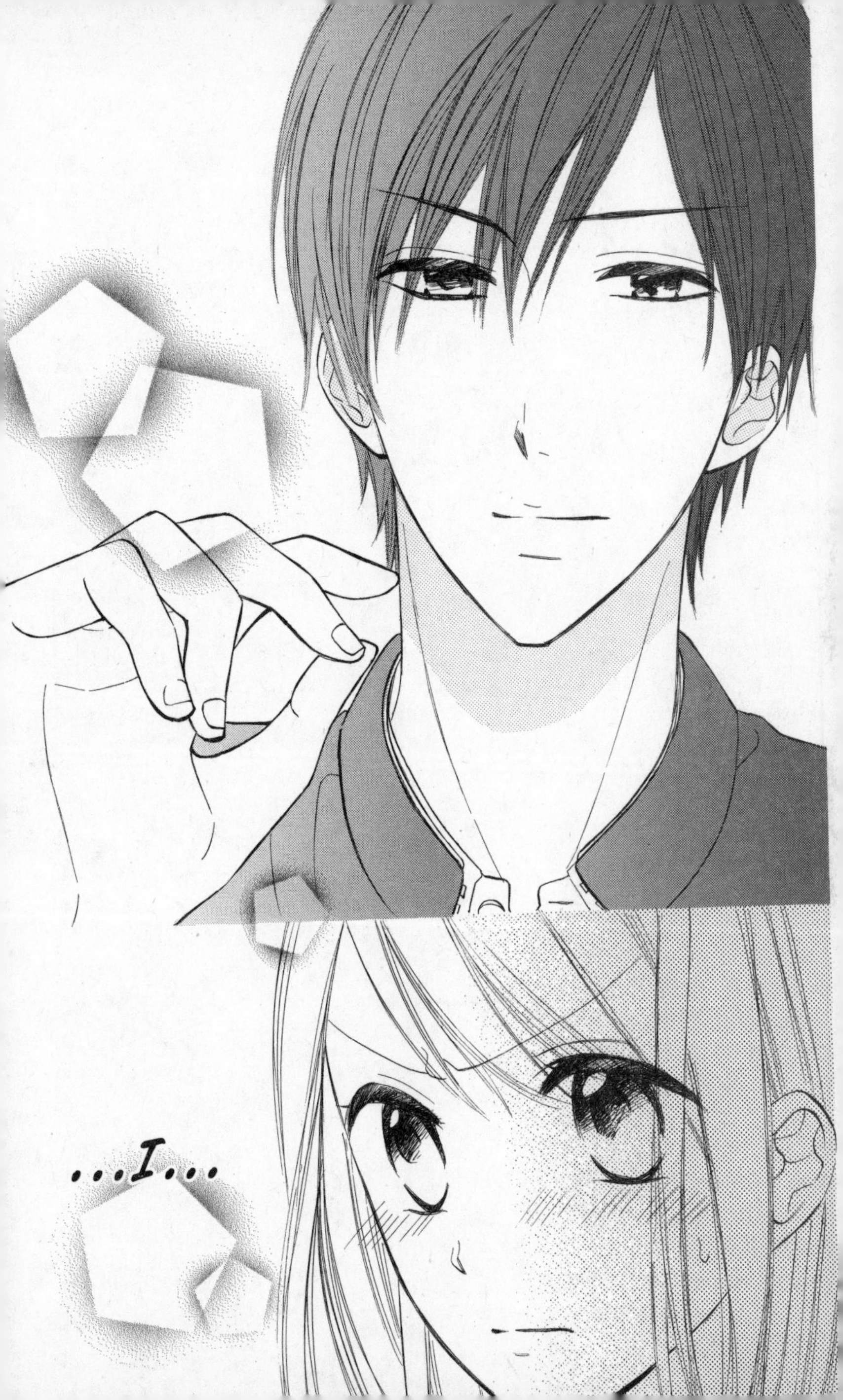
...I...

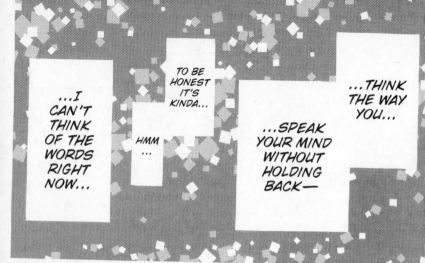

...THINK THE WAY YOU...
...SPEAK YOUR MIND WITHOUT HOLDING BACK—
TO BE HONEST IT'S KINDA...
HMM...
...I CAN'T THINK OF THE WORDS RIGHT NOW...
...BUT ANYWAY, I DON'T...
...DISLIKE THAT ABOUT YOU.
TO TELL THE TRUTH...
...IT'S VERY...
—TA.
MURATA.

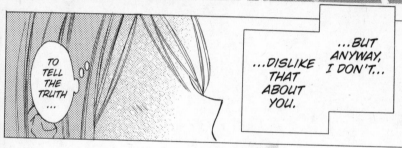

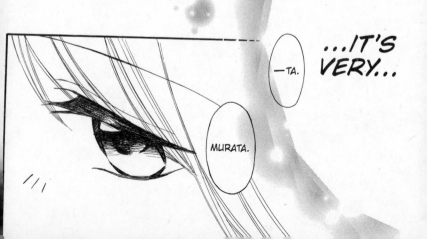

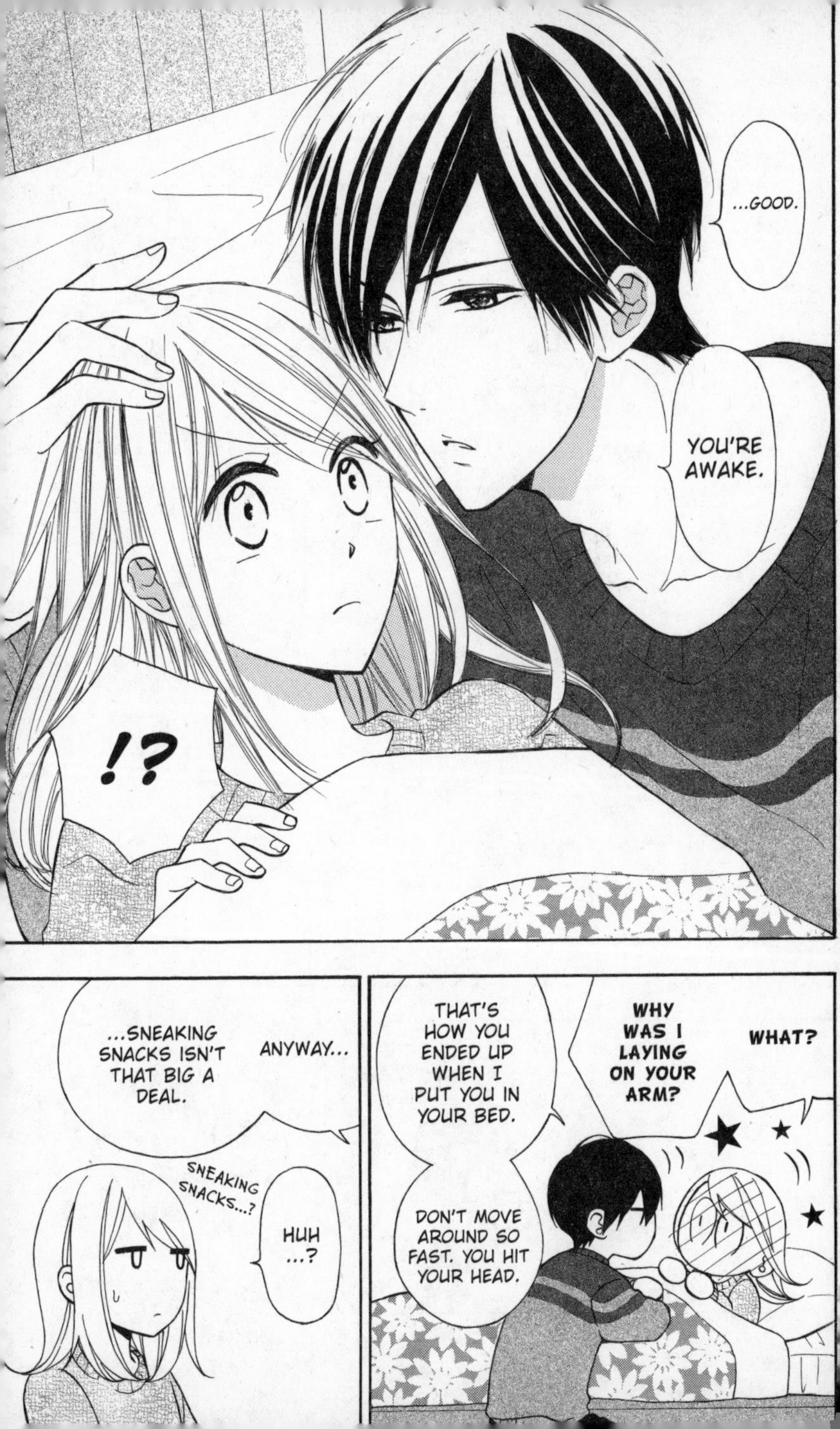
...GOOD.
YOU'RE AWAKE.
!?
WHAT?
WHY WAS I LAYING ON YOUR ARM?
THAT'S HOW YOU ENDED UP WHEN I PUT YOU IN YOUR BED.
DON'T MOVE AROUND SO FAST. YOU HIT YOUR HEAD.
ANYWAY...
...SNEAKING SNACKS ISN'T THAT BIG A DEAL.
HUH ...?
SNEAKING SNACKS...?

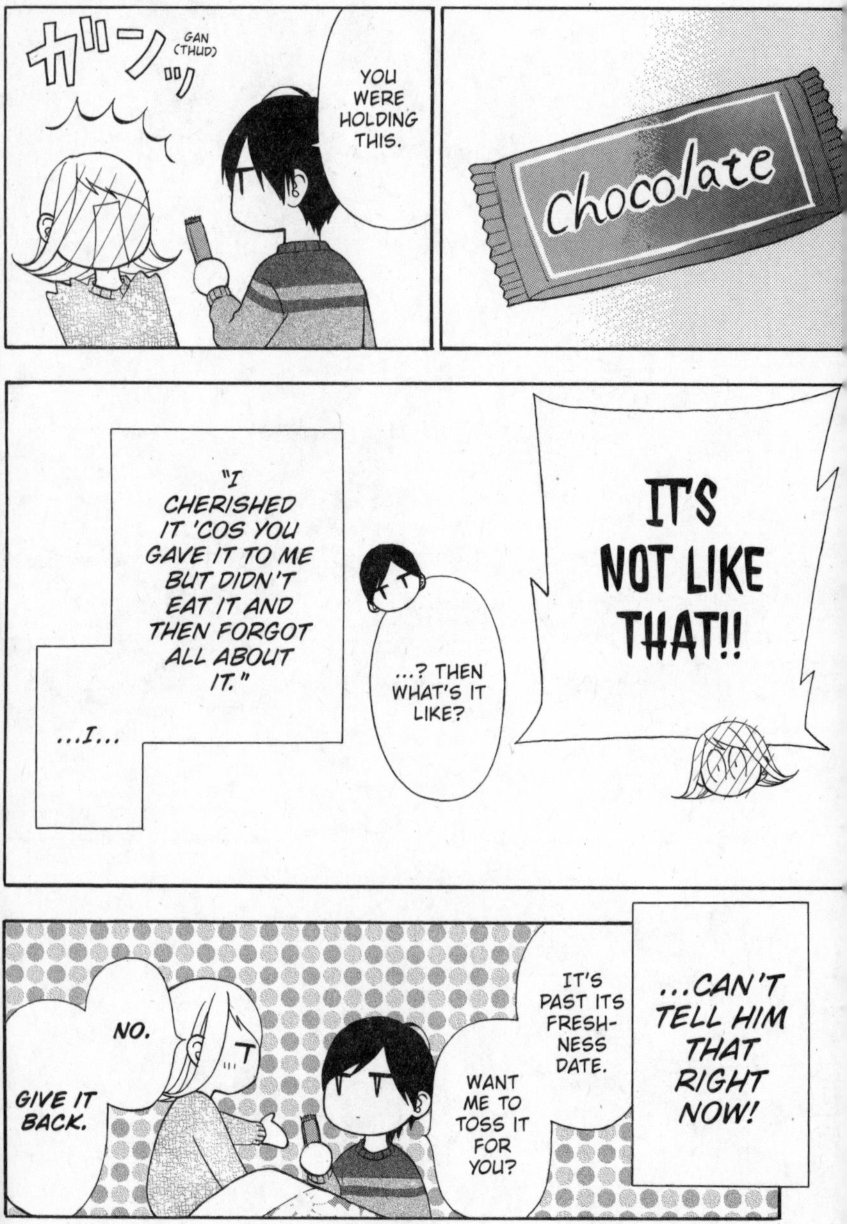
Chocolate
カーンッ
GAN (THUD)
YOU WERE HOLDING THIS.
IT'S NOT LIKE THAT!!
...? THEN WHAT'S IT LIKE?
"I CHERISHED IT 'COS YOU GAVE IT TO ME BUT DIDN'T EAT IT AND THEN FORGOT ALL ABOUT IT."
...I...
...CAN'T TELL HIM THAT RIGHT NOW!
IT'S PAST ITS FRESH-NESS DATE.
WANT ME TO TOSS IT FOR YOU?
NO.
GIVE IT BACK.

Special Story ② End

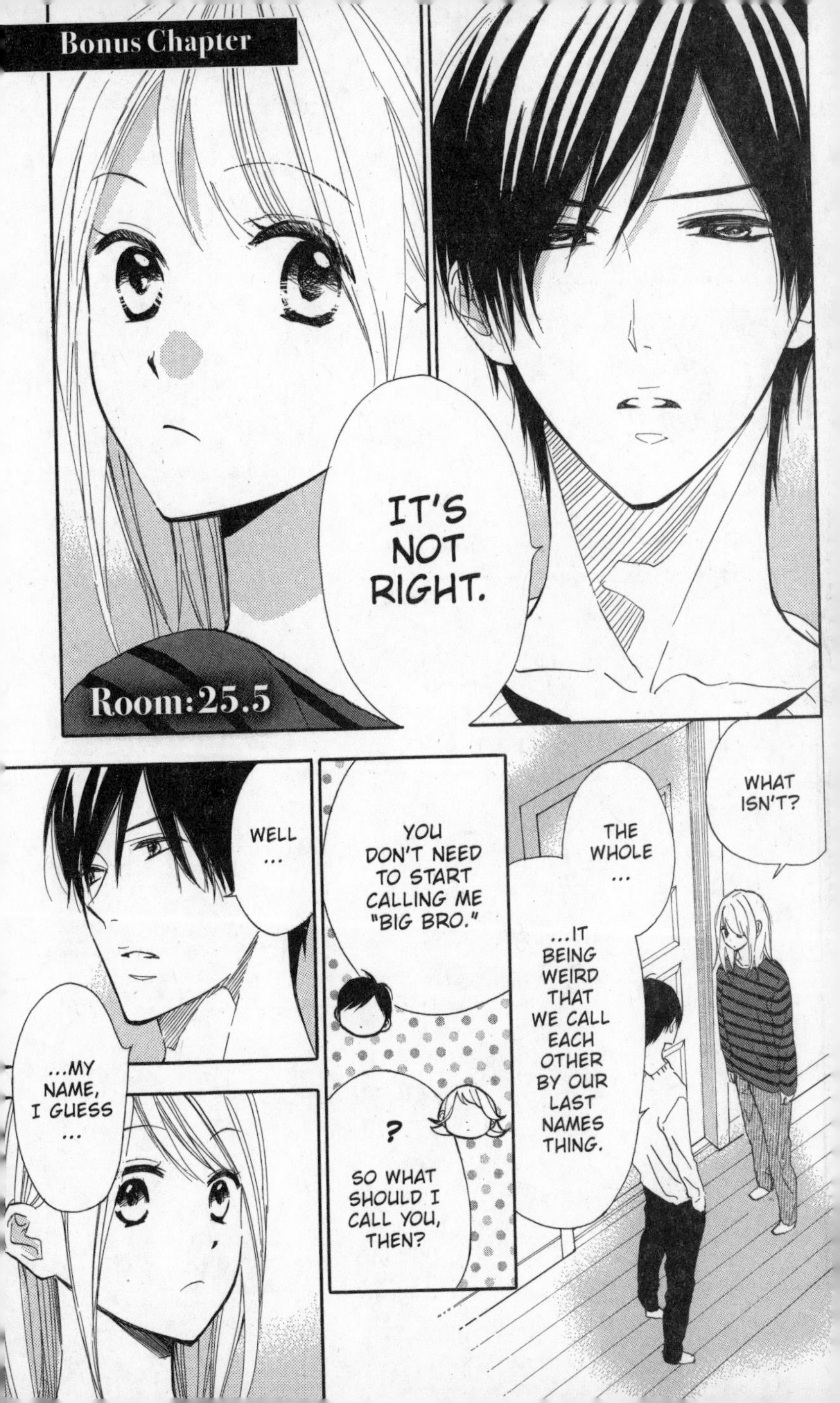
Bonus Chapter
IT'S NOT RIGHT.
Room: 25.5
WHAT ISN'T?
THE WHOLE ...
...IT BEING WEIRD THAT WE CALL EACH OTHER BY OUR LAST NAMES THING.
YOU DON'T NEED TO START CALLING ME "BIG BRO."
?
SO WHAT SHOULD I CALL YOU, THEN?
WELL ...
...MY NAME, I GUESS ...

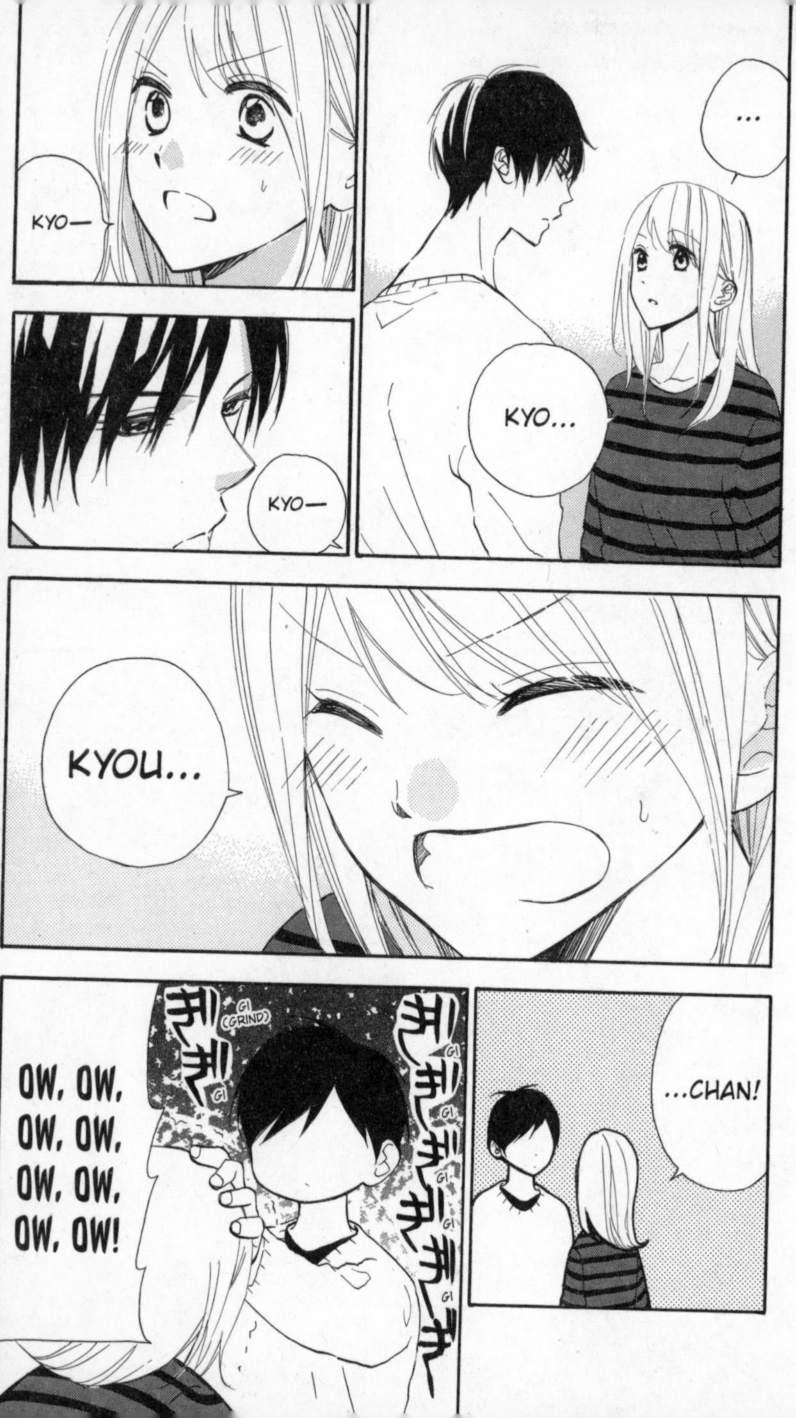
...
KYO...
KYO—
KYO—
KYOU...
...CHAN!
GI (GRIND)
GI
GI
GI
GI
GI
GI
OW, OW, OW, OW, OW, OW, OW, OW!

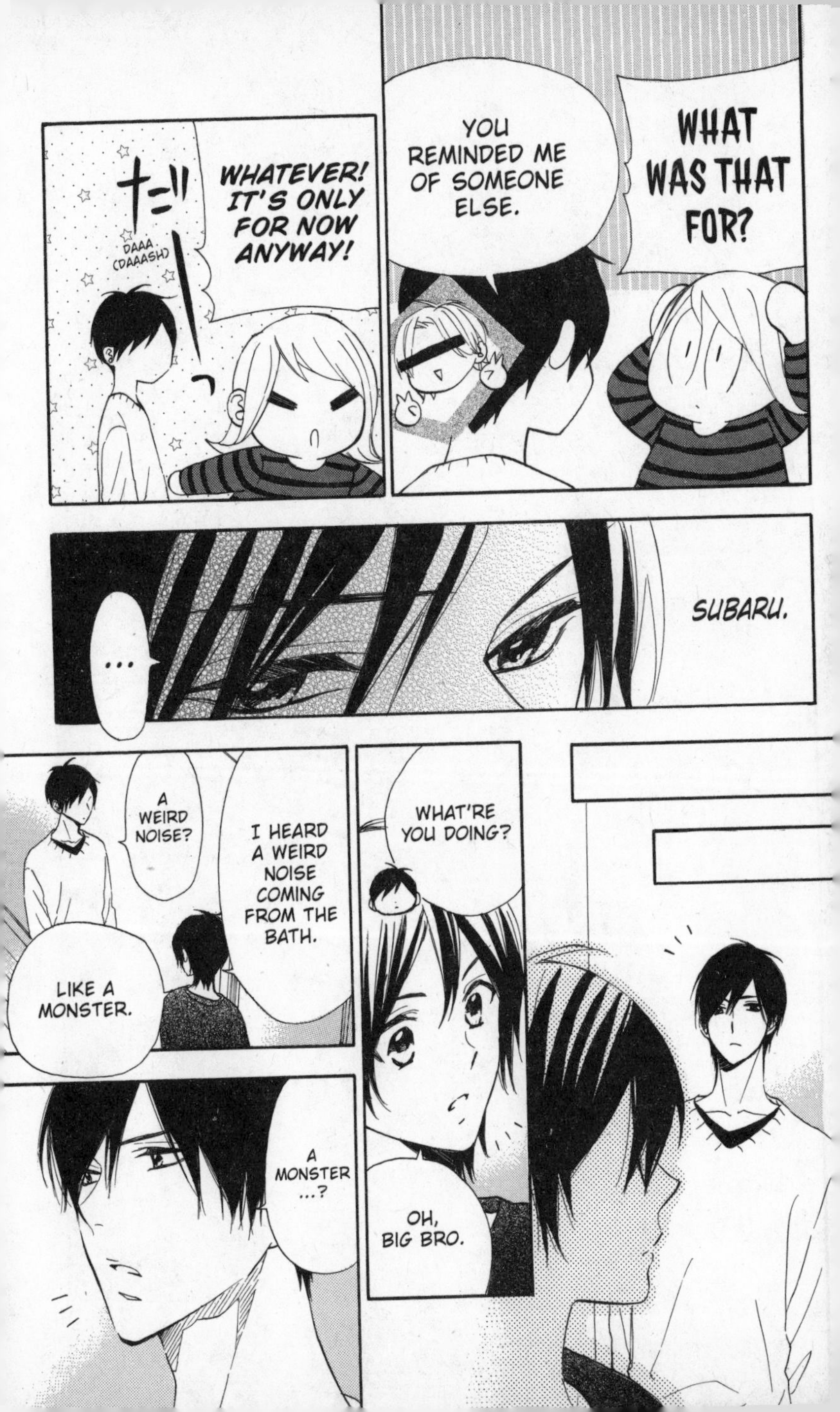

WHAT WAS THAT FOR?
YOU REMINDED ME OF SOMEONE ELSE.
WHATEVER! IT'S ONLY FOR NOW ANYWAY!
DAAA (DAAASH)
SUBARU.
...
WHAT'RE YOU DOING?
OH, BIG BRO.
I HEARD A WEIRD NOISE COMING FROM THE BATH.
A WEIRD NOISE?
LIKE A MONSTER.
A MONSTER ...?

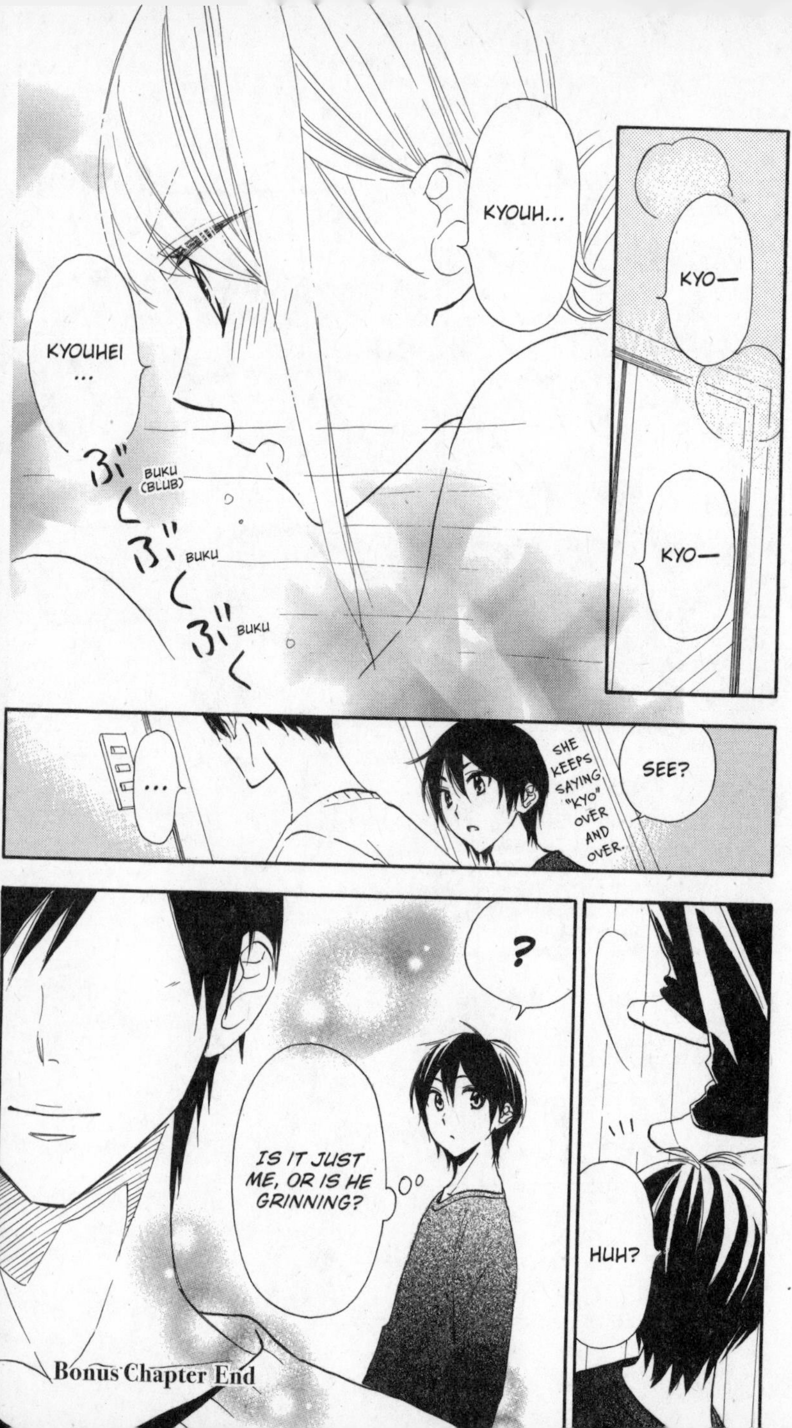
KYO—
KYO—
KYOUH...
KYOUHEI ...
ぶく
BUKU (BLUB)
ぶく
BUKU
ぶく
BUKU
SEE?
SHE KEEPS SAYING "KYO" OVER AND OVER.
...
HUH?
?
IS IT JUST ME, OR IS HE GRINNING?
Bonus Chapter End

TRANSLATION NOTES

Common Honorifics

-san: The Japanese equivalent of Mr./Mrs./Miss. If a situation calls for politeness, this is the fail-safe honorific.

-kun: Used most often when referring to boys, this indicates affection or familiarity. Occasionally used by older men among their peers, but it may also be used by anyone referring to a person of lower standing.

-chan: An affectionate honorific indicating familiarity used mostly in reference to girls; also used in reference to cute persons or animals of either gender.

-senpai: A suffix used to address upperclassmen or more experienced coworkers.

no honorific: Indicates familiarity or closeness; if used without permission or reason, addressing someone in this manner would constitute an insult.

Page 20

Futon: In Japan, some families sleep on futons instead of Western-style beds. Unlike the Western version, Japanese futons usually consist of a thin mattress covered by a heavy blanket. The bottom right panel depicts a futon that has already been laid out for the night. In the morning, they are typically either aired out or stored out of sight until night falls.

Page 40

Last name: First names are usually reserved for close friends, family members, and romantic partners in Japan. Strangers, classmates, and coworkers usually use a person's last name instead. Takako implies that their use of last names signals to her that they may see each other in a less-than-familial or romantic light.

Page 132

Safe for you not to hide your belly button: The Japanese god of thunder, Raijin, allegedly has a fondness for children's belly buttons. According to the superstition, belly buttons are supposed to be hidden during thunderstorms—or they may end up as a tasty treat for the aforementioned deity!

Page 143

I: Like Nanami mentions, the Japanese language has several different ways of saying "I" that can tell a bit more about a person. For example, *ore* is considered very masculine, while *boku* is only somewhat masculine. *Washi* is more often used by elderly men, while *oidon* is distinct to the Kagoshima region in Kyushu.

MINT CHOCOLATE

5

MAMI ORIKASA

Translation: Amber Tamosaitis | Lettering: Barri Shrager

This book is a work of fiction. Names, characters, places, and incidents are the product of the author's imagination or are used fictitiously. Any resemblance to actual events, locales, or persons, living or dead, is coincidental.

MINT CHOCOLATE by Mami Orikasa
© Mami Orikasa 2020
All rights reserved.
First published in Japan in 2020 by HAKUSENSHA, Inc., Tokyo.
English language translation rights in U.S.A., Canada and U.K. arranged with
HAKUSENSHA, Inc., Tokyo through Tuttle-Mori Agency, Inc., Tokyo.

English translation © 2022 by Yen Press, LLC

Yen Press
150 West 30th Street, 19th Floor
New York, NY 10001

Visit us at yenpress.com ♥ facebook.com/yenpress ♥ twitter.com/yenpress
yenpress.tumblr.com ♥ instagram.com/yenpress

First Yen Press Edition: March 2022

Yen Press is an imprint of Yen Press, LLC.
The Yen Press name and logo are trademarks of Yen Press, LLC.

The publisher is not responsible for websites (or their content) that are not owned by the publisher.

Library of Congress Control Number: 2020949568

ISBNs: 978-1-9753-2060-7 (paperback)
978-1-9753-2061-4 (ebook)

10 9 8 7 6 5 4 3 2 1

WOR

Printed in the United States of America